Podcasting

3rd Edition

by Tee Morris and Chuck Tomasi
FOREWORD BY **Mignon Fogarty**

for **dummies**®
A Wiley Brand

Podcasting For Dummies®, 3rd Edition

Published by **John Wiley & Sons, Inc.,** 111 River Street, Hoboken, NJ 07030-5774, www.wiley.com

Copyright © 2017 by John Wiley & Sons, Inc., Hoboken, New Jersey

Media and software compilation copyright © 2017 by John Wiley & Sons, Inc. All rights reserved.

Published simultaneously in Canada

For general information on our other products and services, please contact our Customer Care Department within the U.S. at 877-762-2974, outside the U.S. at 317-572-3993, or fax 317-572-4002. For technical support, please visit www.wiley.com/techsupport.

Wiley publishes in a variety of print and electronic formats and by print-on-demand. Some material included with standard print versions of this book may not be included in e-books or in print-on-demand. If this book refers to media such as a CD or DVD that is not included in the version you purchased, you may download this material at http://booksupport.wiley.com. For more information about Wiley products, visit www.wiley.com.

Library of Congress Control Number: 2017952484

ISBN: 978-1-119-41219-9

ISBN (ePDF): 978-1-119-41227-4; ISBN (ePub): 978-1-119-41226-7

Manufactured in the United States of America

10 9 8 7 6 5 4 3 2 1

Contents at a Glance

Table of Contents

Foreword

Your people are out there. Waiting for you. Whether you want to podcast about pop culture, marketing, bass fishing, or vintage wooden button collecting, you will find an audience if you stick with it and produce a quality show by following the advice in this book. The audience is probably bigger for a marketing podcast than a vintage wooden button collecting podcast, but you never know — there's probably less competition for the button collectors.

When the Sirens lure you to the dangerous waters of obsessing over your listener stats, imagine your listeners all sitting together in one auditorium. Listening to you. It's probably more people than your voice has ever reached in your whole life (unless you're a professor teaching a freshman weed-out class). It's amazing and a little frightening, and there's nothing like the thrill of getting your first message from a listener in China, New Zealand, the Philippines, Egypt, or some other distant land you've never seen.

There's something especially intimate about the listening experience too. Listeners imagine what you look like and where you are, and it's usually better than the reality. They feel like they know you because in their imagination, they have created you.

Now, instead of thinking of them as your audience, think of them as your community. Ask them what they want. Ask them what they like (and what they don't like). Feature them on your show.

Go beyond the microphone and make things for your listeners, and let them make things for you. Meet them in person, and once they get over the disappointment that you aren't the perfect person they've imagined (it happens quickly), your lives will be enriched. If you want it to be, a podcast is a magical gateway to a community.

When people start asking questions about podcasting, it's usually about the equipment. What microphone should they use? What software is best? Do they need a mixer? Tee and Chuck will answer these questions, of course, but they'll also address the bigger and more important questions — the questions you don't even know you should be asking, but that will make the difference between a good podcast and a fabulous podcast that you'll look forward to producing and that will become part of your listeners' regular media diet.

I used to tell students and conference attendees that the online world is so crowded — filled with so many people vying for attention — that you need to be relentless because nobody will miss you if you stop posting or publishing, but I was wrong. Podcasting is different. On the rare occasion when I have (gasp) accidentally released my show late, people have pinged me. They have checked to make sure I'm okay. They are my people. A community.

Lots of people start podcasting, and many continue, but for a few people it becomes a lifestyle, a job, or even a small addiction. "I'll start just one more," they think. Tee and Chuck have been podcasting for more than a decade and literally wrote the book on podcasting. You will benefit from their years of experience.

—Mignon Fogarty, *Grammar Girl* and founder of the Quick and Dirty Tips network.

Introduction

Maybe you've been casually surfing the web or perusing your newspaper when the word *podcasting* has popped up. You've heard the word before, but lately, it's been coming up again and again. *Podcasting.* Steadily, like a building wave that would make champion surfers salivate with delight, your curiosity continues to pique as the word *podcasting* echoes in your ears and remains in the back of your mind as a riddle wrapped in an enigma, super-sized with a side of fries and a diet soda to go.

Podcasting For Dummies, 3rd Edition, is the answer to that super-sized riddle-enigma combo, and it even comes complete with a special prize. Beginning with the question at the forefront of your mind — *What is podcasting?* — this book takes you through the fastest-growing technological movement on the Internet. By the time you reach the end of this book, the basics will be in place to get you, your voice, and your message heard around the world — and you can even have a bit of fun along the way.

About This Book

"So what are you up to, Tee?"

"I'm currently making a podcast of my first novel, a swashbuckling tale that carries our heroes . . ."

"Uh . . . what's a podcast?"

Asked by best friends and lifetime technologists, this question continues to crop up over and over again, immediately after the word *podcast* lands in a casual conversation. Just the word *podcasting* carries an air of geekiness about it — and behold, the habitual technophobes suddenly clasp their hands to their ears and run away screaming in horror lest they confront yet another technical matter. Too bad. If they only knew how technical it really isn't. When you peel back the covers and fancy-schmancy tech-talk, it's a pretty simple process to make your own podcast. You just need someone pointing the way and illuminating your path.

This is why we're here: to be that candle in the dark, helping you navigate a world where anyone can do anything, provided people have the tools, the drive, and the passion. You don't need to be a techno-wizard or a super-geek — you need no wad of tape holding your glasses together, and your shirt tail need not stick out from your fly. Anyone can do what we show you in this book, and often more than not people do. Anyone can take a thought or an opinion, make an audio or video file expressing that opinion, and distribute this idea worldwide. Anyone can capture the attention of a few hundred — or a few thousand — people around the world through mobile devices or smartphones, strapped around biceps, jouncing in pockets, or hooked up to car stereos.

Anyone can podcast.

Podcasting, from recording to online hosting, can be done on a variety of budgets, ranging from frugal to Fortune 500. You can podcast about literally anything — including podcasting for its own sake. As blogging gave the anonymous, the famous, the almost-famous, and the used-to-be famous a voice in politics, religion, and everyday life, podcasting adds volume and tone to that voice.

Podcasting is many things to many people — but at its most basic, it's a surprisingly simple and powerful technology. What it means boils down to a single person: you. Some have likened it to online radio but it can do — and be — so much more. Podcasting is communication on a global platform, transmitting your voice and its message around the world without using public airwaves. It is connecting to the Global Village in ways that the creators of the Internet, RSS, and MP3 compression would probably never have dreamed. It is the unique and the hard-to-find content that can't find a place on commercial, college, or public access radio; but sometimes when a chord is struck, podcasts go beyond their humble beginnings.

You're about to embark on an exciting adventure into undiscovered territory, and here you will find out that podcasting is all these things and so much more.

How to Use This Book

Podcasting For Dummies, 3rd Edition, should be these things to all who pick up and read it (whether straight through or by jumping around in the chapters):

>> A user-friendly guide in how to listen, produce, and distribute podcasts

>> A terrific reference for choosing the right hardware and software to put together a sharp-sounding podcast

>> The starting point for the person who knows nothing about audio editing, recording, managing RSS feeds, hosting blogs, or how to turn a computer into a recording studio

>> A handy go-to "think tank" for any beginning podcaster who's hungry for new ideas on what goes into a good podcast and fresh points of view

>> A really fun read

There will be plenty of answers in these pages, and if you find our answers too elementary, we give you plenty of points of reference to research. We don't claim to have all the solutions, quick fixes, and resolutions to all possible podcasting queries, but we do present to you the basic building blocks and first steps for beginning a podcast. As with any *For Dummies* book, our responsibility is to give you the foundation on which to build. That's what we've done our level best to accomplish: Bestow upon you the enchanted stuff that makes a podcast happen.

This book was written as a linear path from the conceptualization stages to the final publication of your work. However, not everyone needs to read the book from page one. If you've already gotten your feet wet with the various aspects of podcasting, jump around from section to section and read the parts that you need. We provide plenty of guides back to other relevant chapters for when the going gets murky.

Conventions Used in This Book

When you go through this book, you're going to see a few ⌘ symbols, the occasional ⇨, and even a few things typed in a completely different style. There's a method to this madness, and those methods are conventions found throughout this book.

When we refer to keyboard shortcuts for Macintosh or Windows, we designate them with (Mac) or (Windows). For Mac shortcuts, we use the "Command" symbol (that funky cloverleaf symbol found on the "Command" key) and the corresponding letter. For Windows shortcuts, we use the abbreviation for the Control key (Ctrl) and the corresponding letter. So the shortcut for Select All looks like this: ⌘+A (Mac) / Ctrl+A (Windows).

If keyboard shortcuts aren't your thing and you want to know where the commands reside on menus, we use a command arrow (⇨) to help guide you through menus and submenus. So, the command for Select All in the application's menu is Edit⇨Select All. You first select the Edit menu and then Select All.

When we offer URLs (web addresses) of various podcasts, resources, and audio equipment vendors, or when we have you creating RSS feeds for podcast clients, also known as "podcatchers" such as iTunes, Downcast, or Juice, we use `this particular typeface`.

Bold Assumptions

We assume that you have a computer, a lot of curiosity, and a desire to podcast. We couldn't care less about whether you're using a Mac, a PC, Linux, Unix, or two Dixie cups connected with string. (Okay, maybe the two Dixie cups connected with string would be a challenge; a computer is essential.) In podcasting, the operating system just makes the computer go. We're here to provide you tools for creating a podcast, regardless of what OS you're running.

If you know nothing about audio or video production, this book can also serve as a fine primer in how to record, edit, and produce media on your computer, as well as accessorize your computer with mixing boards, professional-grade microphones, and media production software that will give you a basic look at this creative field. You can hang on to this book as a handy reference, geared primarily for audio, though we do include some information on video, *in podcasting.* Again, our book is a starting point, and (ahem) a fine starting point at that.

With everything that goes into podcasting, there are some things this book is not now, nor will ever be, about. Here's the short list:

>> We're not out to make you into an übergeek in RSS or XML (but we give you all you need to make things work).

>> We figure that if you get hold of Audacity, GarageBand, iMovie, Final Cut Pro X, or Premiere, you can take it from there (but we give you overviews of those programs and a few basic editing examples).

>> We're not out to teach you how to use an MP3 player, smartphone, or tablet. That's a prerequisite for this book.

For that matter, to dispel one of the biggest misconceptions of podcasting, you will not be told to run out and get an iPod. *You do not need an iPod to podcast — or to listen to podcasts for that matter.*

If you are looking for a terrific start to the podcasting experience, then — in the words of the last knight guarding the Holy Grail in *Indiana Jones and the Last Crusade* — "You have chosen wisely."

How This Book Is Organized

The following sections give you a quick overview of what this book has to offer. And yeah, we're going to keep the overview brief because we figure you're eager to get started. But the fact that you're reading this passage also tells us you don't want to miss a detail, so here's a quick bird's-eye view of what we do in *Podcasting For Dummies*.

Part 1: Podcasting on a Worldwide Frequency

Part 1 goes into the bare-bones basics of how a podcast happens, how to get podcasts from the Internet to your computer, and how to host a podcast yourself — ending up with a few places online that offer podcast feeds you can visit to sample the experience and (later on) to let the world know "Hey, I've got a podcast, too!"

Part 1 also helps you pick out the best hardware and software you need to start podcasting.

Part 2: The Hills Are Alive with the Sound of Podcasting

Consider this part of the book *Inside the Actor's Studio* — part TWiT, and part WKRP (with your host, Dr. Johnny Fever . . . *booooouuugaaar!!!*). This is where we offer some techniques the pros use in broadcasting. Podcasting may be the grass-roots movement of homespun telecommunications, but that doesn't mean it has to sound that way (unless, of course, you *want* it to sound that way). From preshow prep to setting your volume levels to the basics of audio editing, this is the part that polishes your podcast.

Part 3: So You've Got This Great Recording of Your Voice. Now What?

The audio file you've just created is now silently staring at you from your monitor (unless you're listening to it on your computer's music player, in which case it's just defiantly talking back at you!), and you haven't a clue what your next step is. We cover the last-minute details and then walk you through the process of getting your podcast online, finding the right web-hosting packages for podcasts, and getting a good working handle on the RSS and XML used in podcast feeds.

Part 4: Start Spreadin' the News about Your Podcast

"I wanna beeee a part of it. Podcasting, babeeeee . . .
If I can get on Daily Source,
Then I'll have no remorse for pod—cast—in . . . podcasting . . ."

Sorry. Sinatra moment.

Anyway, you have the podcast recorded, edited, and online, but now you need to let people know you have this great podcast just waiting for them — and that's what we explore in Part 4. With the power of publicity — from free-of-charge word-of-mouth (arguably the most effective) to investment in Facebook Ads, you have a wide array of options to choose from when you're ready to announce your presence to the podcasting community.

Part 5: Pod-sibilities to Consider for Your Show

The question of *why* one should podcast is as important as *how* to podcast. We cover some basic rationales that many folks have for sitting behind a microphone, pouring heart, soul, and pocket change into their craft each and every day, week, or month. What is the endgame? Sponsorship? Patreon? Or just for the love of it? These questions have no right or wrong answers, but our hope is that this part offers pointers to convey you safely through the thought process behind podcasting.

Part 6: The Part of Tens

Perhaps the toughest chapters to write were these: the *For Dummies* trademark Part of Tens chapters. So don't skip them because we'll be über-miffed if you fail to appreciate how hard we busted our humps to get these chapters done!

Right — so what do we give you in our Part of Tens? We give you a list of the most influential people in podcasting, some of them still podcasting to this day. We also offer suggestions for the beginning podcaster — such as what kind of podcasts should be on your MP3 player, just to give you an idea of what's out there, how they sound, and how you can benefit from them. And we wrap it all up with a list of reasons why you should podcast — we're sure you'll find something that resonates with you.

Icons Used in This Book

So you're trekking through the book, making some real progress with developing your podcast, when suddenly these little icons leap out, grab you by the throat, and wrestle you to the ground. (Who would have thought podcasting was so action-packed, like a Daniel Craig-Bond movie, huh?) What do all these little drawings mean? Glad you asked.

TIP

When we're in the middle of a discussion and suddenly we have one of those *"Say, that reminds me . . ."* moments, we give you one of these tips. They're handy little extras that are good to know and might even make your podcast sound a little tighter than average.

REMEMBER

If the moment is more than a handy little nugget of information and closer to a *"Seriously, you can't forget this part!"* factoid, we mark it with a Remember icon. You're going to want to play close attention to these puppies.

WARNING

Sometimes we interrupt our train of thought with a *"Time out, Sparky . . ."* moment — and this is where we ask for your completely undivided attention. The Warnings are exactly that: flashing lights, ah-ooga horns, dire portents. They're reminders not to try this at home because you'll definitely regret it.

TECHNICAL STUFF

These icons illuminate the *"So how does this widget really work . . .?"* moments you may have as you read this book. The Technical Stuff icons give you a deeper understanding of what the wizard is doing behind the curtain, making you all the more apt as a podcaster. But if you want to skip the nitty-gritty details, that's perfectly fine, too.

Beyond the Book

In addition to what you're reading right now, this book comes with a free access-anywhere Cheat Sheet. To get this Cheat Sheet, simply go to www.dummies.com and search for "Podcasting For Dummies Cheat Sheet" by using the Search box.

This book also comes with a companion podcast. Go to your browser, surf to http://podcastingfordummies.com, and subscribe for free weekly audio commentary from Tee Morris and Chuck Tomasi about concepts in this book explored in greater detail, from the difference between good and bad edits, when too much reverb is too much, and the variety of methods you can use to record a podcast.

Where to Go from Here

At this point, many *For Dummies* authors say something snappy, clever, or even a bit snarky. We save our best tongue-and-cheek material for the pages inside, so here's a more serious approach.

We suggest heading to where you're planning to record your podcast, or just plant yourself in front of a computer, and start with Chapter 1, where you're given a few links to check out, some suggestions on applications for downloading podcasts, and directories to look up where you can find Tee's and Chuck's (many) podcasts, and other podcasts that can educate, inspire, and enlighten your ears with original content.

Where do we go from here? Up and out, friends. Up and out . . .

1
Podcasting on a Worldwide Frequency

Understand the fundamentals of creating, uploading, and distributing your podcast for others to enjoy.

Explore various podcast directories to find content that interests you, and compare and contrast how others produce their shows.

Find the right hardware, software, and accessories that fit your budget.

Take your podcast recording on the road with mobile devices and processes.

Chapter **1**

Getting the Scoop on Podcasting

S ometimes the invention that makes the biggest impact on our daily lives isn't an invention at all, but the convergence of existing technologies, processes, and ideas. Podcasting may be the perfect example of that principle — and it's changing the relationship people have with their radios, music collections, books, education, and more.

The podcasting movement is actually a spinoff of another communications boom: *blogs.* Blogs sprang up right and left, providing non-programmers and designers a clean, elegant interface that left many on the technology side wondering why they hadn't thought of it sooner. Everyday people could chronicle their lives, hopes, dreams, and fears, and show them to anyone who cared to read. And oddly enough, people did care to read — and still do.

Then in 2003, former MTV VeeJay Adam Curry started collaborating with programmer Dave Winer about his enhancement to RSS (which stands for *Really Simple Syndication*) that not only allowed you to share text and images, but media attachments which included compressed audio and video files. Soon after, Curry released his first podcast catching client. Thus, the Age of Podcasting began.

Podcasting combines the instant information exchange of blogging with audio and video files that can be played on a computer or portable media device. When you make your podcast publicly available on the Internet, you are exposing your craft to anyone with a computer or mobile device and a connection capable of streaming data. To put that in perspective, some online sources report the global online population is over 3.4 billion users. In the U.S. alone, more than 198 million people own a podcast-ready device, and every one of them can play your content!

This chapter is for the consumers of the content (the audience) and those who make the content (the podcasters) alike. We cover the basic steps to record a podcast and lay out the basics of what you need to do to enjoy a podcast on your media player.

If you're starting to get the idea that podcasting is revolutionary, groundbreaking, and possibly a major component of social upheaval, great. Truth is, some have made their marks in society. But not all podcasts are so deep. In fact, many of them are passion projects inviting you to join in on the experience!

Throughout the book, we discuss audio and video podcasts. Don't be alarmed when we refer to the audience as *listeners*. We're not leaving out viewers intentionally. It's a bit like that gender-neutral pronoun for he/she. Unless otherwise stated, the information we provide is applicable to audio and video productions.

Deciding Whether Podcasting Is for You

Technically speaking, *podcasting* is the distribution of specially encoded multimedia content to subscribed devices via the RSS 2.0 protocol. Whew! Allow us to translate that into common-speak:

> Podcasting allows you to listen to stuff you want to hear, or watch stuff you want to see, whenever and wherever you want.

Podcasting turns the tables on broadcast schedules, allowing the listener to choose not only what to listen to, but also when — often referred to as *time-shifted media*. And because podcasts are transferred via the Internet, the power to create an audio program isn't limited to those with access to a radio transmitter.

The simplest reason to podcast is that *it's just plain fun!* We've been podcasting since the beginning, and we're still having a blast, continuing to get out messages to our worldwide audiences and challenging ourselves with new tricks and techniques in creating captivating media. So, yeah, for the fun of it? Heck of a good reason.

The following sections cover other reasons podcasting is probably for you.

WHAT'S IN A NAME, WHEN THE NAME IS PODCASTING?

As with most items that make their way into the conventional lexicon of speech, the precise origins and meaning behind *podcasting* are somewhat clouded. Although the domain podcast.com was originally registered back in 2002 (nothing was ever done with it, as far as we know), and Ben Hammersley suggested that and many other terms in February 2004 (www.guardian.co.uk/media/2004/feb/12/broadcasting.digitalmedia), it's generally accepted in the podcast community that the first person to use the term as a reference to the activity we now know as podcasting was Dannie Gregoire on September 15, 2004 (http://groups.yahoo.com/group/ipodder-dev/message/41). Although some assert the name has connotations to Apple's popular iPod, Dannie didn't have that in mind when the phrase was coined. Regardless of the intentions, the term has been *backronymed* (that is, treated like an acronym and applied to a variety of plausible existing meanings). We've heard possibilities like *Portable On-Demand casting*, *Netcasting*, and several other similar attempts. Like the practice of podcasting, exact definitions don't seem to really matter as much as the spirit of what you are doing.

You want to deliver media content on a regular basis

Sure, you can include audio, video, and PDFs content in your blog if you have one. Many bloggers record special media segments and insert them as links into the text of their blogposts. Readers then download the files at their leisure. However, this approach requires *manual* selection of the content blog hosts want readers to download. What sets podcasting apart from blogging is that podcasting automates that process. A listener who subscribes to your podcast is subscribed to all your content, whenever it's available. No need to go back to the site to see what's new! Once you subscribe to a podcast, the content is delivered to you in the same way as when you subscribe to a print magazine. New content, delivered to you.

You want to reach beyond the boundaries of broadcast media

In radio, unless it is satellite radio, the number of people who can listen to a show is limited by the power of the transmitter pumping out the signal. Same thing with broadcast television, depending if you are using antenna, cable, or satellite dish to receive programming. Podcasting doesn't rely on or utilize signals, transmitters, or receivers — at least not in the classic sense. Podcasts use the Internet as a delivery system, opening up a potential audience that could extend to the entire planet.

No rules exist (not yet, anyway) to regulate the creation of podcast content. In fact, neither the FCC nor any other regulatory body for any other government holds jurisdiction over podcasts. If that seems astounding, remember that podcasters are not using the public airwaves to deliver the message.

WARNING

Just because the FCC doesn't have jurisdiction, you're not exempt from the law or — perhaps more important — immune to lawsuits. *You're personally responsible for anything you say, do, or condone on your show.* Additionally, the rules concerning airplay of licensed music, the distribution of copyrighted material, and the legalities of recording conversations all apply. Pay close attention to the relevant sections in Chapter 5 to avoid some serious consequences. When it comes to the legalities, ignorance is not bliss.

You have something to say

Generally, podcasters produce content that likely holds appeal for only a select audience. Podcasts start with an idea, something that you have the desire and knowledge, either real or imaginary, to talk about. Add to that a bit of drive, do-it-yourself-ishness, and an inability to take no for an answer. The point is to say what you want to say, to those who want to hear it.

Podcasts can be about anything and be enjoyed by just about anyone. The topics covered don't have to be earth-shattering or life-changing. They can be about do-it-yourself projects, sound-seeing tours of places you visit, or even your favorite board games. There are a few rules and guidelines in common practice, but there may be times when you find it necessary to bend the rules. (That can be a lot of fun in and of itself!)

Some of the most popular podcasts are created by everyday people who sit in front of their computers for a few nights a week and just speak their minds, hearts, and souls. Some are focused on niche topics; others are more broad-based.

You want to hear from your listeners

Something that is a real perk with podcasting: accessibility. On average, most audiences have a direct line of contact between themselves and the podcast's host or hosts. Podcast consumers are more likely to provide feedback for what they listen or watch than for a favorite radio or television show. That's probably traceable to the personal nature of a podcast. Podcasts offer their audiences — and makers — more control, options, and intimacy than traditional broadcast media can. Of course, the radio is much harder to talk back to than a computer with an Internet connection and email.

REMEMBER

When you ask for feedback, you're likely to get it — and from unusual places. Because geography doesn't limit the distance your podcast can travel, you may find yourself with listeners in faraway and exotic places. And this feedback isn't always going to be "Wow, great podcast!" Listeners will be honest with you when you invite feedback.

Creating a Podcast

There are two schools of thought when it comes to creating a podcast: The "I need the latest and greatest equipment to capture that crisp, clear sound of the broadcasting industry" school of thought, and the "Hey, my computer came with a microphone, and I've got this cool recording software already installed" school of thought. Both are equally valid positions, and there are a lot of secondary schools in-between. The question is how far you're willing to go.

But allow us to dispel a few misconceptions about podcasting right off the bat: You're not reprogramming your operating system, you're not hacking into the Internal Revenue Service's database, and you're not setting up a wireless computer network with tinfoil from a chewing gum wrapper, a shoestring, and your belt — regardless if *MacGyver* showed you how. Podcasting, as mentioned earlier, is not rocket science. In fact, here's a quick rundown of how you podcast:

1. Record audio or video and convert it to a download-friendly format.

2. Write up a description of what it is that you just created as a blog post.

3. Upload everything to a host server.

Yes, yes, yes, if it were that simple, then why is this book so thick? Well, we admit that this list does gloss over a *few* details, but a podcast — in its most streamlined, raw presentation — *is* that simple. The details of putting together a single episode start in Chapter 2 and wrap up in Chapter 8; then Chapters 10, 11, and 13 walk you through all the geek-speak you need to make the media you create into a podcast.

Looking for the bare necessities

You need a few things before starting your first podcast, many of which you can probably find on your own computer. For these beginning steps, we're going to focus on audio podcasts. Here's what you should keep an eye out for:

>> **A microphone:** Look at your computer. Right now, regardless of whether you have a laptop or desktop model, Windows or Macintosh, your computer

probably has a microphone built into it — or guaranteed a USB port for plugging in an external mic. You might even luck out and find an included external mic packaged somewhere among the manuals, cables, and such. Yes, even your mobile phone has a microphone or it wouldn't be much of a phone, now would it? Many earbuds even have a microphone in the cord with the earbuds.

Position the microphone in a comfortable spot on your desk or table. If you're using a laptop, it should be somewhere on your desk that allows for best recording results without hunching over the computer like *Young Frankenstein*'s Igor (That's *EYE*-gor.) Check the laptop's documentation to find out where the built-in microphone is located in the unit's housing. For the mobile phone, hold the device as if you are making a call, the way it was intended. Speaking in to it end-on or holding it any other way can degrade the audio quality. If you are using the microphone-earbuds set included with the phone's purchase, you may need to do some experimentation.

TECHNICAL STUFF

Usually the built-in microphone in a laptop is located close to the edge of the keyboard or near the laptop's speakers. Some models tuck it in at the center point of the monitor's base.

>> **Recording software:** Check out the software that came with your computer. You know, all those extra applications that you filed away, thinking, "I'll check those out sometime." Well, the time has arrived to flip through them. You probably have some sort of audio-recording software loaded on your computer, such as RecordIt (PC) or GarageBand (which comes preinstalled with many new Macs).

TIP

If you don't already have the appropriate software, here's a fast way to get it: Download the version of Audacity that fits your operating system (at www.audacityteam.org), shown in Figure 1-1. (Oh, yeah . . . it's free.)

>> **An audio interface:** Make sure your computer has the hardware it needs to handle audio recording and the drivers to run the hardware — unless, of course, you have a built-in microphone.

TIP

Some desktop computers come with a very elementary audio card built into the motherboard. Before you run out to your local computer vendor and spring for an audio card, check your computer to see whether it can already handle basic voice recording.

For tips on choosing the right mic and audio accessories, be sure to check out Chapter 2. Chapter 3 covers all the software you need.

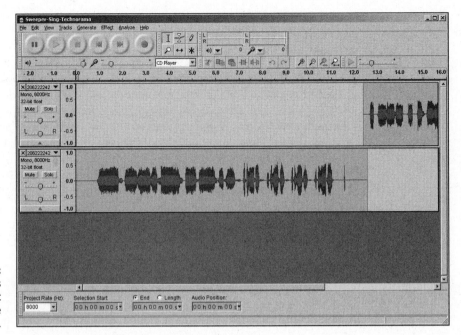

FIGURE 1-1:
Audacity allows you to edit audio and create MP3 files.

Recording your first podcast

When you have your computer set up and your microphone working, it's time to start recording. Take a deep breath and then follow these steps:

1. **Jot down a few notes on what you want to talk about.**

   Nothing too fancy — just make an outline that includes remarks about who you are and what you want to talk about. Use these bullet points to keep yourself on track.

   All this — checking your computer, jotting down notes, and setting up your recording area — is called *preshow prep,* discussed in depth in Chapter 5 by other podcasters who have their own set ways of getting ready to record.

2. **Click the Record button in your recording software and go for as long as it takes for you to get through your notes.**

   We recommend keeping your first recording to no more than 20 minutes. That may seem like a lot of time, but it will *fly* by.

TIP

3. **Give a nice little sign-off (like "Take care of yourselves! See you next time.") and click the Stop button.**

4. **Choose File ⇨ Save As and give your project a name.**

   Now bask in the warmth of creative accomplishment.

Compressing your audio files

Portable media devices and computers can play MP3 files as a default format. While there are many other audio formats in existence, MP3 is quite common and the preferred format for podcasting. If your recording software can output straight to MP3 format, your life is much simpler. In Audacity's case, you need to download an add-on file. If you are using a different audio editor and can't export directly to MP3, another option is Apple iTunes at www.apple.com/itunes. (The iTunes window is shown in Figure 1-2.) It does many things for the podcaster, including converting a wide variety of audio file formats to MP3. Yes, it's from Apple, but the Apple folks made sure to create a version for Windows also.

FIGURE 1-2:
Apple iTunes, available for both Mac and Windows platforms, can create MP3 files from a variety of audio formats.

After launching iTunes, follow these steps to convert your audio file:

1. **Choose File ➪ Add File to Library.**

   Or you can press ⌘+O (Mac) or Ctrl+O (Windows).

2. **Browse for the audio file you want to convert and then click Open.**

   Your file is now in the iTunes Library.

3. **Find the audio file in the iTunes Library and click to select it.**

4. **Choose File ⇨ Convert ⇨ Create MP3 Version.**

Your file is converted to the MP3 format. Figure 1-3 shows the progress screen that indicates your file is being converted.

TECHNICAL STUFF

The default file format for iTunes file import is AAC. If your menu doesn't have a Create MP3 Version option, go to iTunes Preferences (File ⇨ Preferences on a Mac, or Edit ⇨ Preferences in Windows), under the General tab, Import Settings button, and change the Import Using option to MP3 Encoder. The Settings should be at least Good Quality (128 kbps); if you include a lot of audio design in your podcast, select Higher Quality (192 kbps). Now your files will be imported and converted to MP3.

FIGURE 1-3:
Under your Preferences tab, you can select what degree of compression you desire for your MP3 files.

Congratulations — you just recorded your first audio podcast! Easy, isn't it? This is merely the first step into a larger world, as Obi-Wan once told Luke.

Uploading your audio to the web

An audio file sitting on your desktop, regardless of how earth-shattering the contents may be, is not a podcast. Nope, not by a long shot. You have to get it up on the Internet and provide a way for listeners' podcatcher software to grab that tasty file for later consumption.

If you already have a web server for your blog, company website, or personal website, this process can be as easy as creating a new folder and transferring your newly created audio file to your server.

If that last paragraph left you puzzled and you're wondering what kind of mess you've gotten yourself into . . . relax. We don't leave you hanging out in the wind. Chapter 11 covers everything you need to know about choosing a web host for your podcast media files.

TECHNICAL STUFF

We've been focusing a lot on audio at this point, and we will do that throughout the book. Just remember, though, a podcast *media* file can be any sort of media file you like — audio, video, interactive PDF. While our primary attention is on audio, you can use all the tips we give here to handle other types of media.

After you upload your episode, you need to have an RSS file (*Really Simple Syndication*) generated to deliver it. That happens automatically on a blog. The RSS describes where to find the media file you just uploaded. Check your blog software (like WordPress) for the details. Nearly all software for blogging (called *blog engines*) support RSS, but not all support podcasts. You may need to add a plug-in, a downloadable extension that make podcast support a simple affair. This generated RSS file is your *podcast feed.* People who listen to your podcast can subscribe to your show by placing a link to this podcast feed in their *podcatching client* — a fancy term for software that regularly checks one or more podcast feeds for new content.

Yes, we know . . . this all sounds really complicated. But we assure you it's not. Some hosting companies such as LibSyn (www.libsyn.com) specialize in taking the technological "bite" out of podcasting so you can focus on creating your best-sounding show. With LibSyn (shown in Figure 1-4), moving your episode to a web server is as simple as pushing a few buttons, and the creation of the RSS 2.0 podcast feed and even the accompanying web page are automatic.

If you want to take more control over your website, podcast media files, and their corresponding RSS 2.0 feed, look at Chapters 11 and 13. In those pages, we walk you through some essentials — not only how to upload a file but also how to easily generate your RSS 2.0 file using a variety of tools.

Grabbing listeners

With media files in place and an RSS 2.0 feed ready for podcatcher consumption, you're officially a podcaster. Of course, that doesn't mean a lot if you're the only person who knows about your podcast. You need to spread the word to let others know that you exist and that you have something pretty darned important to say.

Creating show notes

Before you pick up a bullhorn, slap a sandwich board over yourself, and start walking down the street (virtually, anyway), you have to make sure you're descriptive enough to captivate those who reach your website. First, you're going to want to describe the contents of your show to casual online passers-by in hopes of getting them to listen to what you have to say. That blogpost you created to help deliver your media is that place. This is where *show notes* take form and give people a rundown of what you're talking about.

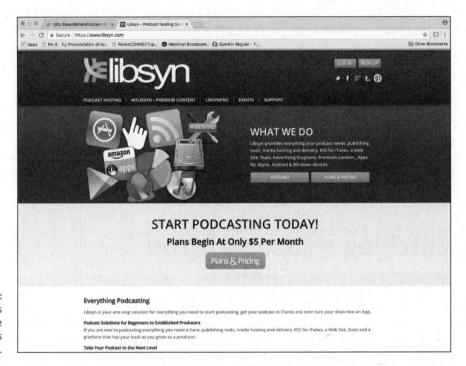

FIGURE 1-4: LibSyn handles many of the technical details of podcasting.

REMEMBER

You can easily glance at a blog and get the gist of a conversation, but an audio file requires active listening to understand, and it's quite difficult to skim. In effect, you're asking people to make an investment of their time in listening to you talk, read a story, or play music. You need some compelling text on a web page to hook them.

Show notes are designed to quickly showcase or highlight the relevant and pertinent contents of the audio file itself. A verbatim transcript of your show isn't always necessary, but we do recommend more than simply saying "a show about my day." Chapter 12 discusses ways to create your show notes and offers tips and tricks to give them some punch.

Getting listed in directories

When you have a ready media file and a solid set of show notes, you're ready to take your podcast message to the masses. You can get listed on some directories and podcast-listing sites, such as iTunes, Google Play, Stitcher, and BluBrry (explained later in this chapter). Potential listeners visit literally dozens of websites as they seek out new content, and getting yourself listed on as many as possible can help bring in more new listeners to your program.

WARNING

A huge listener base is a double-edged sword: More demand for your product means more of a demand on you and the resources necessary to keep your podcast up and running. We recommend working on your craft and your skills, as well as getting a good handle on the personal and technological requirements of podcasting, *before* you embark on a huge marketing campaign. When you're ready, Part 4 has more details about marketing.

Part 4 spends a lot of time talking about the various ways you can attract more listeners to your show and ways to respond to the ideas and feedback that your listeners inevitably provide. Many podcasters are surprised at the sheer volume of comments they receive from their listeners — but when you consider how personal podcasting is (compared to traditional forms of media distribution), that's not surprising at all.

Catching a Cast with Your Podcatching Client

So, you have the MP3 file, an RSS feed, and accompanying show notes. You're all set, but ask yourself, "How do podcasts get from the web to my preferred listening device?" To access all this great, new content, you need a *podcatcher,* an application that looks at various RSS feeds, finds the new stuff, and transfers it from the Internet to your computer or mobile device automatically. In this section, we look at some of the different podcatching clients available for your listening and viewing needs.

REMEMBER

You may think you need an iPod for all kinds of reasons, but you really don't need one to podcast. Allow us to state that again: *You do not need an iPod to listen to or create a podcast. You don't even need an iPhone to listen to or create a podcast with, either.* As long as you have an MP3 player — be it an application on a Mac, an application on a PC, mobile phone, or any portable device you can unplug and take with you — you possess the capability to listen to podcasts. Depending on the MP3 player, you may even be able to create your podcast on the device as well — but to listen, all you need is a device that can play audio files. This includes your computer.

The following sections represent only a starting point for getting access to podcasts. Any attempt at a comprehensive list would be instantly obsolete. Podcasting continues to grow in popularity, and new podcatching clients and players are coming out all the time. And remember, you can listen to podcasts on all sorts of devices besides computers — smartphones, tablets, AppleTV, Roku, and more!

For more information and product comparisons, we suggest heading over to Wikipedia (`https://en.wikipedia.org/wiki/List_of_podcatchers`) and exploring more podcatching clients. Bottom line: At this point, you should easily be able to subscribe to the podcasts of your choice.

The catcher that started it all: Juice

Juice (shown in Figure 1-5) started life as a product called iSpider, then was branded as iPodder, and later became iPodder Lemon. In November 2005, as if searching for a new identity in the community, the package was rebranded as Juice. Inspired by a script written by the podfather himself, Adam Curry, Juice promotes itself as an *open-source* (free to use) application that downloads audio files from RSS feeds of your choice directly to your Mac or PC. You can then sync your portable player with your computer's media player, and now you're podcasting-on-the-go.

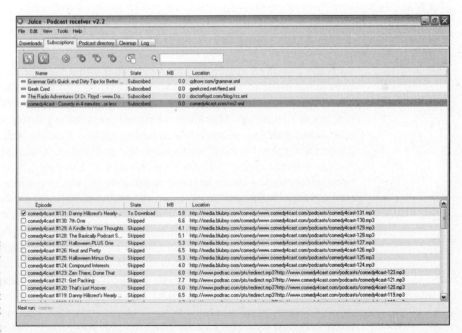

FIGURE 1-5:
The ground-breaking, trendsetting, and all-around-first podcatching client — Juice.

Download Juice from `http://juicereceiver.sourceforge.net`. After you install it, subscribing to feeds is a simple process.

1. **Click the Subscriptions tab.**

2. **On the Subscriptions pane, click the little green button with a plus symbol on it.**

    The Add a Feed window opens.

3. **On your favorite podcast website, look for a small icon, typically orange, that says RSS, RSS 2.0, or something similar.**

     The icon may not even say RSS, but simply be a symbol like the one in the margin.

4. **Right-click the icon to copy the link location.**

5. **Paste the copied information into the URL field of the Add a Feed window.**

    Or, type it in — just be very careful with your typing! If you get it wrong, you won't get your downloads.

Congrats! You now know how to use Juice to subscribe to any podcasts you happen to come across in the future.

The turning of a corner: iTunes

With the launch of iTunes in June 2005, podcasting went from what the geeks were doing in the basement of the Science Building to the next wave of innovation on the Internet (which was, of course, developed by the geeks in the basement of the Science Building). There was plenty of contributing factors that help push podcasting mainstream but iTunes opening its own directory and allowing for an easier subscription method was a huge step forward. As always, such a step into the mainstream market brought some dismay to the original podcasters, finding themselves overshadowed by larger media entities. Now, recognizable studios like NPR, Disney, ESPN, BBC, and so on dominate the iTunes Music Store podcast directory (shown in Figure 1-6). What about the indie podcasts — the ones that started it all? Would they be forgotten? Go unnoticed? Languish unsubscribed? Well, at first, it seemed that many of the original groundbreakers that the pod-casting community knew and loved (*Comedy4Cast, Career Opportunities, Coverville, GrammarGirl*) might get lost in the stampede. But not yet, as it turns out.

Apple's iTunes (available for download at `www.itunes.com`) lends an automatic hand to people who don't know where to find podcatchers, where to find blogs that host podcasts, and which podcast directories list the shows that fit their needs and desires — now they too can enjoy a wide range of podcast choices.

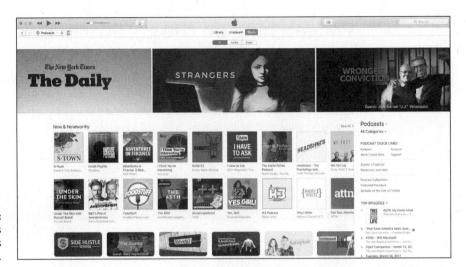

FIGURE 1-6:
The Apple iTunes Music Store's Podcast directory.

TIP

Apple now offers for people's mobile devices a podcast app simply called Podcasts. If you want your music management and podcast management all on the go and away from your computer, you can search, subscribe, and manage your podcasts from here.

With its June 2005 edition, iTunes became a one-stop shop for all your podcasting needs; subscribing to a podcast with iTunes is just as easy, if not easier than with Juice. Follow these steps to do so:

1. **Select Podcasts from the drop-down menu located on the left side in the top section.**

2. **Find the podcast of your choice.**

You can do that by

- Browsing the list of iTunes top episodes and podcasts featured on the right side of the iTunes window.

- Clicking See All on any category or listing.

- Searching by using the Search box in the upper right. Note, make sure you select Store in the top center so you aren't just searching your own library!

3. **When you get to the podcast page (and available podcasts) in iTunes, click the Subscribe button.**

After your podcast finishes downloading, you can find the new episodes by going to the Podcasts section in the left column of iTunes. The new episodes are marked to let you know that you have fresh content waiting for you, and iTunes remembers where you left off in a podcast if you pause or zip over to another podcast or playlist.

Podcatching on the go: Stitcher

As smartphones and tablets became more and more prevalent, the notion of having "an app for that" grew in demand. Finding and subscribing to podcasts in the early days of iTunes on a mobile device was possible, but a bit clunky. The stage had been set for a new kind of podcatcher that was just as easy and elegant to use on your mobile device as it would be on a computer.

Enter Stitcher, shown in Figure 1-7.

FIGURE 1-7:
Stitcher Radio, bringing podcasts and talk radio to your mobile device in a feed that customizes to your listening habits (left), can organize subscriptions on a Favorites list (middle), and gives you control over the episode playing through your smart device (right).

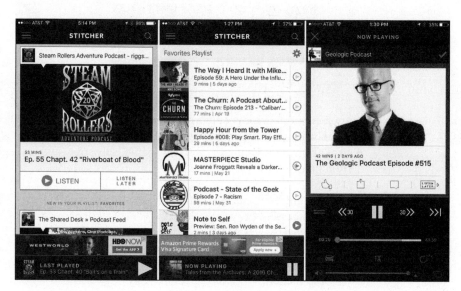

Stitcher Radio (www.stitcher.com with an app available for both iPhone and Android) debuted in 2008 and has quickly become a must-have for not only podcasts, but for radio shows coast-to-coast and around the world. On the app or on their computer, members of the Stitcher community "stitch" together on-air feeds from radio stations and podcasts both from professional and amateur studios into personalized stations all readily available on your mobile devices. Stitcher has become so popular, it joins Pandora as part of featured entertainment options in newer model cars.

Once you set up a free user account on Stitcher, finding a podcast for your personal feed is only a few taps away:

1. **Launch Stitcher on your mobile device.**

2. **Find the podcast of your choice.**

    You can do that by

- Tapping on the Search icon in the top right corner.

- Tapping on the Menu option in the top-left corner and tapping Browse Shows, which offers a variety of categories and sub-categories of interest

- Swiping up through the offered feeds on your Front Page. (The more you use Stitcher, the more shows matching your interests will appear here.)

3. **When you get to the podcast page (and available podcasts) in Stitcher, click the Listen button.**

4. **When the podcast plays, you should see a plus sign (+) to the right. Tap that, and the podcast now appears on your Favorites Playlist (see Figure 1-8).**

FIGURE 1-8: Tapping the plus sign next to the title of the podcast adds it to your Favorites Playlist.

Now you have your podcast feeds on a mobile device that can either play through your device, or through the media center of your car. Stitcher makes the portability of podcasts a piece of cake. It's an app you should have on your mobile device in order to make podcasting happen anywhere.

Podcasting with the G-man: Google Play

As mentioned earlier, Apple iOS users have their own app specifically dedicated to listening to podcasts. Not to be outdone, the diversified search engine service Google, along with Google Drive, Google Docs, and Google Voice, which we discuss later on, offers Google Play (at `https://play.google.com/store` with an app available from the same location) for Android users. It's just as good as it sounds: Google Play is Google's version of the iTunes Music app and the Pocasts app, all in one (see Figure 1-9).

FIGURE 1-9: Google Play, an alternative for Android users.

Google Play works with the Google Play Music app to bring podcasts to you in the same way Stitcher and Podcasts do. There are a few extra steps involved in getting podcasts subscribed and playing on your phone. Once you download Google Play Music and sync it up with your Google account:

1. **Launch Google Play Music on your mobile device, and then tap on the Menu option in the top left of the app screen.**

2. **Select Podcasts from the options.**

3. **Find the podcast of your choice.**

   You can do that by

   - Tapping on the Search icon in the upper-right corner.

   - Tapping on the All Categories option to reveal the top-rated podcasts of categories and sub-categories of interest.

   - Swiping through Top Charts, podcasts that are either promoted or popular. This is the main page of Google Play Music's Podcasts directory.

4. **When you find the podcast you want to listen to, click the Subscribe button.**

5. **Google Play Music will then offer a series of options for you to complete before subscribing.**

   - Select Auto-download if you want the latest content to update automatically.

   - Opt-in for a push notification when new content downloads.

   - Select a Playback Order if you want podcast episodes to go from oldest to newest, or newest to oldest.

6. **Tap Subscribe again.**

As seen by the Subscription process, Google Play Music's app is like many of Google's apps — it's a work-in-progress. With more people podcasting, there will probably be future editions of Google Play Music that will be smoother in their execution. Granted, if your loyalties are not to one operating system, Stitcher works for both iOS and Android users. Regardless of which app best suits you and your digital lifestyle, it's good to know options are out there and available for you.

Quest for Podcasts

Now that you have your podcatching client, it's time to take a good listen to what's happening in the podcasting community. If you're going to podcast (and with you picking up this book, it's a safe assumption that the interest is strong), it's a good idea to look around the podcasting community and see what other podcasters are doing.

Many podcatching clients have internal directories of podcasts, and you can access their listings from another directory or listing site maintained elsewhere on the Internet. Other aggregators maintain their own lists based on how many listeners have used their podcatcher to subscribe to particular shows.

Some of the more popular directories where podcasts can be found include:

> » **iTunes:** iTunes makes finding podcasts easy. The directory includes not only show information — searchable in a myriad of ways — but also the ability to listen to specific episodes, subscribe to a podcast with one click, visit the show's website, leave comments, and see the podcast picks of other people who share an interest in the show you're viewing.

>> **Stitcher:** The directories of both the website and mobile app are similar in that you can search top ranked or by categories for new podcasts. In the mobile app, however, individual episodes offer you the chance to Like an episode, share the episode across a variety of means (text messages, social media, and so on), or leave a comment specifically for that episode. You can also tell Stitcher you'll Listen Later, and it highlights the episode in your directory as a priority for another time. Figure 1-10 shows the Stitcher app.

FIGURE 1-10:
Use the Stitcher app to leave comments for podcasters, rate a show, or share the episode with friends online.

>> **Google Play Music:** While the actual online Google Play directory only features apps for podcasting, the actual Google Play Music apps offer you the ability to find listed podcasts. You can also share podcasts like you can with Stitcher, but the process is not necessarily as quick and easy as Stitcher. (Remember that whole work-in-progress we mentioned earlier?) You can have a look at your options with podcasts through Google Play Music at www.androidcentral.com/how-use-podcasts-google-play-music-android.

>> **Apple's Podcasts:** A separate app from the Music app, the Podcasts app for all Apple mobile devices allows you to search, subscribe, and manage your various podcasts. You can access show notes, share shows across a variety of platforms (like Stitcher), and even follow links referenced in show notes

to other locations. It is a robust app, and offers a lot of hidden options. (Tap through options offered, and you find out this is a layered app.) Figure 1-11 shows the Apple Podcasts app.

FIGURE 1-11: The Apple Podcasts app brings blog posts directly to your mobile device, and offers you options to share an episode across social networks.

>> **PlayIt:** Set up in a fashion like Stitcher, Play.It (`http://play.it`) offers podcasts in various categories ranging from Top Ranked to Shows of Interest. Unlike some directories that offer interaction, PlayIt keeps it simple with show art, show description, and brief episode descriptions. There are a few social share options, but brevity is the soul of wit with this directory.

REMEMBER

If you want people to find you on Stitcher Radio, you need to register your podcast in their network. Just registering a podcast on iTunes isn't enough. Same with Google Play. Each directory offering podcasts through its app may ask that you register with its network. Usually, it's a free service. All it costs you is time. It would not be a bad idea to have this information documented in a separate file so all you need to do from directory to directory is copy and paste.

We give you a few other places to get started in the following sections — directories, podcast-listing services, and even podcast-specific search engines. (Check out the various sources mentioned in Chapter 18 as well.) So where are these directories? Fire up your browser and, as Edgar Winter says, "Come on and take a free ride. . ."

TIP

There are so many directories for podcasts that Rob Walch of Podcast411 has put together a directory of directories (`http://podcast411.libsyn.com/directories`).

Other Podcast Resources

It goes without saying that this book is a snapshot in time, and you will likely want to keep up on the latest news and information of the podcasting world. We have a few suggestions to get you started. Perhaps, as you gain experience in podcasting, you'll share some of your pearls of wisdom with the community by contributing back to the vast universe of podcasting that many people like to call the *podosphere.* We recommend trying out these:

>> **Meetup.com:** When you go to `https://meetup.com` and enter *podcast,* you might be surprised to find others in your area doing podcasts as well. Meetup.com is a great place to organize anything from a meetup at a coffee shop to a group of 200 in a rented hall. If you don't spot anything, why not set up a podcast get together and see who responds.

>> **PodCamp:** Held around the world, a full schedule found at `http://podcamp.pbworks.com`, PodCamp is a community-based, community-driven, open-air conference. It is called PodCamp but these events are geared toward enthusiasts and professionals into podcasting, blogging, vlogging, and social networking. These PodCamps have been happening since 2006 and, *in most cases,* are free to the public.

>> **#TryPod:** At the time of this writing, a special event hosted by podcasters from all parts of the world is taking place. The event is called #TryPod (`http://legacy.wbur.org/about/blog/2017/03/03/trypod`). Podcasters are turning to social media platforms to share their shows with new and pod-curious listeners. By the time this book reaches print the event will be done, but looking up #TryPod may just introduce you to some fantastic online talent.

>> **Podcasts about podcasting:** Rob Walsh has one. Elsie Escobar has one. Daniel J. Lewis also has one. Heck, we have one for this book! Podcasters love talking shop so why not search for podcasts on how to podcast? It sounds pretty meta, sure, but if Tom Felton can deliver *Harry Potter* and *Planet of the Apes* references with a straight face while guest starring on CW's *The Flash,* then searching for podcasts on how to podcasts shouldn't be a challenge for anybody.

Chapter **2**

Getting the Gadgets That Make a Podcast Go

N ow that you're effectively hip as to what podcasting is and what it's all about, you need to start building your studio. This studio can come in a variety of shapes, sizes, and price tags. What you're thinking about doing — podcasting — is like any hobby you pursue. If it's something to pass the time, then keep your setup simple. A modest setup with little to no investment is ideal if you want to see whether you like playing with audio. If, on the other hand, you find yourself tapping into a hidden passion or (even better) talent, you might want to upgrade to the audio gear that's bigger, better, and *badder* than the basics.

If you suddenly decide you — yes, you — have a message you want to share, your next plan of action will be one of two options: picking up a digital recorder, reading the instruction manual, and then downloading some free audio-editing software — or watching the DIY Network for methods of soundproofing the basement and looking at industry-standard equipment that might require some extra homework to master.

This is the beauty of podcasting. In the long run, it doesn't matter whether your podcasting studio is a smartphone with a plug-in microphone or comprised of the latest mixing boards, audio software, and recording equipment. Both approaches to podcasting work and are successfully implemented on a variety of podcasts.

So which one works best for what you have in mind? That's what we look at in this chapter, discussing the options, advantages, and disadvantages of each setup.

Finding the Right Mic

It's easy and affordable to make your computer podcast-capable. Your first order of business is to find the right mic. If you already have a microphone built into your laptop (and you don't mind starting out basic), you can just download Audacity (described in Chapter 3) and take advantage of the fact that it's free. That's all there is to it! (For openers, anyway.)

However, if your desktop computer didn't come with a mic (or you're just not happy podcasting Quasimodo-style), you're going to want to shop around. While microphone shopping, consider the following criteria:

>> **What's your price range?** In many cases, especially with inexpensive mics, you get what you pay for in quality of construction and range of capabilities. You want the most affordable model of microphone that will do the job for you and your podcast.

>> **Do you plan to use the mic primarily in the studio or on location?** A high-end shockmounted model isn't the best choice for a walk in the park, and a lapel mic might not provide you with the quality of sound expected for an in-studio podcast. Before you purchase your mic, consider your podcasting location needs.

REMEMBER

There are many different types of microphones and microphone connections (or jacks). Some mics are meant to plug in to mixers while others connect directly to your computer's USB port. If you're thinking of starting with an inexpensive mic, you may not be able to plug it in to your "upgraded" rig later. Depending on your needs, you may find yourself upgrading more than just your microphone down the road.

>> **What do you want this mic to do?** Record sound? Yeah, okay, but what kind and in what surroundings? Some mics offer ease of handling for interviews. Some are good at snagging specific outdoor sounds. Others may be better at capturing live music. You need to consider multipurpose mics, guest mics, and on-location recording devices, or any kind of condition your podcast provides for you.

Even after narrowing your options, there are so many microphones on the market. After a while, the manufacturers, makes, and models all start to give you that kind of brain-freeze you get when you eat ice cream too quickly. The sections that follow give you the lowdown on the mic that's right for your budget and even make a few *sound* recommendations along the way.

TIP

In Season Three of this book's companion podcast, *Podcasting For Dummies: The Companion Podcast,* Tee and Chuck host several episodes concerning microphones, including one where they test several makes and models, comparing the sound of each. To find out more about microphones, gadgets, and concepts, listen to *Podcasting For Dummies: The Companion Podcast,* available at www.podcastingfordummies.com.

Mics on the cheap

Most of the economical microphones on the market use USB (Universal Serial Bus) hookups. Figure 2-1 shows two types of USB plugs, which you may have used for attaching a digital camera or an MP3 player. You can go online to any of the computer equipment retailers and type **USB microphones** in their respective search engines. Make sure you include **USB**, because a search for microphones can bring up many more alternatives, including video cameras, high-end mics (which we talk about next), and other devices that might be way out of your budget.

REMEMBER

You don't have to sacrifice your retirement fund to get started with a USB microphone. Prices start under $20 for a simple desktop microphone. The phrase "you get what you pay for" doesn't always apply in podcasting. We've heard some amazing sounds out of very inexpensive microphones.

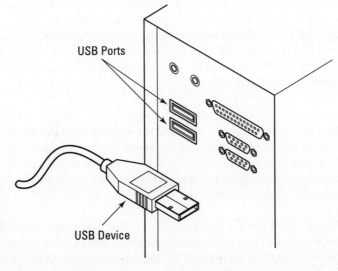

FIGURE 2-1:
The USB ports and connectors on both the computer and the mic.

When shopping for microphones, you'll hear a lot of terminology like *omnidirectional* and *unidirectional.* These multisyllabic words may look cool to type and are impressive to say, but when you read them or they're spoken to you, they can be a little intimidating. In the next two sections, we demystify these terms and explain how effective these various mic types are for podcasting.

Omnidirectional mics

Most microphones that come preinstalled in laptops are *omnidirectional* — they pick up sounds from all directions at once. You can find a fair number of omnidirectional microphones that plug in to your mobile phone for under $10. Omnidirectional mics pick up your voice, along with the television in the background, the traffic outside, the rustling of clothes, the ceiling fan . . . basically, if it makes noise and is within range of the mic, it's recorded.

Although omnidirectional mics are ideal for *sound-seeing tours* (audio tours that incorporate surrounding sounds for ambiance) they may not be ideal for all in-studio podcasting because they don't capture your sound in detail — even when your mouth is so close that your lips brush against the mic's screen. They tend to add a sharp, tinny quality to your voice and cut out on harsh, sudden sounds such as consonants (especially *p*s and *t*s). That's partly because basic omnidirectional mics vary widely in quality and partly because of the limits imposed by their construction. The built-in models, for instance, are sometimes crammed into leftover nooks in their devices, where they're awkward to use and can pick up internal noise.

The most basic of omnidirectional desktop mics available would be Audio-Technica's ATR-4750, currently retailing for about $13, compatible with both Mac and Windows platforms, and connecting with a 3.5 mm stereo (1/8″″) mini-plug. There are omnidirectional mics that come with headphones. Logitech (www.logitech.com) offers a wide variety of headsets built with microphones beginning at just under $30, offering you the ability to record and monitor yourself as you do so.

One advantage headsets have over a desktop microphone is that your mouth is always the same distance away from the actual part of the microphone that picks up sound. If you're an animated podcaster like your authors, this may be useful. On the other hand, they can be very sensitive to breathing sounds. If the mic boom is in the wrong position, the slightest breath from your mouth or nose will sound like an EF5 tornado passing by.

REMEMBER

Although purchasing a USB headset is a monetary plus because you're getting both headphones and mic together with one purchase, this isn't all you need to monitor yourself as you record. To self-monitor your recording, you need software that offers you an on-screen mixer, a mixing board, or the option to monitor the incoming audio signal.

Installation for these inexpensive investments can be a breeze. Find a USB port your Mac or PC, plug in your new headset or microphone, and set up your au preferences in your recording software. You're ready for recording.

Unidirectional mics

Unidirectional mics, unlike their omnidirectional brethren, pick up sound from only one direction: the direction they're pointing. What makes unidirectional mics a good choice for podcasting is in how by design they filter out surrounding sounds, reproducing only the sound directed to it. For in-studio podcasting, interviews, and quality recording, unidirectional microphones are the best option.

If you want to know exactly what a unidirectional mic is and what it can do, take a look at the Brian DePalma film, *Blow Out.* John Travolta plays a Foley Artist, a guy who collects random sound effects and then enhances them for particular moments in whatever film he's working on. One night, he takes a stroll through the park with a *shotgun microphone,* a certain kind of unidirectional mic that picks up only sounds located where it is pointing. This microphone is so particular that it concentrates on recording along the line of sight — so it records not only the sound of a tire blowing out, but also the gunshot that causes it to happen.

If you're out shopping for a unidirectional microphone, watch for the term *cardioid.* It relates to the pattern and sensitivity of the microphone. And if you have a podcast that's out in the field and want to be able to surrender the mic to guests and subjects without worry, look no further than the *MXL 770* (see Figure 2-2). This mic, like many in the Marshall line, offers fantastic audio results for an economic investment. Podcasters can pick up the MXL 770 for under $100 and get years of reliability and quality out of it.

FIGURE 2-2:
Dr. Stacia Kelly of
the *Geek Wolfpack
Podcast* relies on
the MXL 770 for
all her recording
needs.

Investing in a high-end mic

So you can go cheap and pick up a microphone for as little as ten dollars, but let's be honest here — you're going to sound like you've been recorded by a ten-dollar microphone. Say, however, you really want that sharp, professional sound for your podcast, and the cheaper microphones just aren't cutting it for you. As you shop for an upgrade, you see mics ranging in price from an inexpensive $70 and reaching up to $3,600! (No, you're not seeing a typo involving an extra zero.) So what defines a microphone? Price? Manufacturer? Look?

What truly defines a microphone is how you sound in it and how it reproduces the sound coming in. Based on how mics work, prices vary, but as you can see from our recommendations, plenty of high-quality microphones that are out there can pick up nuances and details and remain in the range of affordability.

WARNING

When you purchase a higher-end microphone, keep in mind that you probably will receive no additional cables for hookup, a jack that does not fit into your computer, and no stand. That's because you're upgrading to professional equipment. The manufacturer is assuming that you already have the tools, bells and whistles, and extra do-dads to make this mic work for you. For the lowdown on what accessories you need to hook up your new mic to your computer, check out the "Accessorize! Accessorize! Accessorize!" section later in this chapter.

Remember those three questions a few pages back? Question #2 — *Do you plan to use the mic primarily in the studio or on location?* — helps narrow your search even more for the microphone that's the right investment for you. At this level, there are two kinds of mics you will hear people talk about: *dynamic* and *condenser* mics.

REMEMBER

Although dynamic microphones are marketed more for on-location recording and condenser mics are considered best for in-studio recording, these aren't fast-and-hard rules for what mics should be used where. Sometimes, podcasters use condensers in outdoor settings, and some podcasters prefer the sound of dynamic mics in studio over condensers. When picking a microphone, you want a mic that not only suits your needs but also makes you sound good. *Really* good.

Dynamic mics

Dynamic mics are what you see everywhere from speaking engagements to rock concerts. In fact, when someone mentions the word *microphone*, the image that comes to mind is probably a dynamic microphone. These mics work like a speaker in reverse. Sound entering a dynamic mic (by speaking directly into it) vibrates a *diaphragm* (a small plate) attached to a coil. This is located within proximity of a magnet, and the vibrations that this Wile E. Coyote setup makes create a small electric current. When this signal runs through a preamp or mixer, the original sound is re-created. This system sounds complicated (and if you've ever looked inside of a microphone, it is), but the internal makeup of dynamic microphones is such that they can take a lot of incoming signal and still produce audio clearly. They're also rugged in build so they can be manhandled, making dynamic mics exceptional for outdoor recording.

If you're working in-studio, consider working with Heil Microphones' PR40 (pictured in Figure 2-3). This mic offers up a clean, rich sound and picks up incredible details for a dynamic microphone. For microphones you may want to use out in the field, the Røde Reporter (`www.rode.com/microphones/reporter`), is specifically designed for handheld interviews, and delivers broadcast-quality results within any environment.

FIGURE 2-3: Brandon Kelly, co-host of *Happy Hour from the Tower: A Destiny Podcast*, records his own deeds in the Crucible on the Heil PR40.

Condenser mics

When podcasting happens in studio and you're looking for the subtleties and nuances of the human voice in your recording (the more detail you get, the better!), you may want to shop for studio *condenser* microphones. The anatomy of a condenser microphone is very different from a dynamic one. In the condenser, a diaphragm (similar to the dynamic's) is suspended in front of a stationary plate that conducts electricity. As a signal enters the microphone, the air between the diaphragm and the plate is displaced, creating a fluctuating electrical charge. Once given a bit more power (*phantom power*, which is explained later in this chapter), the movement becomes an electrical representation of the incoming audio signal.

A SHURE-FIRE INVESTMENT

If you were born after 1980, do yourself a favor and find on Netflix or borrow from a friend the comedy classic, *The Blues Brothers*. Aside from *many* tropes you see in movies now (that started with this movie), there is one joke that — thanks to podcasting — will make sense to you. Jake (John Belushi) turns to Elwood (Dan Aykroyd), after looking over the "new used" car his brother is driving, and asks him what happened to their Cadillac. "I traded it," Elwood replies, "for a microphone." Jake leans forward, a little stunned. "You traded the Bluesmobile *for a microphone?!?*" Then, on reflection, he nods. "All right, I can see that." There are differences between the economic $20 USB microphones and the more expensive dynamic and condenser microphones, and there are even bigger differences between the $100 microphones and the $700 microphones.

The Shure SM7B was the first *industry* microphone Tee ever had in *Imagine That!* Studios. This was a microphone that, for its price, could easily cover two mixers and two high-end microphones, and this was a *dynamic* microphone, a kind of microphone that Tee wasn't accustomed to working with in studio. He had recorded with this mic before though, in locations such as the Washington, D.C. WJFK and NPR affiliates in the DC-metro area. Now, it was in his studio, and after his first recording project, Tee understood — with the mic's clarity and exceptional performance — exactly why Shure microphones are considered the industry standard when it comes to recording equipment, be it in-studio or on location recording.

Microphones can be an investment, worth the trade-in of a car in Jake and Elwood's case. What you invest in a microphone will reflect in the quality of its sound. For Tee, the investment was the right one. But is such an investment right for you? Be sure that you and your podcast are ready for this kind of studio asset. Ask other podcasters what they use — we're happy to brag, er, talk about our gear, try out microphones if vendors allow for such test drives, and take your time before making such an investment.

This setup sounds very delicate, doesn't it? Guess what — it is! This is why condenser mics are transported in padded cases; they're not really built for hand-held use and are best used in a studio application (as shown in Figure 2-4) versus an on-location kind of podcast. If manhandled or jostled around, plates can be knocked out of whack or damaged, causing problems in the pick-ups.

FIGURE 2-4:
The MXL 990 captures professional quality sound in home studio settings for a reasonable investment.

The advantage to this delicate setup is that condenser mics are far more sensitive to sound, and they pick up a wider spectrum of audio. These microphones are so sensitive to noise around them that some come with *shockmounts* — spring-loaded frames that suspend the mic when attached to a microphone stand, providing better reception while reducing any noise or vibration from your microphone stand. Think of a shockmount as a shock absorber for your mic.

TIP

If you plan to have a studio with multiple guests, the sensitivity of several condenser microphones can be a liability and will degrade the overall sound of your podcast. The sound from one person's voice will be picked up not only on that person's mic, but also on the other mics as a "distant" sound. For multi-mic podcasts in the same location, consider dynamic microphones.

Tee is a big fan of MXL microphones, mentioned earlier in this chapter. His first in-studio microphone was an MXL 990, a model he still podcasts with to this day. MXL microphones, along with being affordable, reliable, and popular, often come bundled with *mixer boards* (discussed in the section, "Podcasts Well with Others: The Mixing Board," later in this chapter). Online vendors like BSW (www.bswusa.com) offer podcast bundles featuring another MXL microphone, the BCD-1. With each bundle offering new accessories, cost and features go up, but the quality sound that the MXL line captures remains the same.

USB Studio Condenser mics

Microphone vendors are noting the popularity of podcasting, and now *USB Studio Condenser* microphones are becoming more and more prevalent. Blue's Snowball iCE ($50) and Yeti Pro ($270) are solid examples of what is now available for podcasters working on tight budgets. With these microphone models, podcasters can now record studio quality audio without an additional audio card, a mixer, or any of the go-betweens once considered essential for connecting audio gear to a computer. With USB condenser microphones, the audio signal now has a direct connection to the computer. It makes your podcast production extremely portable.

Two drawbacks of USB microphones:

» **Latency** is the slight echo you hear in your voice as you record. This is your computer trying to re-create the signal in real time for monitoring purposes. The recording itself will sound fine, but as you're monitoring yourself, you may hear yourself echoing, and the echo may progressively get worse the longer you record one session, depending on your computer's performance. A faster computer can reduce the latency but likely not resolve it completely. You can side-step the latency problem by disabling the recording application's monitor or use the built-in headphone jack provided with many USB microphones.

>> **Expandability** is another issue. While USB microphones are quick and easy to set up, there's no good way to connect more than one to a computer at a time. If you are planning to have your best friend as a co-host or have an in-studio interview guest, then consider microphones that connect to a mixing board.

High end is relative. Professional recording studios can spend hundreds of dollars on a single microphone. Fortunately, the MP3 format isn't so finicky. For this book, we're defining *high-end* microphones as those ranging from $100 and up.

Podcasts Well with Others: The Mixing Board

If you're looking to have more people in studio or you want to entertain guests on your podcast, you need more than just a good microphone. (Otherwise there will be the passing back and forth of a mic, and that'll get distracting after a while.) You also need inputs for more microphones and full control over these multiple microphones.

Along with good microphones (and probably *microphone stands*, discussed later in the "Accessorize! Accessorize! Accessorize!" section), you will want to invest in a *mixing board.* What a mixing board (or *mixer*) does for your podcast is open up the recording options, such as multiple hosts or guests, recording acoustic instruments, and balancing sound to emphasize one voice over another or balance both seamlessly.

You see mixers at rock concerts and in behind-the-scenes documentaries for the film and recording industry. They come in all shapes and sizes; Figure 2-5 shows the Behringer Q1202USB mixer. For under $100 you can connect four microphones and several additional stereo inputs and feed them directly in to the USB port on your computer.

Before you take your mixer out of its packing, make sure you have room for it somewhere on the desk or general area where you intend to podcast. Something you'll want to consider is how close you want to be to the mixer. An ideal reach for your mixer is a short one. Whether it's you recording yourself or balancing the levels of those around you, clear off a section within a relaxed reach. You'll be happier because of it.

FIGURE 2-5:
The Behringer
Q1202USB, a
reliable and
fantastic mixing
board for
podcasting.

The anatomy of a mixing board

The easiest way to look at a mixing board is as if you're partitioning your computer into different recording studios. But instead of calling them *studios*, these partitions are called *tracks*.

A mixing board provides mono tracks and stereo tracks, and you can use any of those tracks for input *or* output of audio signals. No matter the make or model, mixing boards are outrageously versatile. If you're podcasting with a friend, you can hook up two mics through a mixer so you won't have to huddle around the same microphone or slide it back and forth as you take turns speaking. Multiple microphones are the best option when you and your friends gather around to record. A real advantage of the mixer is that it allows you to adjust the audio levels of those multiple inputs independently so they sound even.

You may also be wondering about all those wacky knobs on a mixing board. Some of the knobs deal with various frequencies in your voice and can deepen, sharpen, or soften the qualities of your voice, and perhaps even help filter out surrounding *background noise* (which is the sound of an empty room because even in silence, there is noise). The knobs on the mixing board that are your primary concern are the ones that control your volume or *levels*, as the board labels them. The higher the level, the more input signal your voice gains when recording. If one of your tracks is being used for output, the level dictates how loud the playback through your headphones is.

TIP

Heavy-metal legends Spinal Tap may prefer sound equipment that "goes to 11," but cranking your mixing board way up and leaving it that way won't do your podcast much good. The best way to handle sound is to set your levels before podcasting. That's what's going on when you see roadies at a concert do a mic check. The oh-so-familiar "Check One, Check Two, Check-Check-Check . . ." is one way of setting your levels, but a better method is just rambling on as if you were podcasting and then adjusting your sound levels according to your recording application's volume unit (VU) meter. For more on setting levels, hop to Chapter 7 for all the details.

ANALOG VERSUS DIGITAL

So you decide to go mixer shopping and you see a lot of these mixers going for $40 or $50, and in some cases the same number of inputs at two to three times the cost. What gives?

Before rushing off and making a purchase you may regret later, understand the major types of mixers and the features they have. The two different types of mixers are *analog* and *digital.* What makes a digital mixer a digital mixer is how it processes the signals internally before it gets sent to your computer or recording device. Analog mixers have the benefit of being simple to set up, configure, and in the case of those with USB or FireWire interfaces — yes, analog mixers can have digital outputs — easy to connect. The drawback is they are 'hard wired' in their configuration and any additional signal processing needs to be done with additional hardware.

What kind of processing, you ask? Compression to bring up low spots and dampen loud spots, or a gate which can set a threshold (a minimal noise level) before getting through to the mixer. These are nice features to help clean up the audio, but not mandatory. Digital mixers take the inputs from microphones, instruments, and other devices, and turn them in to a digital signal inside the mixer. They often have on-board compressors and gates for each channel and often complex input and output routing configuration.

Most podcasters don't need this level of sophistication, but Chuck Tomasi isn't most people. After his Tascam DM-4800 mixer gets done processing everything, the audio still comes out the back and connects to his Zoom H6 recorder with an analog jack. Yes, it has an option for a FireWire card, but he's never opted to get it.

In the case of mixers, you *do* get what you pay for. Cheaper mixers often have inferior audio output because of cheap pre-amps or other components. They often are poorly constructed and don't last as long. For something that sits on the desk, it's amazing how much abuse a mixer can take. When considering how much to spend, use the same rule with mixers as computers — get as much as you can afford. Having a professional microphone with a low-end mixer can put your overall quality at risk.

(continued)

(continued)

Hooking up a mixer to your computer

Now that you have your desk cleaned off (mind the dust bunnies!) and a perfect place for the mixer, set your mixer where you want it. And then make certain you can see the following items:

>> Your USB or FireWire mixer

>> A power supply

>> A USB or FireWire cable

TIP

Before hooking up the new mixer, check the manufacturer's website for any downloads (drivers, upgrades to firmware, patches, and so on) needed to make your digital mixing board work.

USB and FireWire mixers are so similar in setup that we can give the same steps for both kinds of mixers. Regardless of where you fall in the Mac/PC debate, you can follow these steps to hook up your mixer board:

1. **Shut down your computer.**

2. **Connect the power supply to the back of the mixer and to an available wall socket or power strip.**

3. **Find an available USB or FireWire port and plug your mixer-appropriate cable into the computer.**

   If your computer's ports are maxed out, we recommend investing in a PCI card that gives your computer additional USB or FireWire ports. Do not run your digital mixer through a hub because that will affect the quality of the audio.

   A direct connection between your mixer and computer is the best.

REMEMBER

4. **Plug the USB or FireWire cable into the back of your mixer.**

5. **Connect your input devices (microphones, headphones, monitors, and the like) to the mixer.**

6. **Power up your mixer by turning on the Main Power and the Phantom Power switches. See Figure 2-6.**

FIGURE 2-6: Power switches for the board and for phantom power can be found on the backs and channels of mixing boards, depending on model (Mackie Onyx 820i, pictured here).

7. **Start your computer.**

8. **Install any drivers your USB/FireWire mixer may need.**

   Follow the instructions according to the manufacturer's enclosed documentation. Restart your computer if necessary.

THE G-TRACK: THE BEST OF BOTH WORLDS

So far we've been talking about microphones and mixers as being two separate entities, but Samson Technologies decided to take the audio equivalent of chocolate and peanut butter and combine them into one sweet device: *The G-Track,* shown in the figure.

This microphone is a lot more than just a studio condenser mic. The G-Track has inputs *built directly into the mic* for an additional audio source (labeled as *Instrument* but it can really be for any audio input) and for headphones. With the mic's basic interface, you can now mix in secondary audio with little to no crossbleed from whoever is on the mic. All this, and the microphone is completely USB-powered, the latency kept at a minimum as the headphone jack is closer to the signal than a computer's or mixer's headphone jack. The G-Track is a completely portable studio condenser mic solution; for a pod-caster into music, mixing, or simply on-the-go, this mic's potential can really get the audiophile's creative juices going.

And that's it! You're ready to record with your USB or FireWire mixer. Now with headphones on your head and some toying around, you can set levels on your mixer good for recording.

TIP

Before filing away the reference manual that came with your mixer, be sure you know how things work. Buttons like the *Mix to Control Room* suddenly make sense to you as opposed to being "that button that needs to be down when I record." Getting a grasp of how things work on your mixer only makes you a better podcaster, so keep that reference manual close by and set aside a few pockets of time to clock in some reading time with it.

Accessorize! Accessorize! Accessorize!

A microphone and a mixing board are just the beginning when it comes to putting together your audio suite. You now need to add the final touches, as Martha Stewart would no doubt tell you if she were helping you with this process. Now when it comes to accessories, Martha might make suggestions like a doily for the mic stand or a sweet, hand-knitted cover for the mixer. When we talk about accessories, we have something different in mind. Here are some optional add-ons that can help you produce a rock-solid podcast:

TIP

>> **Headphones:** Headphones help you monitor yourself as you speak. That may seem a little indulgent, but by hearing your voice, you can catch before playback any odd trip-ups, slurred words, or missed pronunciations.

We suggest you invest in good headphones before you spend a lot of money on a better mic, or else you won't know how good the microphone is. Good headphones are nice to have for monitoring, but really show their value during the editing and mastering process.

Another advantage with headphones is they have better sound quality than your computer's speakers as well as reduce ambient noise around you if you purchase what are called *closed-ear headphones*. Keep it simple for your first time out with a pair of the *Sennheiser HD202* closed-ear headphones for around $35. These headphones end in a ⅛-inch jack but come with an adaptor that makes them a ¼-inch stereo male jack (as shown in Figure 2-7), plugging directly into your mixing board.

FIGURE 2-7:
A ¼-inch male connection, which is needed to connect headphones to a mixing board.

Bose Noise Cancelling stereo headphones, going for $300, promise the highest quality for audio listening. Note, we say *listening*. Not *recording* and *editing*. Any headphones you see listed as noise-cancelling are going to be terrific for listening to audio, but those headphones aren't the best for recording and editing. You want to be able to hear the noise that these headphones cancel out so that you can eliminate it before a word is recorded. The best noise reduction and elimination happens before and during recording, not afterward. For podcast production, stick with closed-ear headphones sans the noise-cancelling feature.

>> **Cables:** As mentioned in the section "Investing in a high-end mic," earlier in the chapter, your newfangled microphone may arrive without any cable — and buying the wrong cable can be easy if you don't know jack (so to speak). So check the mic's connector before you buy. With many high-end mics, the connectors aren't the typical RCA prongs or the ¼-inch jack shown in Figure 2-7; instead, you use a three-prong connection: a 3-pin XLR male plug. It connects to a 3-pin XLR *female* plug, as shown in Figure 2-8.

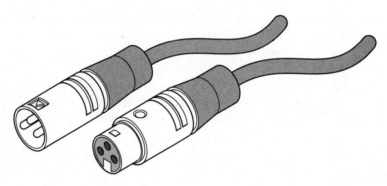

FIGURE 2-8:
XLR male and female plugs, standard plugs for phantom-powered microphones.

To plug a microphone into your mixer, you want to specify a *3-pin XLR-to-XLR male-to-female* cord; the female end connects to the mic, the male end to the mixer. These cables begin at $9 and work their way up, depending on the length of the cord and quality of the inputs.

>> **Microphone stands:** On receiving the microphone and possibly its shock-mount, you may notice the attachment for a mic stand . . . but no mic stand comes with your new mic. It's your responsibility to provide one, and although that may sound like an easy buy, your options for mic stands are many, each with its advantages.

A simple *desktop mic stand* can run you around $10 and is the most basic of setups. When shopping for the right height and make, you'll notice other stands like a *boom mic stand* around the $100 range. The type of mic stand that is best for you depends on what you want it to do and how you want to work around it. With the inexpensive desktop stand, you're ready to go without the extra hassle of positioning and securing a boom stand to your desk. The boom stand, though, frees up space on your desk, allowing for show notes and extra space for you to record and mix in. Consult your budget and see what works for you.

>> **Pop filters and windscreens:** Go to any music store and ask for *pop filters* and *windscreens,* which are both shown in Figure 2-9. Both devices can help soften explosive consonants (percussive ones like *B* and *P*) during a recording session. A windscreen can also reduce some ambient room noise. Using both on one mic could be overkill, but these are terrific add-ons to your microphones.

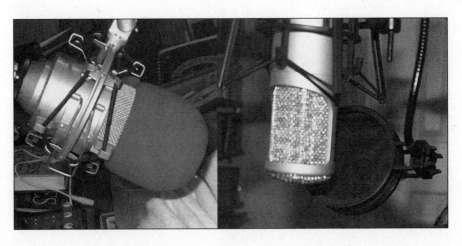

FIGURE 2-9:
Windscreens (left) and pop filters (right) help you control unwanted noise and percussive consonants (such as *P* and *B*) during recording.

WARNING

It is worth mentioning that there are DIY tutorials on YouTube, blogs, and elsewhere that will show you how to make pop filters with a stick and panty hose. Just remember: You get what you pay for. With the time, experimentation, and jerry-rigging to save yourself $10-$20, it's less stress for you to just go and pick up a proper pop filter.

Chapter **3**

Building Your Podcast's Digital Workstation

After you have your recording equipment in place, plugged in, and running, it's time to look at *audio-editing* software packages. These are the applications that help you take that block of audio marble and chisel the podcast hidden within it. (If you are looking to branch into video podcasting or incorporating video segments into your podcasting feed, see Chapter 9 for information about video-editing software.)

As with digital photo editors, DVD-authoring software, and word processors, software for audio comes in all sizes and all costs, ranging from free to roughly an entire paycheck (or three). Like any software package, the lower the cost, the simpler the product and the easier it is to understand, navigate, and use for recording. However, as the software grows more complex (and expensive), the features that offer advantages for pro-level work become abundantly clear. In this chapter, we run down some of the audio recording/editing software that might be right for you.

TIP

When you have software and hardware in place, test your setup to make sure everything works. Check your application's preferences to make sure that your sound input and output are going through your mixer, bring up the volume on the channel on the mixing board that your microphone is connected to, and then listen to yourself through your headphones. Just make sure everything is running as promised so you can jump right in and get recording.

Budget-Friendly Software

Whoever said, "You can't get something for nothing . . ." didn't know about podcasting. It's amazing what kind of product you can turn out with little or no monetary investment.

Audacity: The risk-free option for all

Audacity (shown in Figure 3-1) is a piece of software that quickly became a podcaster's best friend. It's easy to see why: It's free and simple to use. It's available for download at http://audacity.audio.

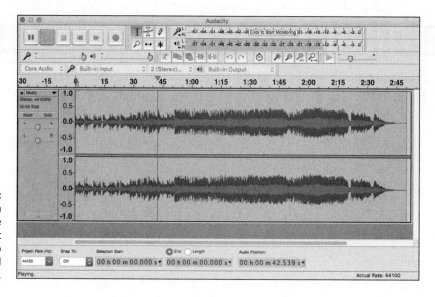

FIGURE 3-1:
Audacity is a freeware application that allows you to edit audio and create MP3 files.

Designed by volunteers who simply wanted to give something cool back to the Internet, Audacity is designed for a variety of audio capabilities such as importing, mixing, editing, and exporting audio. For podcasters, it's become the must-have tool for recording voice straight off a computer. It's also compatible with Windows, Macintosh, *and* Linux. (We want to send a big thank you to the volunteers who went out of their way to show that yes, software can be made available for *any* platform, provided the creators are driven enough to make it happen!)

>> Records live audio through microphones or mixer channels

>> Can record up to 16 channels at once

>> Imports various sound formats for editing and remixing

- » Exports final projects to WAV, AIFF, MP3, and many other audio formats

- » Grants the user unlimited Undo and Redo commands

- » Can create an unlimited number of audio tracks

- » Removes static, hiss, hum, and other constant background noises

- » Offers a wide variety of effects to manipulate your audio (and these effects are expandable via third-party plug-ins)

- » Records at an audio quality of up to 384 kHz

WARNING

Make sure you access the right URL. Remember that the URL for Audacity is `http://audacityteam.org` and *not* `www.audacity.com`. If you happen to enter the latter address in your browser, you find yourself at a banking software consulting service.

Cakewalk's SONAR Home Studio for Windows: A first step in running with the pros

Audacity is an excellent piece of software for the basics, but what if you desire more control over the capabilities and features of your audio-editing package? Are you looking for more recording options, additional audio filters, built-in multi-track recording, and prerecorded music loops? (Gads, what some people will do to set a mood or a tone for a podcast.)

SONAR Home Studio (`www.cakewalk.com/Products/SONAR-Home-Studio`) is the consumer line of Cakewalk's SONAR audio software line. If your computer has the horsepower and the hard drive space, you can buy SONAR Home Studio for around $50. This impressive digital audio workstation (or DAW) is available for Windows 10 and Windows 8 or 8.1.

SONAR Home Studio (shown in Figure 3-2) offers its users some serious goodies:

- » Record audio from a microphone or other media (CD, LP, cassette, or Internet audio stream).

- » Display and edit beat-by-beat with audio waveform displays.

- » Pro-grade audio engineering tools included: Chorus/Flanger, Compressor/ Gate, Tempo Delay, Modifier, Reverb, and other post-production effects.

- » Support for MP3, WAV, and WMA files.

FIGURE 3-2:
Cakewalk's
SONAR Home
Studio provides
the Windows
podcaster with
engineering and
editing options at
an economic
investment.

SONAR Home Studio allows users to record, edit, mix, and produce audio compositions, whether it is an original score for your podcast, a continuous music mix, or just you and your own personal soundtrack. Between its easy audio-editing features and Cakewalk's collection of original audio samples (called *Cakewalk Loopmasters Content Collection*), it's a breeze to set your own themes and special effects.

GarageBand: Moby in your Mac!

SONAR Home Studio is an economic audio package for the Windows user looking to go beyond Audacity, but what about Mac users? For people in the minority of the computer world, it's always a frustration to hear software developers say, "No, we won't be making this product available for Mac users." Sometimes Mac users seem to be denied the coolest toys and utilities because they just aren't offered for the Mac operating system.

Apparently, the Apple crew heard about this injustice, and shortly after the iPod took off, there came a software gem that made it more than cool to be a Mac user — especially one who's into podcasting. Mac-using podcasters call this gem *GarageBand*.

With hundreds of music loops that can easily switch from one instrument to another, GarageBand (shown in Figure 3-3) makes royalty-free music easy to compose. Many of the loops are editable and, with a bit of tweaking, can set the right mood for your podcast. GarageBand has a few new additions:

>> Multitrack recording supports simultaneous tracks recording independent audio sources all in one recording session.

>> With the Multi-Take feature, you can now do multiple readings or segments and save them as separate files. Then you can pick which one you want for the final.

>> You can see a display of the music, with actual notation, in real time.

>> You can choose to record your podcast as a Music Composition (Old School podcasting with GarageBand) or take advantage of the extra features available in the Podcast mode; note the extra track at the top in Figure 3-3.

>> You can save the recordings as loops in the GarageBand library.

FIGURE 3-3:
GarageBand
(pictured here in
the Voice mode)
is easy to use and
easy to have a
blast with.

But perhaps the most amazing aspect of GarageBand, as reported by Arts Technica at https://arstechnica.com/apple/2017/04/iwork-and-ilife-apps-are-now-free-for-old-and-new-mac-and-ios-users, is that GarageBand is now *free* for anyone using a Mac OS or iOS device.

GarageBand's most appealing asset (apart from the fact that it is free now) is its hundreds of sampled instruments available in loops. You can easily edit and splice together these loops with other loops to create original music beds of whatever length you choose. Prerecorded beds range from Asian drum ensembles to Norwegian Folk Fiddles to Blues Harmonica to Emotional Piano reminiscent of films like *The Fault in Our Stars* and *Sense and Sensibility*.

GarageBand also provides a capability — with many (not all) of the samplings — to create your own musical theme. Sure, some instruments may sound better than others, but you might — with a bit of trial and error — create an original melody that serves as the best royalty-free intro and exit for your podcast.

If you're planning to do a bit of composing in GarageBand, be warned. Garage-Band is a lot of fun but can easily soak up free time that you would normally dedicate to recording. So if you need to get in touch with your inner Mozart, set aside a good-size pocket of time to put together your desired riffs. You have many options to choose from; as with podcasting, it's best not to rush the process.

GarageBand is easy to tinker with, navigate, and understand within a short span of time. Plenty of terrific books are available for mastering all the nuances of GarageBand. We cannot praise this application enough — and with expansion packs from Apple that add instruments, riffs, and loops to your GarageBand (always updated and stocked at the App Store), this unassuming software offers a lot to the podcaster.

SHARING WITH THE REST OF THE CLASS

We're particularly keen on GarageBand which gives you the option to organize your final AIFF files in an iTunes playlist. When you're done with that particular recording session (what GarageBand refers to as a *song*), choose Share ⇨ Song to iTunes. Before your final audio is exported, you are offered options to tag your audio with a variety of credits, including your own playlist. Once exporting concludes, iTunes opens with your new playlist. See Chapter 10 for details on adding ID3 tags.

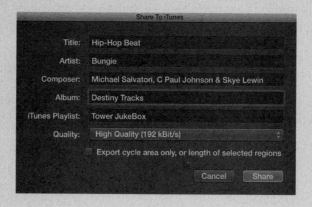

WireTap Studio: Recording and editing made easier

If you're not interested in the musicality of GarageBand, Mac users have another handy application for recording podcasts and it comes with a few features not found in Audacity. WireTap Studio Pro (www.ambrosiasw.com/utilities/wiretap and shown in Figure 3-4) is unique in its ability to record audio from nearly any source — not only coming in from microphones and musical instruments, but also from any audio streaming and live audio chats from Skype and iChat. WireTap even allows you to mix in music from your iTunes libraries!

WireTap sports the familiar features that Audacity, GarageBand, and SONAR possess — such as converting analog music to digital; preparing MP3 files specifically for podcasting (by adding ID3 tags, setting bandwidth, and so on); and supporting audio formats such as WAV, AIFF, and MP3. The latest version of WireTap offers some appealing capabilities:

» Records incoming audio from microphones or other input devices

» Records and encodes audio into a wide variety of file formats, including all the popular ones needed for podcasting (AIFF, WAV, MP3, AAC)

» Simultaneously records two sources of incoming audio (on a per-application basis) into separate tracks

» Provides a lossless/non-destructive waveform editor

>> Offers LivePreview, a monitor mode where you hear your recording at the compression rate and format you select

>> Provides basic ID3 tag editor

>> Offers automated options for scheduling recordings

Retailing for about $70, WireTap Studio is a reliable application for Macintosh podcasters and prides itself in being a one-stop shop for podcasting needs. It's a non-Apple product that can record in Apple's audio-compression formats, easily records streaming audio signals that tend to elude other audio-recording and editing software, and offers editing tools for both audio and ID3 tags so you can create the podcast from beginning to end, making it ready for upload.

The Sky's the Limit: Big-Budget Software

If you're lucky enough to have unlimited funds and resources to build your podcasting studio, this section on software is for you. Most podcasts are working on the bare-bones plan, and so far, the investment in the equipment we've recommended (in Chapter 2) is for a budget of under $500 — provided you feel like making an investment in a professional microphone, mixing board, or software.

REMEMBER

You may hear podcasters say, "content is king," meaning it doesn't matter how good you sound if you don't have anything to say. What makes a good podcast is the same whether you're on a budget of $0, $500, or $Ridiculous.

The difference is in the sound you can get. For the corporate entity, government agency, or professional organization venturing into podcasting, sound quality is crucial as your reputation and experience are now being socially tested. Do you not bother with the details, or do you raise the quality bar? Commercial podcasting demands nothing less than the best in audio quality. Depending on your budget and the future of your podcast, you can purchase and set up the higher-end audio hardware.

If you want to push its envelope and have the bucks, high-end audio software gives you full control over every aspect of the audio you're recording.

Adobe Audition

At one time, a favorite software application was CoolEdit. But when Adobe Systems purchased it and repackaged the software as Adobe Audition (shown in

Figure 3-5), it got even better. Audition (www.adobe.com/products/audition.html) is offered as part of the Adobe Creative Cloud membership for under $20 monthly. Audition's features are nothing short of awesome:

>> 128 tracks available to the user

>> Can record 32 different sources simultaneously

>> Offers 50 digital sound effects to enhance your audio tracks

>> Provides 5,000 royalty-free loops that can be easily edited and compiled to create your own music beds

>> Offers Surround Encoder for 5.1 surround sound mixing for audio only or integration into an Adobe Premiere Pro project

>> Offers audio restoration tools like Click/Pop Eliminators and Noise Reduction that can restore recordings from vinyl and cassette recordings; remedy pops, hisses, hums; and fix clipped audio

FIGURE 3-5: Adobe Audition (formerly CoolEdit) is the professional standard software for editing and engineering audio that gives the podcaster complete control.

What makes Audition so appealing to heavily engineered productions such as P.G. Holyfield's epic *Murder at Avedon Hill* (https://scribl.com/books/P4C82/murder-at-avedon-hill) and the ongoing Secret World Chronicle (http://secretworldchronicle.com) is the complete control users have over the audio. Audition gives you dominion over pitch, wavelength, time-stretching, background-noise removal, and Dolby 5.1 stereo output, making it a staple in the digital audio industry.

Audition runs on Windows and Macintosh platforms. If you know your podcast needs a professional polish and you are ready to make the investment and the jump to higher grade software, Audition may be the option for you.

Apple Logic Pro X

Apple Logic Pro X (www.apple.com/logic-pro) is another software package in the industry that is carving out for itself a place with professionals. Designed to be the next step after GarageBand, Logic Pro X (shown in Figure 3-6) has been given features built for Mac-based podcasters:

>> Supports multitrack recording.

>> Displays multiple audio takes in a single window. After you select your desired takes, Logic Pro X compiles them for a final composite — complete with *crossfades* (the simultaneous fading from one audio source into another) — creating seamless playback for the end result.

>> Copies audio effects and EQ settings from another clip — setting them on an audio clipboard for quick access and application or saving them as a preset for future use.

>> Features specific functions for producing podcasts, such as ID3 tagging.

>> Outputs multitrack audio projects into 5.1 surround sound.

>> Offers multiple audio formats for export including WAV, AIFF, and many others.

FIGURE 3-6:
Apple Logic Pro X is a fantastic tool for podcasters aiming for a professional polish to their production.

Apple Logic Pro X offers incredible options for the audio professional and the up-and-coming podcaster. For $200 from the App Store, you can accomplish a lot with it. Tee does, and swears by it.

Gluing It Together with RSS

The hardware (mics and mixers) and the software (GarageBand and Audacity) are necessary to record audio and create the podcast media file. That's the fun and creative part. But to make your recording a podcast, you need to get your hands dirty on the tedious and technical parts and add one more three-letter acronym to your vocabulary: *RSS.*

We've helped across these editions a huge number of podcasters get started — and in nearly every case, the RSS step is the biggest source of confusion. So, to get the basics out of the way, XML (eXtensible Markup Language) is a *markup language* like HTML (the building blocks of the Internet), and RSS (Really Simple Syndication) is a file format built on XML. XML's purpose is to allow systems such as computers, network devices, and other gadgets to exchange information in a structured format. The RSS file is that bit of information that the podcaster publishes so others can use their podcatching software to check for new content automatically. Without the RSS file, you are not podcasting.

If that somewhat technical explanation doesn't do it for you, try this old school analogy about deliverable content. Consider journalists for publications like *The Washington Post, The New York Times, Vanity Fair*, or *Wired Magazine* as authorities on what is happening within your passions in life. Whether the subject matter covers Apple computers, the Boston Red Sox, or The Beatles, you know these journalists are trusted experts in their fields, or maybe they are fellow fans just as passionate as you are. These journalists, if they are truly worth the ink used in their articles, are always creating new and unique content with every new issue or publication.

IS IT SOUP YET? NOT YET . . .

Regardless of the incarnations of this book or other books published on podcasting, there are people who think if media is posted on a blog or website and a graphic is placed over it that reads *Podcast,* you are podcasting media. No, you're not. If you post a video on YouTube (www.youtube.com) and then circulate that link through a blog, you are still *not* podcasting. Podcasting is a delivery of media from your blog to a consumer using RSS. Without that delivery, you are not casting anything, pod or otherwise. A podcast only happens when you have these three elements in place — a website or blog, some form of media, and an accompanying RSS feed to deliver the media relevant to the website or blog.

What if *you* want that content? Well, you've got options. You can check the news-stand daily. Maybe it's there, or maybe it is sold out on that day so you come back another time to see if the latest issue is there. Another way to get that content is to subscribe to the magazine or newspaper, and the content is delivered to your doorstep.

Here the role of the magazine is filled by the media created by the podcaster, and the RSS is the delivery mechanism that sends your podcast to people who *subscribe*. Just like you would with a magazine or newspaper.

No school like the old school, huh?

As a podcaster, your job is to make sure you keep the RSS updated and current each time you post a new podcast media file. Lucky for you (and us too), plenty of software solutions make this step a breeze.

IT'S ALL ABOUT THE <ENCLOSURE>, BABY

If you already have a blog, you're probably already generating an RSS feed — or can do so. Although podcatching clients can read this existing RSS feed, the feed needs to include the `<enclosure>` tag for podcasting to work.

Dave Winer invented the `<enclosure>` tag in early 2001 for embedding links to large audio, video, or other rich media elements into an RSS feed. At the time, Dave and Adam Curry were trying to solve the click-and-wait problems inherent in big files such as audio and video. Typically, if a user clicked a link to a 30MB file, several minutes would drag by before the file was completely downloaded to the user's hard drive and was usable. Not a good user experience, regardless of what's in the file.

With the advent of the `<enclosure>` RSS element, users could subscribe to places where they expected large files as a regular occurrence and move the downloading of those files to the early hours of the morning, when the users were snug in bed and a ten-minute download was no big deal.

Of course, users back then had to be technically savvy to take advantage of this new RSS element. It wasn't until the summer of 2004 that Adam Curry wrote what most consider the first podcatching client — a simple, user-friendly desktop program that extracted enclosed media files from RSS 2.0 feeds. And behold! Podcasting was born.

Keep it simple and get a blog!

If you're looking to spend the least amount of time dinking around with an RSS feed, look no further than starting up a blog. Easy to set up and often free of charge, blogs make the process of generating and updating RSS feeds insanely easy by doing it automatically.

You can choose from dozens of blog software packages (also called *engines*), each with a variety of bells and whistles that are designed to make your updates (including your RSS feed) as easy and/or customizable as possible. For a crash course in how blogs do what they do, check out *Blogging For Dummies*, by Brad Hill (Wiley). The title can help you choose which blog engine might be right for you. Meanwhile, here are a few options we prefer:

>> **WordPress** (https://wordpress.org): Perhaps the most popular blogging solution in writers' eyes, WordPress has many advantages over other free blogs. Not only is it easy to install and get running, but it also supports podcasting out of the box. When you incorporate the PowerPress plug-in (available at https://wordpress.org/plugins/powerpress), podcasting takes on a whole new level of user-friendly options. There are also thousands of WordPress and user-developed templates that can be used as is or customized to fit your specific look and feel for your podcast. Oh, and it's free. To make incorporation into your website seamless, many hosting companies like DreamHost (http://dreamhost.com) and GoDaddy (www.godaddy.com) offer packages that have WordPress preinstalled or installed with a one-click option. Figure 3-7 shows the WordPress signup page.

   If you choose to go the WordPress route, pay attention to the web address. There's Wordpress.org and Wordpress.com. The .org flavor is where you can download the software and install it on your server of choice and may involve a bit of technical work. The .com site has the software already installed and you just configure it; however, the configuration options are a bit more limited.

TECHNICAL STUFF

   There are two basic options where to put your blog, and prices and products vary from vendor to vendor. The *non-hosted model* blog is where you get to choose the blog engine, a great option if there is a specific engine you want to use. However, there is more work involved with setting it up and maintaining it. The other option, the *hosted model*, keeps things simple. The choice of blog engine is made for you. The trade-off for flexibility is ease of use.

>> **LibSyn** (http://libsyn.com): Don't be surprised if Liberated Syndication turns up quite a lot in this book. LibSyn, still going strong after launching in 2004, is a combined blog/hosting company specifically designed for podcasting. Although it may not address all your needs, its ease of use and all-in-one nature should not be passed up. Some podcasters choose to use

LibSyn as their hosted solution; others use it to store their podcast files while their blog is on a non-hosted solution somewhere else. Either way, we think LibSyn's pricing is quite reasonable, starting at $5 per month.

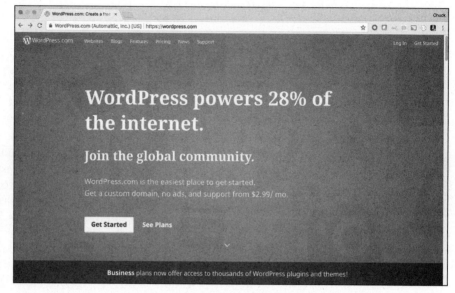

FIGURE 3-7:
WordPress is a popular, user-friendly blogging option that helps podcasters get their shows out into the world.

>> **Podbean** (www.podbean.com): Another popular all-in-one option with the added support of a podcast directory optimized for mobile devices, Podbean combines online hosting packages, podcast publishing tools, and crowdfunding services. Podbean, both in its website and mobile app, offers a user-friendly interface integrating feed and media management, syndication, and analytics, along with promotion through popular social media platforms like Facebook and Twitter. All this is available through affordable, flat-rate hosting plans. If you are starting off with baby steps, and then looking to take a deeper dive into podcasting, then Podbean is the right option for you and your podcast.

Doing it by hand

What's this about podcasting by hand? Are you crazy? No, seriously — generating an XML file in RSS 2.0 format isn't overly difficult. It's just extremely easy to mess up! Sure, you could open Notepad, TextEdit, or any text editor, download a few examples, and generate your own code, but we advise against it.

However, some code warriors — in the same vein of hand-coding HTML, JavaScript, and other markup languages — insist on composing their own code from the ground up. You glutton for punishment, you.

Whether you are running your podcast on a home-spun, handmade RSS feed, or letting WordPress handle the heavy lifting, you're going to want to make sure your feed is solid and ready for prime time. That's when *Feed Validator* is your best friend and harshest critic. Go to http://feedvalidator.org and enter your feed's URL (not the host blog or site, but the *feed* itself) and then click the Validate button. Feed Validator tells you whether your RSS is air-tight. You can also find the full technical specifications for RSS 2.0 and a few answers to questions you may have about RSS. This is a great place to visit not only when you're about to launch a podcast but also when your feed suddenly stops working. When something is borked in your podcast, Feed Validator is the first place you will want to visit.

Podcast Management 101

Unless you already have hosting taken care of, you're going to need a place on the web to put your stuff. You know — your podcast media files, RSS feed, and show notes for your podcast. You also need a way to get them up there.

Getting a hosting provider is a breeze, with hundreds of companies all vying for your precious, hard-earned money each month. The good news is that all this competition has brought down the cost of hosting packages significantly. The bad news is that you must go through a lot of clutter to reach the right selection.

This section covers the basic needs for most beginning podcasts and mentions a few pitfalls to watch out for. In Chapter 11, we get into the process of actually moving your files to your host.

Don't rush into a hosting agreement just yet. We suggest reading the rest of this chapter as well as Chapter 11 before forking over your credit card. We cover lots of good information that can help you narrow your choices.

When you're comparing hosting plans, try not to get bogged down in the number of email addresses, MySQL databases, subdomains, and the like. All those features have their own purposes, but as a podcaster, you have only two worries: how many podcasts the site can hold and how much bandwidth you get.

Size does matter

Podcast media files, especially video files, are big. Unlike bloggers, podcasters eat up server space. Where simple text files and a few images take up a relatively small space, podcast media files tend to be in the 5MB to 50MB range. And that's just for audio. For video, that size can double.

Here are some suggestions for zeroing in on what you need storage-space-wise:

» Think about how many podcasts you want to keep online and plan accordingly. If you have a plan that isn't constrained by storage space, then you don't need to worry about it.

» Consider the amount of server space you'll need to host your blogging software, databases, text, and image files. For example, if Tee wanted to keep all episodes of *The Shared Desk, The Ministry of Peculiar Occurrences,* and *Happy Hour from the Tower* online, he would easily need several gigabytes of space as one of these shows first went online in 2010. Podcasting did help quite a bit in creating a need for server space.

Podcasters should look for hosting plans that include at least 3GB of storage space. As of this writing, several host providers charge less than $10 per month for that much space, and more.

Bandwidth demystified

Of equal importance to storage space is bandwidth, an elusive and often-misunderstood attribute of web hosting that is critical to podcasters. *Bandwidth* refers to the online space needed to handle the amount of stuff you push out of your website every month. The bigger the files, the more bandwidth consumed. Compounding the problem, the more requests for the files, the more bandwidth consumed.

For instance, the bandwidth for Chuck Tomasi's *Technorama* is over 10 terabytes a month — that's impressive. Why so huge? Chuck and his co-host Kreg just celebrated their 500th episode. They've been at podcasting since the very beginning, and at their initial launch, the amount of information exchanged (read: downloads) was modest, but then people started talking. With the rise in popularity (thanks to top-shelf interviews with people in the science and entertainment industries), their downloads increased. So did the demands on bandwidth. Web hosts, in situations like this, must consider when it's time to allocate a larger bandwidth package to handle a show — and that means more cash outlay for you.

And therein lies the double-edged sword of success. Most podcasters want more listeners — and that means more podcatching clients requesting the podcast media files. Bottom line: The more popular your show gets, the more bandwidth is being consumed every month.

To simplify, pretend that you produce one show each week, and your show requires 10MB of bandwidth. You publish the show on Monday, and your 100 subscribers receive your show that evening. You've just consumed 1,000MB of bandwidth ($100 \times 10MB$) for that week. But next week, more people have found out about your incredibly amazing show, and now you have 200 subscribers. Next Monday, your bandwidth increases to 2,000MB, which gets added to your previous week's total to bring you up to 3,000MB. The new listeners were so happy, they also download the previous week's show, tacking on an extra 1,000MB. You've just consumed 4,000MB (or 4GB) of bandwidth for the month. You still have two weeks to go in the month, and if your numbers continue to climb like this, you will be burning through bandwidth (and your web host budget) quickly!

Generally, the longer your podcast episodes are, the more bandwidth you will need. If you find a plan that offers unlimited bandwidth, the problem is solved. Otherwise, you'll want to try and find a plan that's high in the gigabytes. If you have a podcast that's both long and popular, start looking at plans that offer 1TB (that's *tera*bytes) or more.

You have ways to avoid the issue of bandwidth, or at least make it less of a concern even if you have large ambitions — as well as files. Chapter 11 talks about some podcast-specific and some advanced hosting options. Even if you don't think you'll have to worry about bandwidth, it's a section to pay close attention to because you'll likely be more popular — and perhaps wordier — than you think.

Chapter **4**

Go, Go, Power Podcasters!

U p to this point, you have been building your podcast studio with your home computer as the center of your digital audio workstation. You have a mixer plugged with a few mics, and you have your software up and running. Or maybe you have a USB mic hooked up to your desktop computer (directly, and not through a USB hub, remember?), and you have Audacity primed and ready to go. Welcome to your new audio recording studio.

But hold on — what if you want to record someplace else? What do you need to do to pack up the whole recording unit and take this show on the road? What if your podcast isn't about where you are but where you are going?

That's why we're spending some quality time on portability in this chapter. The aim is to be able to pack up your podcast and set up wherever you stop. Yes, yes, yes, we know — podcasts are portable by nature, but we're talking about packing up the studio and working on location. You're not going to have the podcast here. In this chapter, you're taking the studio to go.

TIP

When you have software and hardware in place, especially when you are working remotely, test your setup to make sure everything works. Look at your System Preferences to make sure you are working with the proper sound input and output sources, make certain your levels are solid, and then run a quick sound check through your headphones. It is a good idea to make sure everything is running as promised so you can jump right in and get recording.

Podcasting with Your Laptop

So, you want to have a podcast that has that studio quality sound, but you want more than one microphone, and to be able to have a bit of control over the levels. This is when you would want to invest in a preamplifier or a *preamp*. To understand what a preamp is, you should know a few more technical matters around microphones.

Microphones, be they condenser or dynamic, record their signals at *mic-level*. This is the signal created from the internal diaphragm moving back and forth against a magnet in a wire coil, generating an electrical signal. It's a clean signal, but very weak. The best audio is recorded not at mic-level, but at *line-level*. You get line-level signals coming out of electric guitars, keyboards, and other instruments. To get a weaker mic-level signal boosted to the line-level signal, you need more power. The preamp, sometimes a separate unit or built into a mixer board or a USB microphone, provides that power to bring the mic-level signal to line-level without adding any noise to the original signal.

Now that you know what a preamp is, how about a few options for you to consider?

Mackie Onyx Blackjack

The *Mackie Onyx Blackjack* (shown in Figure 4-1) offers you all the power and reliability of a mixer in a small, compact design. The best part of working with this preamp is it has zero latency when recording. This means there is no delay for when you speak and when you hear your voice while recording. You can adjust the Blackjack's buffer settings to maximize your computer's processing ability as well.

Blackjack also offers podcasters:

>> A preamp bus-powered via USB

>> Two XLR connections delivering 48V phantom power

>> A 25-degree inclination by design, allowing for full view of all controls at all times

>> An all-metal chassis that gives the Blackjack built-like-a-tank durability

>> Onboard analog-to-digital conversion, granting your amplified signal with the lowest noise and distortion possible

FIGURE 4-1:
The Mackie Onyx
Blackjack
provides a boost
to your incoming
mic-level signal in
a compact design,
making it
extremely
portable.

Shure MVi

Shure Audio, a manufacturer we named back in Chapter 2, is no stranger to setting the bar for audio engineering and recording on looking at the prevalence and relevance of their audio gear. With the rise of podcasting, Shure set out to create gear that would capture quality sound, and the *MVi* is a compact, USB-powered preamp ready to power your microphone (or microphones, if you employ a splitter) accordingly. Figure 4-2 shows Shure's MVi.

The MVi offers a podcaster-on-the-go:

>> USB connectivity for easy plug-and-play with optional iOS connectivity with iPhones and iPads

>> Touch-sensitive panel for control over five different DSP presets, headphone volume, and more

>> Built-in headphone jack for real-time monitoring

>> One XLR connection offering 48V phantom power option

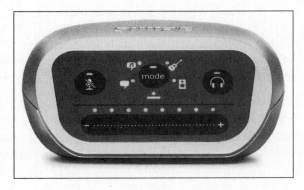

FIGURE 4-2:
Shure's MVi, a
component of
the new MOTIV
series, is a
preamp designed
with desktop
computers and
mobile devices
in mind.

If you want to record on location, you could use Studio Condenser mics which, because of their sensitivity, will pick up a lot of the background, setting a nice ambiance for your podcast. Depending on your environment, though, there might be too much ambiance for your interview. This is why, in most on-location settings, dynamic mics are preferred. You will still get some background noise, but not as pronounced when using Studio Condenser mics.

The Shure MVi can serve as a preamp for up to two microphones, powered by USB, just as the Onyx Blackjack. With an even more compact design, the MVi makes your portable studio even more so.

Podcasting with Your Mobile Devices

Development of mobile devices — smartphones like the iPhone and Samsung Galaxy, and tablets like Apple's iPad and the Windows Surface — has been astounding to watch, especially in the past five years. With cloud computing becoming more and more prevalent not only in personal lifestyles but now in corporate sectors, mobile devices big and small are quickly becoming the new alternative to portable computing. When once it would require an entire backpack and pockets of accessories to replicate the office, mobile devices have reduced portability to a single pocket and a connection to the Internet.

As an example, Nobilis Reed of *Nobilis Erotica* and *This Kaiju Life* has a portable recording rig with a USB microphone, a smartphone, and Dropbox (see Figure 4-3). His sessions are all sent to cloud storage (relieving demands on the phone) and are easily accessed by his editing computer.

Now, leading names in microphone technology are looking to future trends and are releasing new audio gear designed for the portability you come expect from smartphones and tablets.

You may notice the featured photos throughout this chapter are somewhat Mac-centric as both Tee and Chuck are using iPads and iPhones. This does not affect the ability of these innovations to float easily from platform-to-platform. What we showcase here, equipment-wise, does not discriminate from one operating system to another. It's all in the ability to connect.

FIGURE 4-3:
Nobilis Reed of
Nobilis Erotica and
This Kaiju Life has
a portable record-
ing rig with a USB
microphone, a
smartphone, and
Dropbox.

A Shure Thing: The MV5 and MV51

Shure Audio's MOTIV series not only includes a preamp but also a new line of microphones built to be portable, but still able to yield superior audio recording quality Shure is known for.

The MV5

The *MV5* (shown in Figure 4-4) packs a lot of audio punch in its small, sleek, retro design and its economic cost of just under $100. Offering you professional-quality audio when recording, the MV5 provides latency-free headphone monitoring and quick-and-easy plug-and-play capability.

Other features of the MV5 include:

>> Retro-design includes desktop stand and adjustable position for microphone

>> Three digital signal processor (or DSP) presets

>> iOS and USB connectivity

>> Built-in headphone jack and volume adjustment for real-time monitoring

The MV51

The *MV51* (shown in Figure 4-4) is much like its small counterpart, the MV5, in its retro design, ability to capture professional-quality audio, and zero latency when live monitoring. Beyond that, the MV51 is a fantastic addition to your ultra-portable studio because of the additional features found only in this higher model:

>> Quick-and-easy plug-and-play capability

>> Retro-design includes pull-out stand, either for standing independently on a flat surface or fitting into a standard microphone stand

>> Touch-sensitive panel for control over five different DSP presets, headphone volume, and more

>> iOS and USB connectivity

>> Built-in headphone jack for real-time monitoring

>> Large-diaphragm condenser capsule offering wider audio range for recording

The MV51 is more than just a step up from the MV5. It promises to set a new standard in mobile recording. With its capability to capture clean audio, setup and recording is as simple as unlocking your mobile device and recording on your audio app of choice. You are also given advanced options such as either recording with one of the MV51's onboard presets or simply recording flat, uncompressed, unaltered audio, offering you full control over post-production treatment. Whether in-studio or on-the-road, at $200 the Shure MV51 proves itself an asset in your mobile studio setup.

Two for the Røde: The VideoMic Me and smartLav+

Røde Microphones (http://en.rode.com) has made a name for itself in the podcasting circles (or the *podosphere*) since the early days. New Zealand's first podcast author, Pip Ballantine (http://pjballantine.com), won the 2009 Sir Julius Voguel Award for her podcast *Chasing the Bard,* recording her epic fantasy on the Røde Podcaster (http://en.rode.com/microphones/podcaster). Pip still endorses the USB microphone, suggesting it to everyone building a new home studio on a tight budget.

Røde continues to provide podcasters with a complete array of mobile options for podcasters ready to take their recording out of the studio, and go one step further in specializing gear for smartphones. Why smartphones? Particularly in interview situations where sitting is not an option (press conferences, man on the street interviews, and so forth), you need your recording rig to be even more compact than a tablet. That is where your smartphone transforms faster than an Autobot (or a Decepticon, depending on the mobile OS you prefer) and becomes your recording studio.

VideoMic Me

Røde's VideoMic Me (shown in Figure 4-5) at the cost of just under $60 upgrades your on-board smartphone microphone to higher-quality audio. Instead of that tinny quality found in most phone conversations and smartphone recordings, the VideoMic Me picks up a far wider range and frequency, while focusing the direction of the mic, yielding audio of a much higher quality. The accessory also comes with an optional mount for better mic stability and a windscreen to cut down on any unexpected weather elements you might encounter.

WARNING

In turning smartphones into portable recording devices, you may find your recording riddled with intermittent static. This is *RFI,* or *Radio Frequency Interference.* RFI occurs when a disturbance in frequency is generated by an external source — in this case, a second microphone — causing a degradation of a signal. Static. You can try recording in Airplane mode, but this prevents you from doing anything online (such as Facebook Live or Periscope), and even then, it is no guarantee. As always, test your mobile rig before trying to capture that once-in-a-lifetime recording!

smartLav+

For the podcast more about the host or for the interview where the interview host is edited out of the final show and only the subject's voice remains, the *smartLav+* at a cost similar to that of the VideoMic Me offers broadcast-quality audio for a modest investment. The smartLav+ is a *lavalier mic,* meaning it is not held by or pointed at the subject but worn on lapels or the collar of a host or guest's shirt. Unlike other lavalier mics that are connected to a wireless transmitter, the smartLav+ connects directly into a smartphone or tablet headset jack and records using GarageBand, Røde's own Rec app, or any other media-recording app of choice. A small windscreen is included to cut down on both wind noise and percussive vocal elements.

FIGURE 4-5:
Røde's VideoMic Me (top) transforms your smartphone into a handheld recording device.

The smartLav+ also features:

- » A Kevlar reinforced cable, protecting your mic connection from unexpected stretching or fraying
- » High-quality omni-directional condenser mic design
- » A body design no larger than 4.5mm

TECHNICAL STUFF

At the time of this writing, many smartphones in use are still using headphone jacks. Before purchasing these suggested models or other attachments that turn your smartphone into an equally smart recorder, you will want to see how the accessory connects, just to assure you are picking up the accessory that is the right one for you.

When you find yourself in the kind of setting where your podcast studio needs to fit in the palm of your hand, Røde offers options that will not let you down. There is a reason that *Podcasting For Dummies* recommended Røde's products back in the second edition and continues to do so now. We use them, and yield great results on account of that company's work. So, if your tablet is not portable enough, consider Røde or other audio vendors that convert your preferred smartphone into a super-portable recording rig.

Podcasting with Portable Recorders

Up to this point we have gone from podcasting with laptop computers to podcasting with mobile devices. Now we take everything we need to record and reduce it to a fully contained recording studio that fits comfortably in the palm of your hand.

Zoom-Zoom-Zoom: The Handy Recorder Line

In 2006, Zoom Technologies (https://www.zoom.co.jp) introduced its own series of portable recorders that raised the bar for not only portable podcasting but for portable recorders across the market. With each new model, Zoom upped its own game. Now, Zoom offers an entire line of lightweight, unobtrusive, all-in-one solutions for portable podcasting; a new standard arrived.

Zoom H1

The H1 Handy Recorder is the smallest, sleekest of the Handy Recorder series. It also has the simplest of interfaces: one button. And yes, that is the one you use to get the recording underway. Along with ease of use, the H1 offers:

>> Onboard X/Y microphones configuration.

>> Recording formats include both WAV and MP3 in different bitrates and varying quality.

>> Reference speaker and tripod mounts built-in.

>> 1/8-inch external mic input and 1/8-inch stereo line output.

>> Records directly to MicroSD and SDHC cards up to 32 GB capacity.

Zoom H2n

The H2n is the next step up and the evolution from the popular H2 that debuted over a decade ago. The new and improved H2n makes portable recording a piece of cake:

>> Five built-in mic capsules offering multiple recording modes, including stereo, 90° X/Y stereo, 2-channel, and 4-channel

>> Recording formats include both WAV and MP3 in different bitrates and varying quality

>> Built-in studio-grade emulators, including Low-cut Filter, Compressor/Limiter, Auto Gain, Tuner, Normalize, and Surround Mixer

>> 1/8-inch external mic input and 1/8-inch stereo line output

>> Records directly to MicroSD and SDHC cards up to 32 GB capacity

>> 20 hours of operation on two standard AA batteries

Zoom H4n Pro

The H4n Pro (shown in Figure 4-6) sets a new standard for portable podcasting as it delivers a wide array of features building on the previous models. It features

>> Four-channel audio recording, able to record either in stereo or mono

>> Two XLR connections with both 24V and 48V phantom power options

>> Two-Input/Two-Output USB audio interface

>> Built-in studio-grade instrument effects and emulators

>> Onboard X/Y microphones able to emulate a variety of condenser and dynamic microphones

>> Capable of recording up to 140 dB SPL

>> Recording formats that include both WAV and MP3 in different bitrates and varying quality

>> Records directly to SD and SDHC cards up to 32 GB capacity

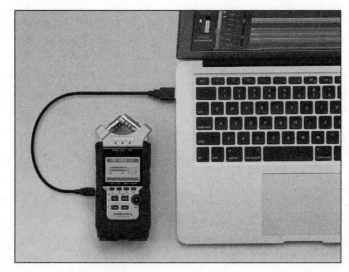

FIGURE 4-6:
The Zoom H4n Pro is the latest portable recorder that sets new standards for recording on the go.

Zoom H5 & H6

Maybe you need more than the H4n Pro offers, and if that is the case you need to look at Zoom's H5 and H6. Both these portable recorders offer all the functionality and features found in the previous models (as you would expect), but the H5 and H6 offer more options for your on-the-go studio.

>> Interchangeable input capsules that can be swapped out as easily as the lens of a camera

>> Multichannel and stereo USB audio interface for PC/Mac/iPad

>> Recording formats that include both WAV and MP3 in different bitrates and varying quality

>> Four-channel (H5) and six-channel (H6) audio recording

IT'S A PREAMP! IT'S A RECORDER! KIDS . . . IT'S A PREAMP *AND* A RECORDER!

The preamp is a terrific way to get studio-quality sound while recording portably. If you want to be able to work on a laptop and still be able to take your studio completely on-the-go, however, the Zoom Handy Recorders have got you covered.

The H4n-H5-H6 models can all operate in the field as recording devices, and you can easily plug in an XLR microphone (the Røde Reporter, for example) and conduct the interview right there on the spot. However, if you have an on-location spot secured and want to set up more XLR microphones for a round-table discussion where participants have their own mics, these models can easily plug in via an available USB port and serve as a preamp for your laptop.

And if that isn't versatile enough, you can attach any of the Handy Recorders to a USB port and use it as a USB-powered microphone.

>> Two (H5) and four (H6) XLR connection ports with various phantom power options

>> Records directly to SD and SDHC cards up to 32GB capacity (H5) and SD, SDHC, and SDXC cards up to 128GB (H6)

>> Mountable to DSLR or camcorder with optional HS-01 Hot Shoe Mount adapter (H5)

There are other portable recorders out there — TASCAM and Roland, for example — but Zoom has established itself as a reliable, durable, and affordable option for field and on-location recording. Depending on what you need for your podcast, you no longer need to worry about remaining tethered to a studio.

TIP

Before recording, always check that you have enough storage on your recording device. Most portable records will have an indicator to show how many hours or minutes can fit on the remaining storage. For mobile phones, go to your system settings and ensure you have approximately 1MB available for each minute of audio you want to record (much more for video). Chapter 10 gets into more nitty-gritty details about settings and storage considerations.

WARNING

As noted earlier, RFI can be a real downer when recording. Even with portable recorders, ensure your mobile devices are a safe distance from your recording device as phone's radio signals can leave a telltale buzzing/beeping noise and ruin your recording. Just ask Ben and Keith of *The Two Gay Geeks Podcast* (http://tggeeks.com) when they recorded a 90-minute interview with Kevin Schindler at the Lowell Observatory in Flagstaff, Arizona in 2016. Keith used his phone to prop up his recorder and it sounded like a video game was being played the entire time. Fortunately, Chuck was there and had a second recording of the same interview which was unaffected and happily shared it — because that's what podcasters do!

From Cloud to Computer: Portable Audio Workflow

Now that you know how portable you want your podcast to be, how exactly will the workflow differ from the usual editing work in a studio? There are a few different approaches to consider when working portably. It's not a dramatic switch. It's more of how to get the audio from your mobile devices to your studio.

Getting audio from your portable recorder

After you finish recording with your portable recorder, you have audio sitting in your portable recorder. How do you get it from the recorder to the computer you are editing your podcast on?

Here's some good news — the hard part of getting great audio for your podcast is done. Getting the audio to the computer? That's the easy part:

1. **Connect the portable recorder to an available USB port.**

   You should have a USB cable that is USB 2.0 A to Mini-B. The A tab goes to your computer. The Mini-B attaches to your portable recorder.

2. **The portable recorder's interface should give you either Storage or Audio I/F as an option. Select Audio Storage from the menu.**

   Audio I/F is the option for using your portable recorder as a USB microphone or preamp for your computer. In Storage mode, as shown in Figure 4-7, the portable recorder (and the SD card inside it) mounts onto your desktop as an external drive.

3. **Once your portable player mounts as a drive, select the drive. Then select the folder labeled in the mode you used for recording.**

   Depending on the model of portable recorders, you may see folders labeled with offered recording modes. That should be where your audio is stored.

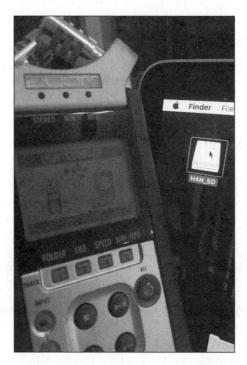

FIGURE 4-7:
Portable
recorders, when
connected to
your computer
via USB, mount
on your desktop
as an external
drive.

4. **Find your latest recording, and then drag it to where you are storing your audio sessions.**

   Whether you are working on an internal drive, an external drive, or cloud storage, you now have copied your audio file source from the recorder to your workspace. You can now begin the post-production process.

TIP

It is typically quicker to transfer files from your portable recorder to your computer directly rather than use USB. If your computer has an SD card reader, you can remove the SD card from your portable recorder and place it in the SD card reader for faster copying. Just be sure you observe good practice and properly eject the media before pulling the SD card out of the computer and returning it to your portable recorder!

Getting audio from your portable device

With your smartphone or tablet, it's a little different environment. Instead of a hard drive or an SD card, you have internal flash memory that will quickly fill up if you are saving audio or video files directly on your device. To work with your audio recorded on your mobile device, you need to transfer it to some sort of cloud storage service. The workflow we created for this section incorporates Dropbox as the cloud service, an iPad for the portable device, and GarageBand for iOS as the audio recorder.

1. **Before transferring audio, check to make sure that your cloud service's app is loaded and synced with your mobile device.**

2. **Launch GarageBand.**

   If you have been working on a project, GarageBand will open on the last project you were working on, or default to an audio recording interface.

3. **If you are in a project, tap on My Songs in the upper-left corner of window.**

4. **Tap the Select option in the top-right corner of the app.**

5. **Find the project you want to export and tap it once to select it.**

   The project(s) you want to export will be highlighted in blue.

6. **Tap the Share option in the top-left corner of the app.**

   The Share function (shown in Figure 4-8) accesses which apps can share the media you are about to export. If you cannot find the app you want to share to, find the More option to add your cloud service app.

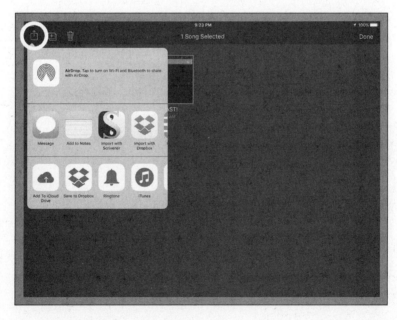

FIGURE 4-8:
From the Share icon (upper left), apps are offered where your media can be shared.

7. **Tap your cloud service app.**

   In the case of Dropbox and iPad, tap the Save to Dropbox option to begin the export process.

8. **Edit the Info for the file and then select Audio Quality from the offered options. Single tap Share to begin the exporting process.**

    In GarageBand, you can select from three formats: MP3, Apple Lossless (m4a), and AIFF.

9. **Select the location where you want to save your media and then tap the Save option in the upper-right corner of the Save window.**

Your media has now been exported on to your cloud service, and is waiting for you to edit or prepare for uploading.

WARNING

While you can record and export audio to MP3, it is never a good idea to make an MP3 from another MP3. It is the audio equivalent of making a compressed JPEG image from another JPEG image. Always strive to record in a raw, uncompressed format such as AIFF or WAV files. It takes more space initially, but produces better results.

2

The Hills Are Alive with the Sound of Podcasting

Understand the steps involved before hitting the record button, such as topic, posting frequency, and episode duration.

Unlock the art of the interview including interview prep, which questions to ask (and not to ask), which software options are available for interviewers, and how to query for interviews.

Record with confidence after sound checks, level checks, and ensure your software is ready to record.

Add production value to your podcast with intros, outros, bed music, and simple editing.

Take your podcast to a whole new level with video.

Chapter **5**

Before You Hit the Record Button

Tune to a classical radio station (and when we refer to *classics* here, we mean Beethoven and Haydn, not The Beatles and Hendrix) and listen to the DJs — oh, sorry, the *on-air personalities* — featured there. You'll notice that they're all speaking slowly and articulately, mellowed and obviously relaxed by the melodic creations of greats such as Mozart, Wagner, and Joel. (Yes, Billy Joel has a classical album — a pretty good one, too!) Although the on-air personalities of your local classical music station all sound alike, they sound dramatically different from the wacky Morning Zoo guys on your contemporary hits radio station who sound as if they're on their eighth cup of espresso.

When you hear people talk about *finding your voice* in broadcasting, that's what they mean. You come to an understanding of what your average audience wants (and to some degree, expects), and then you meet that need. This chapter helps you develop the voice and personality you want to convey when podcasting.

After you discover your voice, you will want to get ready for the show. This chapter shows you what to do to prepare for smooth and easy podcasts that (one can hope) will be glitch-free during the recording process. Preshow prep is essential when making a feed worth catching. Even the most spontaneous podcasts follow a logical progression and general direction, and remain focused on the podcast's intent.

Choosing a Unique Topic for Your Podcast

Before you can think about putting together a podcast, you need to decide what topic you want to cover. At the time of this writing, a sample of what people were podcasting (according to statista.com [http://statista.com/] at the end of 2015) — listed by the top ten categories — looked like this:

Topic	Number of shows (approximate)
Christian	39,000
Music	33,600
Comedy	14,200
TV and Film	12,800
Literature	10,600
News and Politics	10,200
Video Games	7,000
Sports	6,700
Management and Marketing	5,200
Personal Journals	4,300

That's a total of 143,600 podcasts — up from 36,540 from the second edition of this book published in 2008. That's a lot of growth!

The first thing to understand about podcasts is that this activity isn't all about being "number one" in your chosen podcast genre. Granted, some podcasts do vie for top honors on various polls, but instead of worrying about garnering ratings and awards, think about what will make your podcast uniquely worth your effort and your listeners' time. The point in launching a podcast isn't always "I want to do something totally new . . ." but more about "What do I have to say about this topic?"

Here are some ways you can create a unique podcast:

>> **Study other podcasts.** Before you can figure out what will make your podcast unique, check out some other podcasts. The best way to find out what makes a podcast worthwhile is to subscribe to a few feeds that pique your curiosity.

Listen to these feeds for a few weeks (provided they're weekly) and jot down what you like and don't like about them. From the notes you take, you might find your angle. Keep in mind that downloading and listening to other podcasts should be educational and constructive, not a raid for fodder for your own show.

WARNING

Don't steal content, special effects, or unique segments (like "On This Day in Tech History" or "The Loot Crate Lookie-Loo") from another podcast. Approach others' podcasts as you would someone's website. It's okay to be inspired; just don't make your podcast a carbon copy of your inspiration's work. When you have your podcast up, avoid criticizing another podcast in your own. Criticizing someone else's work is no way to better yours. It is better to show support for other podcasts and the podcasting community on a whole rather than insult or trash other people's hard work.

In other words, stay on the pod-sitive side. It's better for you and the community.

>> **Pick a topic you know.** Whether you've decided to take on the topic of music, religion, or technology, the best way to make your podcast unique is to find an angle you're comfortable with (Polka: The Misunderstood Music, Great Travesties of Sports History, Forgotten Greats of Science Fiction). There's also the possibility that your initial show may inspire an additional angle so unique that you'll have to start another podcast specifically to address that audience.

>> **Speak confidently.** Don't apologize for being "yet another podcast on . . ." or point out what you are doing wrong compared to others. What makes a podcast fun is the passion and the confidence you exude when the mics are hot. Address your topic with authority and energy, and enjoy your time recording. If you have a blast making a podcast, your audience will enjoy it along with you. That confidence might even inspire others to podcast themselves. That was how it happened with podcaster Joe Hogan and his first podcast, *Geektitude* (shown in Figure 5-1 and found online at http://geektitude.com). His confidence and passion for the geek lifestyle inspired others like the *Geek Wolfpack Podcast* to launch their own podcasts.

REMEMBER

The content you bring — regardless of what genre it's in — is unique because it is *your* podcast. It's your voice, your angle, and your approach to whatever intent you pursue. Provided you maintain a high confidence level and genuinely enjoy what you're doing, people will tune in and talk to other listeners about what you're podcasting.

Finding Your Voice

The broadcasting industry might not want to admit to this, but podcasting and commercial radio share a lot in common. In the early days of what is now a major radio genre, talk shows were reserved for National Public Radio and news stations. In general, they were pretty dry and lackluster, bringing their listeners the news, weather, and daily topics that affected the world — but nothing particularly unusual or exciting.

Then a guy named Howard Stern came along and changed everything in this once-tiny niche. You can love him, you can hate him — you can claim to hate him when secretly you love him — but Stern completely turned around what was considered AM-only programming. Now talk radio is big business. Some personalities are just out to entertain, other hosts deep dive into lifestyles and subjects of interest, and others use it to voice their political viewpoints.

The majority of podcasting is just that: talk radio. Each podcast has a different personality and appeals to a different market. Finding your voice is one of the most challenging obstacles that you (as a once-and-future podcaster) must clear. Even if your podcast's aim is entertainment, you have a message you want to convey. That message will influence the voice you adopt for your podcast. If you're podcasting an audio blog about life, its challenges, and the ups and downs that you encounter, then maybe a soft tone — relaxed and somewhat pensive — would be appropriate. But if you decide to go political — say you're the Angry Young Man who's fed up with the current business on Capitol Hill — then it's time to fine-tune the edge in your voice. That's what you need for a podcast of this nature.

After you discover the passion your podcast is centered around (see the preceding section for tips on how to do that), here are some ways to *find your voice:*

- » **Record your voice and then listen to what it sounds like.** It astounds us how many people hate listening to their recorded voice. It's a fear akin to getting up in front of people and speaking. When finding your voice, though, you need to hear what your current voice sounds like. Write a paragraph on your show's subject. Then read it aloud a few times and find a rhythm in your words. Expect the following:

  - Talking too fast

  - Swallowing small, one-syllable words like *to, in*

  - Ignoring commas, thereby creating one long, run-on thought

  - Lip-smacking, heavy breathing, and the unavoidable *ahs* and *ums*

  You can edit out some of these problems (see Chapter 8), but you should grow accustomed to hearing your own voice because you'll hear yourself again and again . . . and again . . . during the editing process. The more familiar you are with how your voice sounds, the easier time you'll have editing your podcasts before publishing them online.

- » **Play around with the rhythm of your speech.** You don't have to be an actor to podcast, but you can apply some basics of acting when you're recording. One of these basics, as one of Tee's acting professors told him, is to "make a meal of your words." This means to play around with the rhythm of your speech. When you want to make a point, slow down. If you're feeling a tad smarmy, pick up the pace. Above all, be relaxed and make sure you don't sound too contrived or melodramatic.

- » **Speak clearly.** Another simple trick from the acting world to add to your arsenal is to open your mouth wider. Many people talk with their mouths mostly closed, but by opening your mouth wider, you can gain clarity. So, when making a meal of your words, it *is* good manners to chew with your mouth open.

- » **Speak with confidence.** Yes, we're saying this again, because it bears repeating: Speak confidently about your topic. No one is going to believe in what you say if you don't believe in yourself. It may take a few podcasts to find a groove, or you might hit the ground running and have a podcast that immediately takes off. Just speak with conviction and allow yourself to shine.

>> **Develop your podcasting personality.** After you know what you sound like when you record, here's where you develop your podcasting personality. Is your persona going to be light, fun, and informal, or something a little edgy, jaded? Is your message taking an angle of marketing, politics, or religion? Or are you podcasting a love of music, science, or your Macintosh? Your persona should generally match the theme of your show. If you're doing a show on classical music, a persona of a morning radio DJ probably isn't going to work. If you're taking a light-hearted look at politics, you may want to have a little more levity in your tone and pace than a funeral director.

What If I Hear More than One Voice?

One of our favorite ways to podcast is with guests in-studio or co-hosts where more than one podcaster gets on mic. While there's something to be said for the single voice doing a monologue or perhaps doing interviews, the show dynamics change quite a bit when you get multiple people gathered together over your favorite topic. For one thing, it's a lot easier to carry on a conversation! Another bonus is with the right dynamic between hosts, an energy is created that subscribers see and hear in every episode. Along with the guidelines described in this and other chapters, there are some specific things to be aware of when doing a show with multiple guests.

>> **Have a mixer with enough channels.** In Chapter 2, we talk about gear. Remember the mixer? The mixer becomes a crucial piece of equipment when co-hosts become part of the production. You can try the one mic, two voices approach, but the end result is hard to control and mix in post-production. For the best sound and optimal control, all participants need their own microphones. This means XLR connections, not USB, for microphones. Two hosts and you'll need two channels. Four hosts, four channels. And don't forget, you may want a few extra inputs for music, sound effects, and more. So make sure the mixer can handle the in-studio demands.

>> **Make sure everyone can hear.** You're wearing headphones when you record. So should your guests, especially if drop-ins are included in your recording. It's not only fair, it's practical that everyone hears the same thing. Each guest needs his or her own set of headphones. Before you run out and get a cheap "Y" cable to split the signal, realize that with each split, the audio signal degrades. To keep the investment economical, invest in a stereo headphone amplifier for about $25 that takes the headphone signal and splits (while boosting) it in to four separate channels. Then pick up from BSW a 5-pack of Sennheiser headphones (http://bit.ly/5packphones) for

you and your co-hosts or guests. You'll find this investment will serve you and your podcast well.

>> **Always do your prep work.** Even after a decade of podcasting, there are still gremlins in our audio systems. We can record on Saturday afternoon and come back Sunday night only to find audio levels have been adjusted. Okay, it could be the cats playing with the mixer settings in the middle of the night, but it never hurts to check your audio (and video) settings before each recording.

>> **Have one director.** This is the person in charge of your show's flow, timing, and in some cases coming up with clever segues to jump from one topic to the next. Usually this is the person at the mixer, but not always. It may even be someone off mic (or camera) giving hand signals. In some cases, this may be a baton passed from person to person in the cast. You'll find what works best for your group. The podcaster calling the plays serves as a moderator. It is your job to keep the energy up, the conversation going, and keep the episode on track.

>> **Give everyone some air time.** As with the previous item, the director may need to make sure everyone gives everyone else a chance to talk. Different people bring different things to your show. Some people may be passionate and outspoken (and some may be considered an unstoppable train), while others don't want to interrupt and wait their turn. Encourage your guests to play fair and give everyone a share the air time. We recommend discussing this among your co-hosts before it becomes a problem.

>> **When guests are in-studio or on the line, give them the majority of air time on that episode.** Both Chuck and Tee have seen and heard their fair share of interviews gone bad. It can be something as horrific as the host or hosts not knowing (or caring) to do any research on the guest. Tee recalls one podcast where the co-hosts broke on a tangent between themselves for ten minutes *while the guest remained silent on the line, waiting to be asked another question.* When guests are on the docket, remember that the episode is no longer yours. It's theirs. For more on interview techniques, take a look at Chapter 6, coming soon.

>> **Make sure everyone can see everyone else.** It's been said that as much as 93 percent of our communications is nonverbal. Even if you are doing an audio podcast, you want to be able to see each other during the conversation. Configure your studio to make sure everyone can see everyone else in order to have eye contact, see silent signals to pick up the pace or slow down, and let the director know all have something to say (see Figure 5-2). Being able to read each other's nonverbal cues is made easier when sightlines are clear and unobstructed — well, most of the time.

REMEMBER

Be aware that your show will be longer as you include more guests in the conversation. If you want to keep your show length consistent — a good recommendation in our book — then include fewer topics than you expect. Part of Chuck's Saturday ritual for building out the Sunday night episode is to find out how many people are coming over so he can add or remove topics accordingly. For Tee, it's coordinating with his co-hosts who wants to take the lead on a specific topic. Breaks offer a moment for anyone to say, "Mind if I take the lead in the second half?" If you really don't care about length, then just realize that more guests will make for a longer show and plan accordingly. Communication is essential with co-hosts and in-studio guests.

Deciding Whether You Need an Outline or Script

What method works best for you? A full script and hours of prep time, or a single note card and two clicks of the mouse — one for *Record* and another for *Stop?* Both approaches work, depending on the podcaster's personality. It could be said that there's little difference between a writer and a podcaster: Some writers prefer to use an outline when putting together a short story or novel; others merely take an idea, a few points, and a direction, and then let their fingers work across the keyboard.

If you decide to work with a script, it's a good idea to invest some time into *pre-show prep*, simple preparation for what you're going to say *and* how you're going to deliver it. Depending on your podcast, though, prep time may vary. Here are a couple of examples of how dramatically different prep time can be for different podcasting situations:

>> For their podcast *The Brit and Yankee Pubcast* (`http://thebritandyankee.com`), Phil Clark and his crew do very little prep — usually just enough to get some basic facts about the drink of choice for that show and perhaps set up a location and interview with the brewmaster. After he does minimal orientation with the guest panel, he's ready to record. You really need to know your subject and have good chemistry with your show participants to make a minimal plan like this turn in to a good show, but it can work.

>> On the other side of the spectrum is *The Radio Adventures of Doctor Floyd* (`http://doctorfloyd.com`), a 10-minute show in the style of old-time radio with a modern, educational, comedic spin. Grant Baciocco and Doug Price (see Figure 5-3) have every show carefully scripted. Depending on the historical research required, Grant can spend anywhere from 1 to 3 hours doing preshow prep. The careful scripting comes in real handy when Doctor Floyd has celebrity actors playing a part in the show.

FIGURE 5-3:
The Radio Adventures of Doctor Floyd's Grant Baciocco (left) and Doug Price (right) take their comedy seriously, and that means plenty of preshow prep!

Preshow prep can range anywhere from jotting a few notes on a napkin to writing a complete scripted with full sound effects — regardless of show length. So how far should your prep go technically? That depends on what your podcast needs. Outlines and scripts will keep you on track with what you want to say, serving as roadmaps you use to keep moving smoothly from Point A to Point B.

Whether you're a napkin scribbler, a script writer, or somewhere in between, if you've never done any kind of planning like this, the secret to efficient preshow prep can be boiled down to three disciplines:

» **Habit:** Many podcasters, especially podcasters emerging from corporate offices, prepare for podcasts in the same manner as business presentations. They jot down essential points on note cards to keep the podcast on track, but the points are the only material they write beforehand. You can easily apply your organizational skills from the workplace to the podosphere.

» **Talent:** Some podcasters are truly the Evel Knievels of the podosphere, firing up their mics and recording in one take. These podcasters tend to have backgrounds in live entertainment, deciding in a moment's time when a change of delivery is required. This is a talent of quick thinking, and although it keeps material spontaneous and fresh, it's a talent that must be developed with time.

» **Passion:** For most podcasters, passion is a driving force that keeps their podcasts spur-of-the-moment. With enough drive, inspiration, and confidence in their message, they keep their prep time to a minimum because podcasting isn't a chore but a form of recreation.

Determining a Length for Your Show

If you've been using this chapter to develop your podcast, you've made serious progress by this point in getting your preshow prep done. Now you're ready to podcast, right?

Well, no. First you must consider how long your show's episode is going to run. The following sections give you the rundown on how best to determine your show's length.

TIMING YOUR PODCAST TO THE AVERAGE COMMUTE

You may hear some veteran podcasters say, "Your podcast should never be longer than 30 minutes because that is the time of an average commute." Chuck has heard actual listener feedback asking, "Can you make your show the length of my commute?" Oh boy! Tee's response to this has not changed since 2005: "Obviously, you don't live in the Washington, D.C. Metro area, do you?"

Yes, maybe the average commute from sea to shining sea is 30 minutes, but that should not be a set-in-stone template. There are shows where each episode is 60 seconds, others where the host(s) decide they need to go on for hours (thank you to whoever invented the pause button!), and still others where each episode length is variable.

The bottom line: You decide how long it takes you to podcast, and remember, there are going to be those super-sized episodes that occasionally come along.

The hidden value of the short podcast

There are many podcasts that run under ten minutes where hosts deliver their message and then sign off only moments after you thought they signed on. While on average — and this is more like an understood average, not really a scientific, detailed study of all the podcasts out there — a podcast runs from 20 to 30 minutes per episode. So what about these 10-minute vignettes? Does size matter? Does time matter? (Whoa. Deep.) Is there such a thing as too short a podcast?

Here are some advantages in offering a short podcast:

>> **Shorter production time:** Production time is reduced from a weeklong project to a single afternoon of planning, talking, editing, and mixing. With a quick and simplified production schedule, delivering a podcast on a regular basis — say, every two weeks, weekly, or twice a week — is easier.

>> **Fast downloads:** You can be assured — no matter what specs you compress your audio file down to — that your podcast subscribers will always have fast and efficient downloads.

>> **Easy to stay on target:** If you limit yourself to a running time of less than ten minutes, you force yourself to stick to the intent (and the immediate message) of your podcast. There's no room for in-depth chat, spontaneous banter, or

tangents to explore. You hit the red button and remain on target from beginning to end, keeping your podcast strictly focused on the facts. Shakespeare said, "Brevity is the soul of wit." Considering his words, ol' Bill would probably have podcast under 15 minutes if he were alive today.

Nothing's wrong with keeping a podcast short and sweet. In fact, you might gain more subscribers who appreciate your efficiency.

A little length won't kill you

Now with that quote from the Bard about brevity, you might think, "Shakespeare said *that?!* Before or after he wrote *Hamlet?*" That's a good point because Shakespeare did have more than a few of his characters say, "My lord, I will be brief . . ." and then launch into a three-to-four-page monologue.

What if Shakespeare decided to be brief in his podcast? Would he get any subscribers if his show ran longer than half an hour? What if he broke the 60-minute ceiling? Would the Podcast Police shut down his show?

Podcatchers and subscribers, on reading your show notes and descriptions, should be able to figure out the average running time of your show. On a particular topic, some podcasts can easily fill two or even three hours. It's hard to believe even avid podcast audiences would want to sit and wait for such a mammoth download, but huge productions have some definite advantages:

» **If the show is an interview, you have anywhere from two to three hours with an authority.** It's something like having a one-on-one session stored on your computer or MP3 player. From shows like SyFy Wire's *The Churn* (see the upcoming sidebar, "Free-falling into *The Expanse*"), if a guest is part of the podcast, you can rest assured your podcast will go a little longer than 30 minutes — and sometimes it should.

WARNING

Be careful with this one. Shows and interviews that ramble aimlessly run the risk of losing audience attention. We talk more about good interview practices in Chapter 6.

» **You're allowed verbal breathing room.** Discussion stretching past the 30-minute mark allows you and your co-hosts or guests to break off into loosely related banter, widening your podcast's focus and sparking discussion that can lead in other directions.

REMEMBER

The cost of podcasts longer than 30 minutes is in bandwidth and file-storage — issues that smaller podcasts rarely, if ever, must deal with. See Chapter 10 for a discussion of the bandwidth demands on your server.

FREE-FALLING INTO *THE EXPANSE*

The SyFy channel has been employing podcasting as an "enhanced experience" to its leading shows. In the first and second editions of *Podcasting For Dummies, Battlestar Galactica's* Executive Producer Ronald D. Moore and SyFy (then called SciFi) were featured for hosting hour-long episodes, similar to director commentaries on DVDs, providing an inside look at what went into the episode airing that day. The companion podcast of *Battlestar Galactica* was so successful that SciFi broadened its scope to include script-writing sessions and guest appearances from cast members.

Since then, SyFy continues to use podcasting as a means to bring fans deeper into its most popular shows, and *The Churn* is such a podcast. *The Churn*, hosted by *Fangrrls* Managing Editor Cher Martinetti and Editor-in-Chief Adam Swiderski and writers Ty Franck and Daniel Abraham (who collectively make up the pen name S.A. Corey), take deep dives into *The Expanse,* the books that Franck and Abraham create. Along with getting into the heads of the series creators, *The Churn* also invites actors, visual artists, and special science guests like *Bad Astronomy's* Phil Plait to talk about issues addressed in the show from accuracy of physics to theoretical politics stretching across the solar system. If you are a fan of this incredible science fiction series, *The Churn* is a must-have companion for watching *The Expanse*.

Finding that happy medium

Is there such a thing as middle ground in the almost-completely undiscovered territory that is podcasting? How can you find a happy medium if podcasters can't agree on a standard running time?

The happy medium for your podcast should be a sense of *expectancy* or *consistency*. For example, in Tee's Parsec-winning podcast of *Tales from the Archives*, the running times for each episode are across the board — the shortest clocking in at just over 30 minutes, and the longest weighing in at over an hour. His audience, however, understands this is a *podiobook,* an audiobook presented in a serialized format. Readers understand that chapters and short stories vary in size, so it's no surprise when a podiobook follows suit. Some of the episodes are short and sweet while others push the length limits expected from literature.

Podiobooks aren't the only genre that variable length works well for. If your podcast deals in do-it-yourself home improvement, explaining the construction of a bookshelf will be a far shorter show than one about adding an extension to your deck.

Give yourself some time to develop your show, your voice, and your direction. If you build some consistency and expectation for your audience, it's easier to introduce a little variation or even a happy medium into your running time.

Mark Your Calendar: Posting Schedule

You've got a format for your show. You've got an idea about its running time. Now you have to figure out when your show is going to go live. What is the best pace to set for your podcast? What are the advantages to posting frequently versus posting on occasion? How often will you be dropping your podcast into your feed?

There are four different kinds of posting schedules, some easier to maintain than others. Your podcast, depending on the planning and running-time you set, will dictate how often you post. There is no sure schedule to podcasts. What matters is setting a schedule and maintaining it.

A good way to know what posting schedule works best for you is to sit down and brainstorm on show topics. If you rattle off several ideas, rapid-fire, you may be looking at a frequent schedule. If your ideas are reliant more on current events and their outcomes, you may space out your episodes. See how quickly you can come up with ideas, and from there, make a decision on a reasonable posting schedule.

Posting daily

The demands of podcasting can be daunting between recording, editing, and posting. There are those who have figured out a way to minimize production, whether it is keeping the recordings raw and unedited or employing a studio with a crew or something in between, and posting on a daily schedule. Every day, a new episode appears in your podcatcher. Every day. That's a lot of content to sift through if you subscribe to a long-running podcast. Daily podcasts, though, do not necessarily follow a linear path. In other words, you do not have to go back to Episode 1 to understand the flow and the atmosphere of a podcast. Just jump on in, and enjoy!

If you think podcasting is daunting, podcasters like Nathan Lowell on *Today on My Morning Walk* (`www.nathanlowell.org/tommw`), the high-energy *Geek Radio Daily* (`http://geekradiodaily.com`), and *The New York Times* powered *The Daily* (`https://www.nytimes.com/podcasts/the-daily`) undertake the challenge and produce new content every day. A payoff to answering this challenge is building an audience. With so much content to share, your community should grow quickly.

WARNING

Regardless of your intended schedule, life sometimes deals us an unintended hand. Just let your audience know. They'll understand. We've found that doing this can build loyalty. Let's face it, the majority of podcasters are doing this as a second job. We have family that need attention, day jobs that require business trips, and a host of other things that might crop up, scheduled or otherwise. You don't have to reveal personal details if it's not appropriate; however, a quick message to your audience is always polite.

Posting weekly

Perhaps the most common of schedules for podcasts is weekly posting, like you would with a popular television show. Perhaps not as demanding as the daily schedule, this schedule means a commitment to producing new content at least once a week. You will want to make certain the content is there before you launch, and find workflows that make your production schedule more efficient. You can do this by maintaining a buffer of content, seen often in gaming podcasts like *Steam Rollers Adventure Podcast* (`http://riggstories.com/the-podcast`) and *So Many Levels* (`http://christianaellis.com/so-many-levels-a-dd-podcast`) that record gaming sessions that can last for an hour (or longer) and then present them in a serialized format. Pick a day out of the week, and make that your day. That will be the time your listeners or viewers will be expecting your next episode.

Other podcasts like George Hrab's *The Geologic Podcast* (`www.geologicpodcast.com`, shown in Figure 5-4) and *Grammar Girl's Quick and Dirty Tips* (`www.quickanddirtytips.com/grammar-girl`) seem to just happen spontaneously. There's some planning that goes into these podcasts, but talent also comes to play. If you can get behind the mic and feel right at home, you can keep up with the weekly schedule.

Posting biweekly (or "fortnightly" for our friends in the Commonwealth)

Say you have a reasonable amount of content, but not a whole lot of free time. Or maybe you want to podcast but are concerned that you will burn through the content before you can come up with new ideas and directions for your show. A biweekly posting schedule provides you with a comfortable alternative to the regular demands of a weekly production. This may mean the audience response and the timeliness of your podcasts may be lacking when compared to a more frequent posting schedule, but this schedule is easier to maintain in case a weekly schedule is difficult for you to maintain. Podcasts like *Headshots* (www.headshotspodcast.com) and *The Wekk Podcast* (https://wekkpodcast.com) find a good life-work-podcast balance with the biweekly schedule.

TIP

Whether working daily, weekly, or biweekly, you might find life stepping in the way of your production schedule. This is why having a concept of seasons should be considered for your podcast. In the case of Tee's steampunk podcast, *Tales from the Archives*, seasons are defined by 10 to 12 short stories. If you see a break coming in your production, make sure to let your audience know.

Posting monthly

What are the benefits of a monthly podcast, aside from the relaxed scheduling and production schedule? It's easy to see what is the challenge in working on a monthly schedule: nurturing the audience. Posting only monthly makes it difficult — not impossible, but difficult — to build a community over content that only happens once a month. In addition, the timeliness of a monthly podcast is almost nonexistent as news headlines happening weeks ahead of a recording session are impossible to comment on in a timely fashion.

What does make a monthly podcast schedule appealing? Longer-than-usual running times on topics inspired by the recent weeks' headlines. Such is the case *State of the Geek* (www.stateofthegeek.com/podcast), where hosts Joe Hogan and Kelly Hightower talk about topics that have cropped up in the month's news. These are geeks discussing politics in-depth, voicing their opinions on a monthly inspired topic. As they have a month to prep for recording, both Joe and Kelly have time to gather their resources as well as their thoughts. So if you have a subject that needs time for research and discussion, posting monthly may be a better option for you.

TIP

If you find yourself with an intermittent schedule, avoid apologizing for the absence. Both Tee and Chuck have listened to a number of podcasts over the years that have somewhat random schedules. When we hear from those wayward podcasters, we're excited to hear from them again. It's a bit of a letdown when the first words we hear are "Sorry for not producing a show as often as I would like." Instead, consider telling us how glad you are to be back, or just don't mention it at all. Get right in and start your delivery as if nothing happened. We forgive you!

I Hear Music (And It Sounds like Police Sirens!)

Adding the right kind of music to your podcast can give your show an extra punch or just a tiny zest. Although our skills and tastes range from classical to jazz to rock 'n' roll, both Chuck and Tee appreciate and understand the power of music and what it can bring to a podcast.

Chuck and Tee also understand and appreciate the law. Although you may think it's cool to "stick it to the man" and thumb your nose at Corporate America, the law is the law, and there are serious rules to follow when featuring that favorite song of yours as a theme to your podcast.

WARNING

We want to make this clear as polished crystal: We are not lawyers. We're podcasters. We've looked up the law on certain matters so we know and understand what we're talking about, but we are *not* lawyers. We can tell you about the law and we can give a few simple definitions of it, but we are *not* giving out legal advice. If you need a legal call on a matter concerning your podcast — whether it concerns the First Amendment, copyright issues, or slander — please consult a lawyer.

The powers that be

The government regards the Internet even today as a digital Wild West, an unknown territory that's avoided regulation for many years, granting those who use it a true, self-governed entity where ideas, cultures, and concepts can be expressed without any filtering or editing, unless it comes from the users themselves.

Does this mean we podcasters are free to do as we please? Well, no, not by a long shot. There are some rules and regulations that even podcasts must follow. There are also organizations that both broadcasters and podcasters *must* pay attention to.

The following organizations have influence on the destiny of podcasting, and it's only going to benefit you as a podcaster to understand how their legislation, activities, and actions are going to affect you.

The Federal Communications Commission (FCC)

The Federal Communications Commission, or FCC (www.fcc.gov), is the watchdog of anything and everything that gets out to the public via mass communications. The FCC keeps an eye on technology development, monopolies in the telecommunications industry, and regulating standards for telecommunications in the United States and its territories. It is most commonly known for enforcing decency laws on television and AM/FM radio.

For podcasters, the FCC can't regulate what is said (yet) because it doesn't consider the Internet a broadcasting medium. However, given existing legislation to reduce *spam* (junk email) and the growing popularity of podcasting among mainstream broadcasters (such as Clear Channel, Oprah Winfrey, and ESPN), it may not be long before the law catches up with technology.

The Recording Industry Association of America (RIAA)

Sean Fanning. Does that name ring a bell? Sadly, it was Fanning who lost his battle against the Recording Industry Association of America, also referred to by its more common acronym RIAA (www.riaa.com), when he contested that his file-sharing application, Napster, in no way infringed on copyright laws and was not promoting music piracy. The RIAA led the charge in shutting down the original Napster and continues to protect property rights of its members — as well as review new and pending laws, regulations, and policies at the state and federal level.

The RIAA will have a definite say as to why you cannot use a selected piece of music for your podcast. Simply put, it's not your music. Sure, you own that CD or maybe you have downloaded that album from iTunes, but the music you listen to is under the condition that you use it for listening purposes only. This means you can't use it as your own personal introduction that people will associate with you. And, no matter how appropriate your favorite song is, you cannot use it as background music. Unless you're granted licenses and you pay fees to the record labels and artists, you're in copyright violation when playing music without permission.

TIP

One way of getting music for themes, background beds, and segues is to look into what musicians and podcasters refer to as *podsafe music.* This is professionally produced music from independent artists who are offering their works for podcasting use. The demand for podsafe music has been so high that several sites like the Free Music Archive (see Figure 5-5) have been launched (`http://freemusicarchive.org`), offering a wide array of genres, artists, and musical works. Today several other sources of podsafe music exist including Digital Juice (`www.digitaljuice.com`), Neosounds (`www.neosounds.com`), and Instant Music Now (`www.instantmusicnow.com`). Find out more about podsafe music, the conditions of using it, and how it can benefit your podcast.

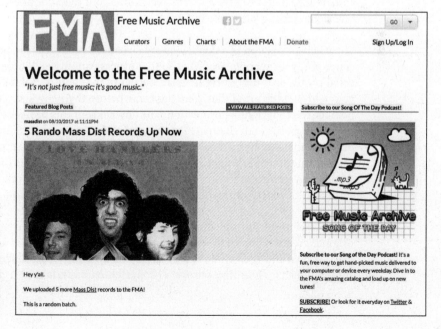

FIGURE 5-5:
The Free Music Archive is an interactive library of high-quality, legal audio downloads directed by WFMU.

The Electronic Frontier Foundation (EFF)

In addition to the big dogs who are passing the laws and legislations to restrain your podcasting capabilities, a group is looking out for you, the podcaster, with Science Fiction author and tech guru Cory Doctorow stepping forward as one of its more outspoken members. The Electronic Frontier Foundation, or EFF (www.eff.org), is a donor-supported organization working to protect the digital rights of the individual; to educate the media, lawmakers, and the public on how technology affects their civil liberties; and uphold said civil liberties if they're threatened.

A good example of EFF's mission is its involvement in various legal cases concerning URL domain registration and *cybersquatters* (individuals who buy desired domains and then hold on to them, waiting for the highest bidder). The EFF stands for the rights of legitimate website owners who happen to own a domain that a larger corporation would desire to use.

The EFF, provided you have a strong case to contradict the findings of the RIAA and the FCC, will stand up for you and give your voice a bit of power when you're standing up to a corporate legal machine.

Creative Commons (CC)

Founded in 2001, Creative Commons (CC) is a nonprofit corporation dedicated to helping the artist, the copyrighted material, and the individual who wants to use copyrighted material in a constructive manner but may not have the resources to buy rights from groups like the RIAA.

Copyright protection is a double-edged sword for many. On the positive side of a copyright, your work is protected so that others cannot steal it for their own personal profit, or if other people make the claim that you're ripping off their work, your copyright is proof that your egg came before their chicken. That's the whole point of the copyright — protection. The downside of this protection is that people now must go through channels for approval to feature your work in an educational or referential manner; and although you're given credit for the property featured, there's still a matter of approvals, fees for usage, and conditions that must be met. Also, many contributors just want to share their work with others on no other terms but to contribute and share with the world. Copyrights complicate this.

This complication of the digital copyright, protections, and desire to exchange original creations brought about Creative Commons (http://creativecommons.org), shown in Figure 5-6. It's dedicated to drafting and implementing via the Internet licenses granting fair use of copyrighted material.

FIGURE 5-6:
Creative Commons offers free licenses for use of original content in podcasting.

In the case of the podcaster, you want to offer your audio content to everyone, not caring whether listeners copy and distribute your MP3. As long as the listeners give you credit, that's all fine and good for you. CC can provide you with licenses that aid you in letting people know your podcast is up for grabs as long as others give credit where credit is due. CC provides these same licenses for artists and musicians who would not mind at all if you used their music for your podcast.

CC licenses are made up of permission fields:

>> **Attribution:** Grants permission for copying, distribution, display, and performance of the original work and derivative works inspired from it, provided credit to the artist(s) is given.

>> **Noncommercial:** Grants permission for copying, distribution, display, and performance of the original work and derivative works inspired from it *for noncommercial purposes only.*

>> **No Derivative Works:** Grants permission for copying, distribution, display, and performance of the original work only. No derivative works are covered in this license category.

>> **Share Alike:** Grants reproduction of the original work and also allows derivative works *if* they are also released under a similar Creative Commons license.

These four fields can be used as stand-alone licenses or can be mixed and matched to fit the needs of the podcaster or the artist offering content for the podcast.

The CC and its website give details, examples, and an FAQ page that answers questions concerning the granting of licenses for use of protected content. Just on the off-chance you don't find your answer on the website, it gives contact information for its representatives. CC is a good group to know and can open opportunities for you to present new and innovative ideas and works in your podcast.

I can name that tune . . . I wrote it!

Using almost anyone else's music for your podcast can be an open invitation for the RIAA to shut it down. This is primarily to protect the artist's rights. Think about it — how would you feel if you were producing a popular podcast, receiving praise from all over the world, and while you're thinking about ways of taking the podcast to the next level, you turn on your radio and hear your podcast being broadcast on a top-rated radio station. Soon, your podcast is all the rage on the broadcasting airwaves — and you haven't made dollar one.

The same thing can be said for artists and their music. They work hard to produce their work, and now podcasters are using their music to brand their shows, not bothering to compensate the artists for their efforts. Artists love to say that they do what they do for the love of the craft but in the end, it's their *work* and artists have to pay the bills, too.

So how can you use a piece of music without suffering the wrath of the RIAA or FCC? Ask permission of the artist? Only if the artist owns the rights to the music and the recordings. Otherwise, you also need to get written permission from artists, musicians, record labels, producers . . .

REMEMBER

The best way to avoid the legal hassles is to avoid copyrighted material that is not your own.

If you want to use published pieces that aren't royalty-free, ask the artist directly (if you can) for permission to use that music on a regular basis. Compensation to the artist may come in the form of a promotion at the beginning or end (or both) tags of the podcast. As long as you have written permission from the artists and the artists have the power to grant it (that is, they haven't signed the power over to their label or publisher), you should be able to use their work to brand your show or feature them on your podcast. (If you're not sure whether you have the appropriate permission, you may want to consult an attorney.) This is usually acceptable with independent artists because, in many cases, they also own the record label. Confirm this with artists. Otherwise, you run into the same legal issues if you were to use music recorded by Queen, Bruno Mars, or U2.

TIP

You can always offer your podcast as a venue for the musician to sell his or her work. Dave Slusher of *Evil Genius Chronicles* (www.evilgeniuschronicles.org) has written permission from the Gentle Readers to use its music as intro, exit, and background music for his podcast; in return, Dave promotes its CD, *Hi, Honey.* This promotion works well for the Gentle Readers as well as artist Michelle Mallone (www.michellemalone.com). After her music was featured on Dave's podcast, her sales spiked — both through her website and on iTunes!

I'll take the First: Free speech versus slander

Words can (potentially, at least) get you in just as much trouble as music. The legal definition of *slander* is *a verbal form of defamation, or spoken words that falsely and negatively reflect on one's reputation.*

So where does podcasting fit into all this? Well, the Internet is a kind of public space. Think about it — before you open your mouth and begin a slam-fest on someone you don't like in the media or go on the personal attack with someone you work alongside, remember that your little rant is reaching MP3 players around the world. Be sure — *before* you open your mouth to speak — that you aren't mis-quoting an article or merely assuming that your word is gospel. Cite your sources, and make certain those sources are not only reliable and authentic, but also that they are confirmed by other credible sources. If you're doing a news podcast or include a news segment in your show, consider citing the source where you got your news. It not only tells your listener that you're not making this stuff up, but it's also a nice way to drive traffic to the website you consider valuable. When expressing opinions, jaded, constructive, or otherwise, have real evidence to back up what you say.

Chapter **6**

Interview-Fu: Talk to Me, Grasshopper

odcasting is empowering. There's something about a microphone in your hand that gives courage. Suddenly, you're not afraid of anything. Oh yeah, you're running with the big dogs now, and like Charlie Rose, Larry King, or even BCC's own Stephen Sackur, you're asking the questions to find out what makes your guest tick.

What sets you apart from those big dogs, though, is skill. James Lipton of *Inside the Actor's Studio* may make interviewing look easy, but make no mistake: Interviews are not easy. It takes skill to host an interview, and hosting a great interview is an art. The good news is these luminaries possessing the gift of gab all had to start somewhere. Podcasting is an excellent venue to hone these skills, but you're going to want a solid foundation to build your skill set on.

Along with helping you schedule an interview, we help you get ready for it by looking at hardware and software tried and true for us, asking good questions to keep the conversation lively and engaging, and giving you examples of bad questions best avoided. Finally, we impart those always-valuable behind-the-scenes technical tips that make the interview go smoothly.

I'll Have My People Call Your People: Interview Requests

The courage to submit an interview request comes simply from your interest in the interview subject. Script or compose an email to ask your favorite author, actor, sports celebrity, game streamer, podcaster, or whomever you want for an interview. You may need to submit the request multiple times, and sometimes you may have to work through numerous people simply to get a "no" as your final reply. That happens. It doesn't mean that individual is mean, a rude person, or otherwise. They just don't do interviews. For every "no," you will find ten others who will enthusiastically say "yes."

Here are some things you should keep in mind when working on the interview request:

>> **Market yourself and your show.** A good deal of marketing is involved with podcasting. Your interview request needs to sell your services to the prospective interviewee. If you're part of a podcasting network, be sure to mention that. Large listenership numbers are always helpful. Have you done interviews before? If so, do some name dropping. If not, a good place to start might be with other podcasters. They're looking to get their names out and grow their listenerships also.

>> **What can I do for you?** The person (or the person's agent) is going ask "What's in it for me (or my client)?" You need to ask yourself questions like: Does he or she have a new book coming out? Perhaps he or she is about to launch a special product? Find an angle and work with it.

>> **Be flexible.** Remember, you're asking for *their* time. There may be restrictions in your schedule and theirs. Sometimes you can get an interview within 24 hours, and other times, you have to schedule it weeks or months in advance. You may have to take time off work from your regular job or rearrange other plans, just like the interview subject who is taking time out of his or her day to chat with you.

REMEMBER

Don't assume the person reading your interview request is going to know your podcast, or even what a podcast is. (Yes, we've been at this for over a decade and there are people who *still* don't know what a podcast is.) You may have to explain your platform using alternative terms or a short explanation.

THE INTERVIEW REQUEST

One of the easiest ways to do interview requests is via email. It's time to put on your marketing hat on top of your public relations hat and consider how you want to represent your show when sending queries. First, putting words like *interview request* or *podcast interview request* in the subject tells readers what you want before they even open the message. Use a warm greeting, "Hello" followed by the person's name is always a good start. Remember, you may not be sending the message to the interviewees directly, but rather must work through their agent or handler.

In the body of the message use the B.L.U.F rule — or Bottom Line Up Front. The first line of your message body should include something along the lines of "I am requesting an interview with Brent Spiner for the *Warp 11 Podcast*" — again, no doubt what you want. Don't dive in to the details about your show yet. We know, it's tempting right after you mention it by name, but remember, this query is about them. You can mention what your podcast is about with a one-liner about what you do ("*Technorama* is a show showcasing the lighter side of the geek lifestyle. . .") or it may be all in the title ("We would love to host an interview with Shohreh Aghdashloo in an upcoming episode of *Happy Hour from the Tower: A Destiny Podcast*"), but right now, the interview subject is your focus.

Explain why you want to speak with that person. Does he have any upcoming books, movies, or appearances he is interested in promoting? This would be a good time to mention how much time you are asking for. Asking someone for 2 hours is a much different consideration (and easier to say no to) than 15 minutes.

Now is when you can get on with describing your show, but don't drone on — a couple sentences and perhaps some other notable names whom you have interviewed ought to be all you need. If you have an audio or video file that describes your show, include a link to that, as well.

Close with a respectful, yet positive salutation such as "I look forward to hearing back from you." Remember, most people are very busy and may not respond back right away so you might need to follow up periodically. In some cases, several times. It took Chuck two years of polite, yet gentle, reminders to get an interview with Dr. Robert Ballard (the man who discovered the *Titanic*), but it was worth the effort.

Preparing for Interviews

There's an approach that all interviewers, be they Barbara Walters or Stephen Colbert, should take in talking to guests — use a simple, basic plan to ask the questions that garner the best responses.

Asking really great questions

Chances are good that if you're new to podcasting, you've never held an interview quite like this — an interpersonal, casual chat that could get a bit thought-provoking or downright controversial, depending on your podcast's subject matter. The interview may be arranged by you, or it may be prearranged for you. There's a science to it, and here are just a few tips to take to heart so you can hold a good, engaging interview:

>> **Know whom you're talking to and what to talk about.** When guests appear on your show, it is a good idea to know at the very least the subject matter on which you will be talking about. Let's say, for example, you are having an author appear on your show. If the author has written over a dozen books, be they fiction or non-fiction, trying to find the time to read all your guest's books would seem an impossibility. So, do some homework. If the author guest has written a popular series, go online and research the series. Visit `Wikipedia. org` and see if the series has a summary there. If you can only find limited information, find websites relevant to the topic of the series. If the series is steampunk, dig up information about the Victorian era. If the series follows a snarky, sentient robot, look up Artificial Intelligence. This has two effects: (1) You sound like you have a clue what the writer is writing about and (2) It allows you to ask better questions. These same rules apply for non-fiction authors, and really for guests of any background.

TIP

It's also a good idea to visit guests' websites (provided they have 'em). You don't have to be an expert on their subject matter, but you should be familiar with it so you know in what direction to take the interview.

>> **Have your questions follow a logical progression.** Say you're interviewing a filmmaker who is working on a horror movie. A good progression for your interview would be something like this:

- What made you want to shoot a horror movie?

- What makes a good horror film?

- Who inspired you in this genre?

- In your opinion, what is the scariest film ever made?

You'll notice these questions are all based around filmmaking, beginning and ending with a director's choice. The progression of this interview starts specific on the current work and then broadens to a wider perspective. Most interviews should follow a progression like this, or they can start on a very broad viewpoint and slowly become more specific to the guest's expertise.

>> **Ask open-ended questions.** To understand open-ended questions, it's simpler to explain closed-ended questions. Close-ended questions are the

kind that give you one-word answers — for example, "How long have you been studying plate tectonics?" Don't count on your interviewee giving a dynamic answer to a question like that. Close-ended questions make the process harder than it needs to be. Instead, rephrase your question like "So what exactly got you interested in plate tectonics?"

TIP

Write down a series of questions that could fill your podcast with brief, one-or-two-word answers. This way, if you find yourself struggling, you have a hidden stockpile of questions to call upon. After a few quick answers, you can always fall back on the "Would you expand a bit on that please?" question.

>> **Prepare twice the number of questions that you think you'll need.** Some interviews you hear grind to a halt for no other reason than the interviewer believed that the guest would talk his head off on the first question. You're certainly in for a bumpy ride when you ask a guest, "Tell the listener a little bit about your experience at WidgetCo" and the guest replies, "It was a lot of hard work, but rewarding." (Yeah, this is going to get painful.)

TIP

Have a pad and a pen on hand, ready to go. In the middle of your interview, an answer may inspire a brand new question you would want to ask your guest about. Jot it down so you won't forget it. Then ask this new question either as a follow-up, or in place of another question you have up and coming.

>> **Never worry about asking a stupid question.** When asking questions that may sound obvious or frequently asked, remember: Chances are good that your audience has never heard them *answered* before. Okay, maybe a writer has been asked time and again, "Where do your ideas come from?" or a politician has heard, "So, when did you first start in politics?" often. When you have a guest present for a podcast, there's no such thing as a stupid question; what's dumb is not to ask a question that you think isn't worth the guest's time. He or she may be champing at the bit in hopes you *will* ask it.

REMEMBER

Leave room for spontaneous questions as mentioned above. Listen to your guest's answers and see if a new path has opened up. She may be tense while answering the same questions for the 50th time, but if you strike a chord and stumble on a piece she is passionate about, abandon the questions for a bit and follow the trail!

Avoiding really bad questions

Before you start percolating and dream up a few questions based on the preceding tips, stop and think about the interviews you've listened to where things suddenly headed south. Usually the interviewers find themselves with guests they know nothing about and they are expected to interview them on the fly, or the host ambushes the guest with questions that dig into something that's out of the guest's scope or none of the interviewer's business. We've piled up the typical gaffes in a prime example of a good interview gone bad.

Every podcaster should know how to turn a pleasant conversation sour (uh, this *is* a satire and not a recipe, okay?), and the following blunders should do it faster than an Uwe Boll movie is in and out of theaters:

» **Ask inappropriate questions.** Keep in mind your podcast is not *60 Minutes, HardTalk,* or even *Jerry Springer.* If you want to fire off hard-hitting-tell-all-mudslinging questions, think about who your audience is, whom you're talking to, and whether the question is within the ability of the guest to answer honestly and openly. If not, an awkward moment may be the least of your worries. Inappropriate questions can also be those irrelevant, wacky, off-the-wall, and far-too-personal questions for your guests. "Who was the rudest person you have ever worked with on a set?" could put a stunt performer's career into jeopardy if answered earnestly. "What's the worst book you've ever read?" could drop a writer into hot water with colleagues. Asking athletes "You are in fantastic shape. Do you sleep naked?" could easily derail an interview quickly. Maybe these wild card questions work for shock jocks, but when you have an opportunity to interview people you respect in your field, do you really *want* to ask them something like, "Boxers, briefs, or none of the above?" Think about what you're going to ask before you actually do.

» **Continue to pursue answers to inappropriate questions.** If a question has been deemed inappropriate by a guest, don't continue to ask it. Move on to the next question and continue forward into the interview. Podcasts are by no means an arena for browbeating guests into submission till they break down in tears and cough up the ugly, sordid details of their lives.

   Are there exceptions to this exception? We would say, yes, depending on the content of your podcast. Say after reading — and enjoying — *Podcasting For Dummies,* you decide to become the Zach Galifianakis of podcasting, complete with the foliage as your backdrop. Of course, if you're after irreverent material for your show and push that envelope as far as you can, your guests may not want to play along — especially if they don't get the joke. If that's the case, expect your guests to get up and walk away. Even in the most idyllic situations, guests can (and do) reserve the right to do that.

» **Turn the interview into the Me show.** Please remember that the spotlight belongs to your guest. Tee recalls a podcast where — no kidding — the three-person crew invited a guest on their writing podcast to talk about their books and their methodology of writing . . . only to launch into a ten-minute discussion between themselves on a completely unrelated topic, leaving the guest on the other side of their mic. Silent. *For ten minutes.*

   Yes, it is your podcast, but when a guest is introduced into the mix, you're surrendering control of the show to him or her, and that isn't necessarily a bad thing. Let guests enjoy the spotlight; your audience will appreciate them for being there, which adds a new dimension to your feed. One way to avoid the me-factor is to think of yourself as a liaison for the listener. Ask yourself, "As a listener, what questions would I ask or information would I be looking for from the guest?"

>> **Disrespect your guests.** This has happened to Tee as an interview subject. He's answered some questions that made him uncomfortable, and requested podcasters to please edit out the question and related awkward response. In most cases, the podcast respected his request. The others who did not bother to edit their podcasts? Well, he no longer fields queries from them. With that experience, Tee extends the same courtesy to his guests. Why? He wants to avoid blacklists. Also, interview subjects talk to their friends. You want them to speak positively of you and your podcast. Show them respect, and those guests worth your time will do the same.

Feelin' the synergy

One final note on preparing for interviews: We've heard some guests say, "I'm doing these interviewers a favor by going on their show." And we've been told by other show hosts, "We're doing you a great favor with this chance to showcase your work on our show."

Both opinions are not just arrogant, they're just flat-out wrong.

The reality is that host and guest are working together to create a synergy. The interviewer has a chance to earn a wider audience and display mastery of journalistic techniques. The guest has a chance to get into the public eye, stay in the public eye, and talk about the next big thing he or she has coming in sight of said public eye. Working together, guest and host create a seamless promotional machine for one another.

If you decide to take on the art of the interview, keep these facts in mind; you and your guests will have your best chance to work together to create something special.

REMEMBER

If your format allows it, ask your guest for an ID that you can drop in from time to time. You've probably heard these before on radio stations "Hi, this is Rex Kramer, danger seeker. You may remember me from such films as *Airplane* and *The Kentucky Fried Movie,* and you're listening to *The Shameless Self-Promoting Podcast.*" If the interview guests want to be more creative, let them. These are a great self-promotion tool, a whole lot of fun, and a way to remind your listener of previous accomplishments. Remember to ask politely, and be aware that not everyone will (or can) comply.

Recording Interviews with Skype

Unless you're conducting in-person interviews, your podcast just got a bit more technically complicated. You need to have the appropriate software to record your interview over the phone.

One option of recording your interviews is with Skype (www.skype.com). What makes Skype appealing to podcasters is its expandability of the application, available for Windows, Mac, and Linux. Skype is the vehicle to make your calls, but it lacks the feature to record them. You can record Skype conversations with various methods and use downloadable software to monitor levels and volume as you record. You can also use Skype with a little more hardware for similar results. We discuss all your options — whether software or hardware — in the following sections.

WARNING

As stated in Chapter 5, there are legal restrictions concerning the recording of telephone/Skype calls, and these restrictions vary from country to country, state to state, and region to region. Compliance with these laws is the responsibility of the podcaster. Always ask for permission (or better yet, get it in writing) before recording phone calls.

Recording using software

Recording using software or hardware — once again you're faced with choices. Software solutions are typically less complex to set up and use and cost less; however, they can put more load on the computer's CPU. If the CPU is too busy, it could impact the quality of the recording. The following sections cover some software options for recording Skype calls.

Call Recorder

Call Recorder for the Mac from eCamm Network (www.ecamm.com/mac/callrecorder) is a handy little piece of software with a simple interface that allows you to record Skype audio and video and save it to one of many formats for later editing. The only downside of Call Recorder is that the file is recorded as a robust MOV file. To reduce its size (for archiving purposes or to produce a smaller MP3 from), you need to run it through a media player like QuickTime Pro, producing a streamlined AIFF or WAV file. However, this step isn't necessary if you're using GarageBand or Logic Pro. If you don't have the money for a mixer and second computer (or portable recording device), the $29.95 investment is a great deal.

SoundTap

For Windows users, SoundTap, from NCH Swift Sound (www.
soundtap/index.html), lets you record just about any audio that
your Windows computer. Simply install the software and turn it c
sound played on or through the PC, including Skype calls, will be recorded as WAV
or MP3 files. All audio is tapped by a virtual driver, so the process is perfect digital
quality. Current pricing for SoundTap is $29.99.

WireTap Studio

As mentioned in Chapter 3, WireTap Studio from Ambrosia Software (www.
ambrosiasw.com/utilities/wiretap) lets you record just about any audio that
plays through your Mac and allows you to record from a second source such as
your mixer, iTunes, or another media player.

As for the steps involved in recording a Skype interview with WireTap Studio, it's
a piece of cake:

1. **Launch WireTap Studio and make sure the Controller window (shown
   in Figure 6-1) is visible. You can access it either by choosing Window ⇨
   Controller or by pressing ⌘+0.**

2. **From the Controller's top menu, select one incoming source of audio.
   From the menu underneath it, select your second input source.**

   The image on the right in Figure 6-1 shows you the input menus for the
   running applications that can serve as an audio input source.

FIGURE 6-1:
WireTap Studio's
Controller
window (left)
allows you to
select two
separate
incoming sources
of audio on your
Mac (right) for
recording and
mixing.

3. **Choose File ⇨ Preferences to access the Preferences of your WireTap
   Studio Pro application.**

   The Preferences window appears, as shown in Figure 6-2.

4. **Click the Source button at the top of the Preferences window. Have your interview subject (on Skype) talk as you check your own levels (on the mixer, USB microphone, and so on).**

FIGURE 6-2:
The Preferences window in WireTap Studio gives you an opportunity to do a quick sound check before recording.

5. **Click the Format option to select an audio format.**

   You can record your audio as an AIFF, a WAV, or another uncompressed digital audio format or it can go directly to MP3 to the compression settings of your choosing.

6. **Close this window and then return to the Controller. The large, dark circle is the Record button. Single-click that to begin recording.**

7. **When the interview is concluded, end the recording by clicking the Stop button (the dark square).**

   Automatically WireTap Studio pulls up a window with the waveform of your newly recorded audio (see Figure 6-3). Here you have tools available for editing, creating loops, and creating basic audio effects. For more on the capabilities of these tools, review the online tutorials for WireTap Studio at www.ambrosiasw.com/utilities/wiretap/videos.html.

8. **When your recording is ready, you can select it from WireTap's Library window and then click either the iTunes or the Local Disk button from the Send To options at the bottom of the window.**

   If the Library window isn't displayed, choose Window ⇨ WireTap Studio Library to display it. Check out Figure 6-4.

   Your WireTap recording is then sent to your desired location either for ID3 tag editing (see Chapter 10) or for further editing.

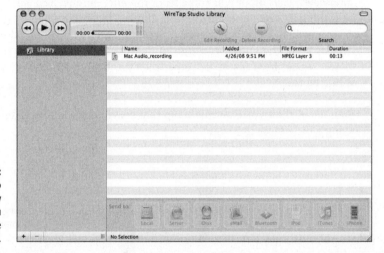

FIGURE 6-3:
After you make
your recording,
the final product
is pulled up in a
window, allowing
you to review or
edit what you've
recorded.

FIGURE 6-4:
WireTap Studio
Library window
allows you
to manage
your clips.

WireTap Studio is the pricier of the software options at $69, but when you consider its capabilities of mixing in two separate audio sources, editing, ID3 tagging, and exporting options, it's an easy and reliable recording resource for those important Skype interviews.

TIP

Skype uses VoIP (Voiceover Internet Protocol) to do what it needs to do to help you host and hold audio and video conferences. If you have a good Internet connection and want an all-in-one solution, consider looking into Zencastr (http://zencastr.com) as a possible solution for recording interviews. It will require that your interview subject on the other side of the website has audio hardware hooked up on her end, but the result is audio so cleanly recorded, you would think both host and guest are in the same room together.

Recording using hardware

If recording using software has your head spinning, using hardware may simplify things a bit. The key to the operation is a device called a *mixer*. (You can find more details on mixers in Chapter 2.) You've probably seen mixers at music concerts or television studios — those are for the big boys and tend to be quite expensive. Fortunately for you, there are less expensive options that cost as little as $50.

The idea behind a mixer is to take multiple inputs and mix them to create an output. An input can be a microphone, a computer, an MP3 player, an electronic keyboard, or just about anything with an audio output to feed in to the mixer. For interviews, *your* input will come from the microphone, and your interviewee will be coming from a computer running Skype. The output needs to go to a recording device such as an MP3 player or a second computer. Why do you need a second device? Well, the output can't go to the machine running Skype, or your inter-viewee would hear his or her own voice (probably with annoying lag), and that would be bad.

Figure 6-5 shows an example setup that provides the ability to record Skype calls using a little more hardware.

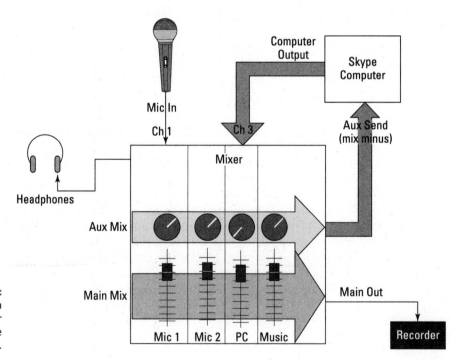

FIGURE 6-5:
Use a mixer and a recorder for recording remote guests.

For standard studio recording, the mixer is quite simple — microphones, computers, perhaps an MP3 player in the input port (or channels), and your main output going to a recording device. Of course, because we're talking about interviews, who wants simple?

Alright, it's not that complex. Whether you have a basic four-channel mixer or something the size of a cruise ship, most mixers have the same basic layout and features. Plugging in a microphone to a single audio channel is straightforward. Adding the stereo output of a second computer is also simple (given you have the right connecting cables). The real fun begins when you need to get your output back to the Skype machine and the recording device. This is where you need to take advantage of your mixer's *aux send* (sometimes called *effects send*) port. This is an output port that you will feed back to your Skype machine. So, the question now becomes, how do you get your microphone input sent out the aux send?

You see, most mixers can create multiple mixes. The *main mix* is what you typically record, but there are often hidden mixers, called *buses,* that let you create an alternative mix. How cool is that? You thought you were just buying one mixer, and you got yourself one (or more) for free! To make use of this additional output mix, locate the row of knobs on your mixer labeled Aux, which often are red in color. (If you have more than one row of Aux knobs on your mixer, each row corresponds to a separate aux send channel.) These are the volume controls for your aux send. If you turn up the volume on your microphone, whatever is connected to listen to the aux send output will hear it.

For example, if your Skype computer is connected to input channels 3 and 4, you want the red knobs on those channels turned all the way down so that input isn't fed back to the output on the aux send channel. This is called *mix minus 1* because you're taking the entire mix minus one input (the Skype machine). For a short video tutorial, watch the video at `https://www.youtube.com/watch?v=au47Ferbxfc`.

Prepping Your Green Room for Guests

A guest could be your dad, your mother-in-law, your best friend, or the man on the street. It could also be the friend of a friend who can get you on the phone with your favorite author, actor, or athlete. When you're interviewing, you have a second party to worry about.

Removing the "technical difficulties" element usually means either taking the show to the guests or bringing the guests to the show. This kind of interview not only is the most fun to do, but also gives you direct contact with the subject so you can observe body language, facial expressions, and reactions to questions and answers.

Welcoming in-studio guests

When you have guests visit your facilities — and because you're podcasting, this is probably your house — make them feel at home. Offer them something to drink. Offer to take them on a tour of your humble abode. Introduce them to your family. The point is to be polite. You don't have to cook dinner for them, but offering a hint of hospitality, be it a glass of water (or a beer, if you've ever worked closely with the *Binary Studio* crew), is a nice touch.

If you're having in-studio interviews, it's also a good idea to get your home and yourself ready to receive guests. Sure, Tee has recorded quite a few podcasts in his pajamas, but because he's working with his wife or recording short stories for his podcast, he's allowed. If fantasy and science fiction authors Terry Brooks and Catherine Asaro ever come over to his house for an interview, don't think he'd be greeting them in his Avenger jammies and Stone Brewery slippers.

Okay, maybe he *would* greet them wearing the Stone slippers, but he would be bathed and dressed and have his teeth brushed and hair combed. The key word here is *guest*. Treat them as such. Be cool, be pleasant, be nice. And if you're a guest on someone else's podcast, the same rules apply. Don't prop your feet up on the furniture, don't demand hospitality, and don't be a jerk during the interview.

The in-studio visit is an audition for both guest and host. If the guest is abrasive, abusive, and just plain rude, chances are good that the guest will never be invited back, no matter how well the previous interview goes. If a host asks unapproved questions, continues to pry into personal matters that have nothing to do with the interview, or seems determined to take over the interview spotlight as if trying to impress the guest, said guest may never return, even if extended an invitation.

Meeting guests on their own turf

Be cool, be pleasant, be nice. These same rules apply when you take your podcast on the road. You may find yourself at a person's home, place of business, or some other neutral place. You're now practicing — for the lack of a better term — guerilla journalism, ambushing unsuspecting people with questions that may not strike you as hard and probing but could be to people who don't expect them. Make certain to show respect to your guests, wherever you are when the interview takes place.

A good approach for getting good interviews is to ask permission of your guests, be they passersby or experts at their place of business, to interview them. Shoving a microphone in someone's face and blurting out a question is hardly a great way to introduce yourself and your podcast to the world. If the guest you want to interview has a handler or liaison, it's good protocol to follow the suggestions and advice of the guest's staff.

If you start out with a warm, welcoming smile and explain what you're doing and why, most people open up and are happy to talk.

TIP

When interviewing people on the street or in the moment, there are some easy ways to identify yourself. Michael Butler of *The Rock and Roll Geek Show* (http://www.americanheartbreak.com/rnrgeekwp) uses a *mic cube* around his microphone — these are sometimes called *mic flags*. The classic cube usually has a logo identifying a network, a show, or an organization affiliated with the interviewer. You can find mic cubes online (unprinted) starting around $25. There's also the simple greeting, "Hi, do I have your permission to record this for a podcast?"

REMEMBER

Just as with the phone and Skype interviews, test your equipment. You're now out of the controlled environment of your home studio; you must deal with surrounding ambient noise and how well your interview is recording amid uncontrolled background variables. Set up your equipment; power up your laptop, mixing board, and mics; and record a few words. Then play back your tests and set your levels accordingly. When you have your setup running, you're ready to get your interviews.

Ensuring Trouble-Free Recordings

When it comes to recording conversations, here are a few points to keep in mind before asking the first question:

>> **Get permission to record conversations, even if the interview is prearranged.** Laws (both federal and state) prohibit the recording of conversations without permission, and further restrictions limit broadcasting these conversations. If you plan to record *and* publish a conversation, get the subject's consent (for both) beforehand, both verbally and in written communication (even email) to make sure your legal issues are covered.

>> **Test the calling equipment.** If you have arranged a phone-in (or Skype-in) interview with someone for your podcast — say, a favorite musician or politician — prepare for the interview ahead of time. Skype (or phone) a friend to conduct a mock interview and make sure the recording setup not only works but also sounds good.

The bandwidth demand increases the more people you conference through your computer. Reception will be affected, so if you know more than one person will be involved in this interview, it's a good idea to test how many people you can effectively conference in one call.

>> **Check your batteries.** If you're using a portable recorder (such as the Zoom H4n Pro), make sure your batteries are charged and you have spares. (Check the spares, too.) If you're really paranoid or live in an environment with periodic electrical problems, you can also pick up an uninterruptable power supply in case your main power cuts out.

>> **Check your storage space.** Hard drives and solid-state devices are getting bigger and cheaper, but that doesn't mean they're infinite. Audio files can be big — especially if you're recording to a raw format like WAV or AIFF! If you run out of space in the middle of recording a show or an interview, you lose time; lose pace; and in the case of interviews, lose face with your interviewee. If you're recording to a portable recording device, it's basically the same idea. Know how much storage you have, in megabytes or gigabytes, and how long you can record at your current bitrate. Don't worry; we talk more about bitrates in Chapter 10.

TIP

If you're doing an interview with multiple Skype participants (known as *conferencing*), it's often best to have the person with the highest-power CPU host the meeting. That person should initiate the call and invite the other attendees one at a time. The better the CPU, the better the conference will run and the better your recording will sound. Also, the conference host may or may not be the same as the person recording the call. Remember, your goal during an interview is to try and minimize the chances for problems.

And although this may sound a bit pessimistic, be ready for things to go wrong. Guests might not show up for interviews. Also, new high-tech toys, if not given a proper preinterview shakedown, may not come through. Prepare to have plenty of topics to discuss on your own, and then your podcast can continue following a quick disclaimer. In podcasting, sticking to a regular schedule is reassuring to your listeners because they know you'll offer new feeds consistently and punctually.

Chapter **7**

So What Are You Waiting For? Record, Already!

O kay, you've most likely gone through the hardware and software gadgets from Chapters 2, 3, and 4. In this chapter, we make the bold assumption that you've made your purchasing selections, hooked up all the hardware according to the supplied documentation (you *did* read the documentation, right?), chosen your software, and gotten everything ready to record. This is it! You have a microphone pointing in the direction of your mouth, just waiting anxiously for you to begin podcasting.

Okay then. What's stopping you?

Perhaps you have no clue how you sound to your recording equipment, or perhaps you're still trying to understand why your smooth and sultry voice sounds like you just finished a dozen espressos. The problem could be in your audio application's sound settings. Too much pep in the voice, and you sound like Rob Zombie crooning a goth's delight. Too little amplification, and you'd be better off if you just went out to your front porch and shouted your podcast's content.

Before the podcast gets underway with your single-click or touch of the Record button, you must *set levels.* That's a very fancy-schmancy way to say *fiddling with knobs and sliders* on your mixing board or your audio-editing software. Setting levels ensure that the signal you're sending through the microphone is loud and clear. Once the technical side is running smoothly, give some thought to your voice — things like timing and enunciation — as how you say your message directly impacts the listeners' interest in what you're saying.

Did Your Sound Check Clear the Bank?

If you show up early enough for a rock concert, you see those roadies setting up microphones, playfully waving to the crowd as they speak quickly into a microphone "Check one, check two, check-check-check!" It's a staple for rock 'n' rollers to do such a mic check because the fans expect a good performance — it needs to be done.

With podcasting, your own mic check should be more involved. In Chapter 5, we recommend you perform such an audio diagnostic just to assure yourself (and, if applicable, your guests) that the equipment is working and sound is, in fact, reaching your computer. The goal is not only to confirm that your mic is picking up sound, but also to check the volume of the voices — yours and that of whoever else is involved in this podcast.

Understanding dB levels

Setting levels is quite easy, provided you know where your *decibel (dB) input levels* are displayed on your software. The *decibel* unit is used to express the intensity of sound, beginning at -9 dB for the least perceptible sound to approximately 130 for an intensely loud sound level. Your readout measures how *hot* you are (in this instance, that's the power of your voice, not how good you look) on the microphone. Audio *signal strength* (measured in decibels) is the amount of power that goes into the signal, which affects how clearly it can be heard and how hard it hits the ears. "Loud and clear" is good; too much signal strength causes distortion, and that's a pain to listen to.

In vintage radio and audio equipment, this dB display was a *VU (volume unit)* meter — the little needle that bounced in response to your voice. Later, the needle was replaced by lights that reacted when you spoke into a microphone, going from green to yellow to orange to red. What the lights said was pretty easy to translate:

>> **Green:** Well, I can hear you, but wow, are you quiet!

>> **Yellow-Orange:** You're coming in loud and clear.

>> **Red:** You're in danger of hitting the distortion level (clipping).

>> **Red with double bars:** Your audio is going to sound distorted.

Across hardware and software, the volume meters appear different (Figure 7-1 shows the volume meter display for Audacity), but they all serve the same purpose: to make sure your content is heard clearly. Your aim, as you speak and watch the indicators speak back, is to keep your dB levels bouncing in the high level (low red) without lighting up those double bars. When you attain that average, your voice is rising and falling within a good balanced dynamic range. Try to keep things a little lower — in the red and orange range — with only the high points (when you raise your voice) going in to the red occasionally. You can always bring up the low spots with some simple post production tips (described later in this chapter).

Input level meters

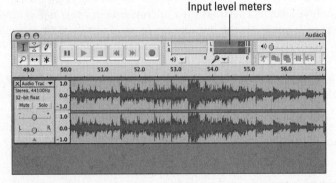

FIGURE 7-1:
The input level meters for Audacity (shown in the upper-right corner) respond to your voice and allow you to monitor how loud you are when recording.

Because microphones, audio-capture cards, and mixing boards all work at different sensitivity levels, it's best to test your voice before you record. If your levels are in the green, it means you're loud enough to be heard by your equipment but still so soft that people will have to crank up the volume on their computers or portable MP3 players, consequently blowing out their eardrums on the next podcast or playlist.

If your recording is too loud (or "hot"), it tends to cause problems for listeners. Listeners have their MP3 players set for a pleasant, comfortable volume . . . and suddenly your show begins with guns blazing and pipes blaring. As your levels reach deep into the red, listeners fumble for their players and try to turn down the sound so the program can be understandable through its own distortion. Sadly, the modulation is such a problem that your voice crackles and growls as it tramples the volume limits of your recording equipment, even at the lower volume. Worse yet, some programs and microphones will even cut the signal from the mic for a second, leaving you with chunks of missing audio — and you may not discover this until after your precious recording is over!

CALLING IN THE CREW

It'd be great to set your levels so that "0 dB" is always where your lights remain, but recording is a real-world activity. Sometimes your meter may never reach yellow, and other times it might hit the double red bars. If your goal is to maintain perfect levels from the beginning to the end of a recording session, an audio crew can work with you in rehearsal and performance, adjusting levels when you go loud and when you go soft.

The downside of hiring a crew is an added expense to producing your podcast. Even if the crew is a collection of audio geek friends, it can still cost you sending for a *lot* of pizza every time you record.

WARNING

You want to try to avoid *clipping* to prevent that distorted sound. Clipping is when you're feeding too much signal to your equipment. It can come from many sources, including incorrect settings on a microphone or other audio input, incorrect settings on a mixer, or the preferences in your software. Once audio is clipped, you can't get the original (or intended) quality back.

In achieving a balance in your audio, you could spend the day setting and resetting those levels in quest of dB nirvana. That's time spent, but not *well* spent. It makes more sense to practice until you get a pretty good sense of what your best working level is and get comfortable speaking into a mic at that level. Time to go mano-a-mano with setting the levels.

Setting your levels

Your mission, should you choose to accept it, is to keep your levels about 0 dB, dipping and spiking when necessary. For podcasting, consistency is key. You have your mixer turned on (if you have one), your mic is plugged in and turned on — check — and your software is running. Now follow these steps to check levels:

1. **Begin talking into the mic about your podcast topic or plans.**

You can do a scripted test read or just talk off the top of your head, but be sure to speak in the manner and mood of your podcast.

Instead of speaking to thin air in the vague direction of the mic (or the person next to you), speak in the exact direction of the mic, pointing your voice directly at the recording device (as shown in Figure 7-2). Even if the mic isn't omnidirectional (meaning it picks up sounds from all directions at once), it can pick up your voice better this way.

FIGURE 7-2:
Set your microphone at a comfortable distance, close enough to overpower ambient noise, but far enough to avoid microphone contact.

TIP

If you speak directly into the microphone, you might hear some sounds — particularly *p*s and *b*s — causing an effect known as *popping*. An investment of less than $20 in a windscreen or pop filter can fix that. This device is a foam or nylon filter that stops the wind made by your mouth from hitting the microphone's diaphragm and causing distortion.

2. **While you're talking (or if you're monitoring by playing back your test takes), keep an eye on your dB levels on the computer screen.**

   If the levels are spiking into the double-red/red area or remaining in the green, check your input volume settings on your mixing board or audio-editing software. This might require a bit of multitasking on your part, but continue to adjust the input levels while talking, as you watch the input meters.

3. **Rerecord your voice at the new settings.**

   Try to speak in the same manner and inflection as you did on the first recording.

4. **As you review the second take, watch the dB input levels and adjust accordingly.**

   When in doubt, err on the side of caution on the input levels. Record your volume a little low. You can always correct it in post-production. One way to increase the volume later, using Audacity, is to select your audio and use the Effects ⇨ Amplify feature to bring it up. Another is to save your audio to WAV format and use a tool called The Levelator (http://conversationsnetwork.org/levelator) to fix the levels.

THERE'S A RIGHT WAY AND A WRONG WAY . . .

Time for a confession.

When Tee got his MXL990, it was his first studio condenser microphone. He was so excited about this microphone he failed to check the small slip of paper included that told him how to talk into it. Perhaps it was the excitement of venturing into new frontiers of creativity that made him hook up the equipment without reading the directions. Maybe it was a bold assumption that he knew what end to talk into with a mic as he had worked with (dynamic) microphones before. Whatever the reason, Tee was speaking into the microphone incorrectly (left image). His friends in the podosphere, on seeing Tee in action, didn't really have the heart to tell him so — or didn't know any better themselves.

Fortunately, Evo Terra of *The Opportunistic Travelers* (https://www.theopportunistic travelers.com) is a heartless evil mastermind. He told Tee he was doing it wrong, as any heartless evil mastermind would. On a podcast, naturally.

All microphones do not behave the same, and condenser microphones work best when speaking into them properly (right image), with the microphone pointed straight down. Tee, reflecting on Evo's "kind" advice, positioned the mic accordingly and continues to do so to present day. When hooking up microphones, refer to the enclosed documentation for additional and essential information on getting the best sound out of your microphone.

You, too, can avoid the embarrassment (caught forever) that published photographs may deliver upon you . . . regardless of how good the content it generates for your podcast.

TIP

After you set your levels, make a note of the settings somewhere other than your computer (using, say, a smartphone or its retro ancestor — a legal pad and pen), in case your preferences are lost or fiddled out of whack by somebody's child or best friend playing spaceship in your studio. (Yes, even adults enjoy playing spaceship with super-cool-looking equipment!) That way, even if something awful happens to your application's preferences or your mixing board, you always have your last known settings to reference.

Noises Off: Capturing Ambient Noise

Part of the charm that is podcasting is just how varied the content is, as well as how spontaneous the shows tend to be when the Record button is hit. Some podcasters believe that a "true" podcast (whatever *that* is!) must record everything in one take and deliver its content to listeners completely unedited. This supposed mark of authenticity includes any background noise (also called *ambient* noise) you happen to capture while recording — from comforting sounds like rustling trees and birdcalls, to the more grating one like pounding car stereos and jackhammers.

Hey, if that's the style of your show, that's great. However, if you're trying to take listeners to a place in their imagination, read on to find out how to reduce or eliminate ambient noise.

Identifying ambient noise

As we discuss in both Chapters 4 and 8, how much you edit depends on what kind of content you're presenting. For example, if you're doing an off-the-cuff, off-the-wall podcast about your life and a typical day in it, you may just grab the VideoMic Me, plug it into your iPhone, and head out the door, recording every step along the way. This kind of podcast can be (note we said *can be*) easiest to record. You're podcasting a slice of Americana . . . or Britannia, if you're in the United Kingdom . . . or Kiwiana if podcasting from the Land of Hobbits, Championship Rugby, and Pavlova. Especially if your goal is to capture the look and feel of your culture, ambient noise is not only welcomed, but desired. Up to a point.

Some podcasters cringe at the mere mention of ambient noise — ambient noise like . . . well, what was in Tee's very first podcast. When he podcasted *MOREVI: The Chronicles of Rafe & Askana* back in 2005, he worked to create a magical setting with voice, story, music, special effects . . . a world that was completely shattered by real-world interference like school buses, kids at recess, UPS trucks, the Virginia Commuter Rail system, and air traffic from two nearby airports. Even if you love the *source* of the ambient noise, sometimes it just doesn't fit what the podcast is trying to do.

TIP

The best noise reduction happens in preproduction. If your podcast could do without input from the outside world, strategically scheduling recording sessions is the start of your production. Try recording at night or early morning. You'll find that traffic is lighter, the kids are in bed, construction crews aren't running those earlier-mentioned jackhammers, animals typically are less active — all adding up to less ambient noise, hence fewer takes on the mic.

Minimizing ambient noise

To reduce the intrusion of the outside world, record anytime during the day, and still maintain a budget, some creativity is in order.

Truth be told, there really isn't an easy solution to podcasting in a noisy world. One not-so-cost-effective answer is to rent a studio and record your podcast there. Unless you have a sponsor who bankrolls your costs, your hobby could easily max out credit cards and cast a hungry eye upon your nest egg. (Let's not even go there.)

A somewhat-less-expensive option is to soundproof your home-based recording room. That may sound simple, but it can involve a lot of home improvement before you have one room in which you can be sure the only sound is yours. But is it impossible or impractical? Not really. P.G. Holyfield of the podcast novel *Murder at Avedon Hill* (https://scribl.com/books/P4C82/murder-at-avedon-hill) built his own studio for podcasting.

Holyfield's do-it-yourself adventure began with a house hunt, so a studio in a finished basement was on the list of what the house needed. The studio eventually came about from a large storeroom, a few new walls, and the addition of an air vent. The newly created 7-x-8-foot room was then soundproofed with foam tiles that cost around $500. Holyfield found the effort worthwhile. "The studio is working out great. It was amazing to hear the difference as the foam went up. Now I have a completely silent room, except when the A/C turns on, which I can turn off most times, since the basement is pretty cool." Figure 7-3 shows the process he went through: the arrival of acoustical foam (left), measuring twice and cutting once (center), and the studio (right). The advantage of being in the basement is far less outside noise entering through the walls. The advantage of the acoustic foam is to reduce sound waves bouncing off the walls and creating unwanted effects.

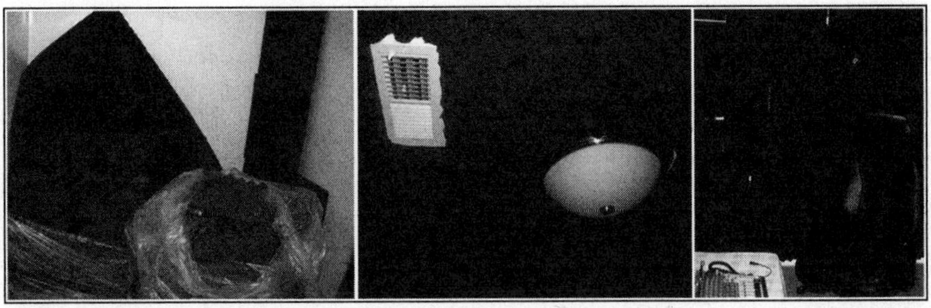

FIGURE 7-3:
The Voices of
Cairn Studios
started as
P.G. Holyfield's
dream project.

Renovation, especially if you're a fan of the DIY Network, makes this kind of home-built studio a possibility, but still may not be a practical solution for all homeowners. And this kind of aggressive home improvement is seriously frowned upon if you're renting an apartment.

You can keep this home renovation affordable and within the lease agreement terms:

>> **Stuff towels under the door.** It decreases the amount of sound from inside your house filtering into your recording area.

>> **Keep the microphone as far away from your computer as possible.** Its fan (if audible) simply becomes part of the natural ambiance for the podcasting room.

>> **Turn off any ceiling fans, floor heaters, additional air conditioners, or room ionizers.** With fewer appliances running, you have less chance of additional ambient sound being created.

>> **If you do encounter ambient noise that you don't want in your podcast, simply give it a few moments.** Wait until the noise subsides, pause, and then pick up your podcast a few lines *before* the interruption. That's for the sake of post-production: With a substantial gap in your podcast activity, you can easily narrow down where your edits are needed.

TIP

When noise interferes with your podcast, leaving gaps of silence so you know where to edit isn't exactly a foolproof method. Always set aside enough time to listen to your podcast — and *really* listen, not just play it back while you clean the office or call a friend. Make sure levels are even, no segments are repeated, and the final product is ready for uploading and posting.

Many podcasts rely on ambient noise to set a mood, but sometimes reality just doesn't cut it. If you want to put more craft into the setting for your podcast, the ideas in this section should help you keep the background down to a dull roar.

When holding podcasts on location, make sure the ambiance — be it a particularly busy crosswalk at a street corner, a frequented bar, or backstage at a concert — does not overwhelm your voice. Background noise belongs in (well, yeah) the background. Its intent is to set a tone for the aim of the podcast, not to become the podcast itself. It would also be a good idea, if possible, to do a few test recordings in the space to see how much volume you'll need and how close to the mic you must be to be heard.

Now Take Your Time and Hurry Up: Pacing and Clock Management

Podcasts, whether short and sweet or epic and ambitious, all share something in common: the need for *pacing.* As a rule, you don't want to blurt out the aim or intent of your podcast in the opening 5 minutes and then pad the remaining 10 or 15 with fluff. Nor do you want to drone on and on (and on . . .) till suddenly you must rush frantically into why you're podcasting on this day about this topic. Give yourself ample time to set the mood comfortably and competently and make it to the intent without dawdling. Enjoy your podcast but respect your listeners' time. Make certain you don't overstay your welcome. The trick in pacing is to understand how much time you have to get your message across.

The big question is how to really grasp how much time you really have. Where to start?

It's a good idea to get a grasp of how much time you really have in one whole minute. To do this, find a clock, watch, or a stopwatch and for 1 minute (and *only* 1 minute) sit quietly and do nothing, say nothing, and remain perfectly still. That 1 minute will feel like a short eternity. Now imagine that 1 minute times 15. (No, no, no — do *not* repeat this exercise for 15 minutes. There's a fine line between an exercise and a complete waste of time.)

Fifteen minutes (for a start) is a good amount of time on your hands, so you should make certain that in your podcast you take your time to get to the message. The journey you take your listeners on doesn't necessarily have to occupy all that time — be it 15, 20, or 30 minutes — but you have time to play. That's the most important thing to remember as you set your best podcasting pace.

Take the potato out of your mouth and enunciate

It isn't out of the ordinary to fire up the mic and launch into your podcast with enough energy and vitality to power a small shire in England. Nothing wrong with that — until you go back and listen to yourself. Your words, phrases, and thoughts are running together and forming one turbulent, muddy stream of thought. Yes, that is your voice, but even you're having a tough time understanding what the podcast is about and what the podcaster is saying . . . and you're the podcaster!

One way of getting a grip on pacing yourself through a podcast is *enunciation* — pronouncing your words distinctly, explaining your topic clearly — and there is no better way to do that than to slow your speech slightly and listen carefully to certain consonants (for example, the *t*, *s*, and *d* sounds). Proper enunciation can help you set a comfortable pace and keep you from rushing through your presentation. In fact, it isn't a bad idea to *over*-enunciate. In the excitement of recording, over-enunciation forces you to slow down, clean up your pronunciation, and make your voice easily understandable. That same excitement is likely to increase your pace of speaking. Again, if the rapid pace is part of your presentation, stick with it, but if you're doing anything like a narration for an audio book, slow down. If you think you're speaking just a little too slowly, you're probably going just the right speed.

TIP

Speaking a few tongue-twisters before going on mic helps your enunciation and warms up your voice and prepares it for the podcast you're about to record. Here are some easy ones that emphasize the problem consonants lost when speaking too quickly:

>> Toot the tin trumpet, Tommy, in time.

>> Pop prickly pickles past the peck of parsley.

>> See sand slip silently through the sunlit seals.

>> The sixth sheik's sheep is sick.

>> Will Wendy remember wrecking the white rocker?

If you perform a search online for tongue twisters, you can find a wide variety of classic and original warm-ups for the voice. You can also take the twisters you find and compose your own.

And now let's take a break for station identification

Ever notice that certain podcasts suddenly break in with a show ID or take some other marked break and then (if they're lucky enough to have sponsors) play their sponsors' spots? They're trying to emulate — and maybe make themselves easily syndicated by — conventional radio. You know — the broadcasting industry. *Clock management* is the careful, standardized interruption of a typical radio broadcast — usually every 15 minutes in a one-hour slot — for such necessities as station identification, show identification, public-service announcements (PSAs), and (of course) commercials.

Another nice bonus of following clock management is you have several points in your show to give a quick *show ID* (something like "You're listening to *Technorama* with Chuck and Kreg . . .") that lets people know who you are. This show ID is great to catch the attention of people who may be walking into the middle of your podcast, and just as they ask the podcast listener "What are you listening to?" the show ID drops. Although show IDs are usually expected at the top of the hour and on the half-hour, you can drop in a show ID anytime you feel like it.

A good rule of thumb for clock management for each hour is:

» :00 — Programming break, station identification, show ID, PSAs, advertisements

» :15 — Programming break, PSAs, advertisements

» :30 — Programming break, station identification, show ID, PSAs, advertisements

» :45 — Programming break, PSAs, advertisements

These breaks vary in length but can last anywhere from two minutes to five minutes. No surprise that this is where hardcore podcasters (anyone podcasting since before early 2005) get a bit restless. They find clock management and show ID redundant, if not frivolous. Why bother to break or even drop in a show ID? People have downloaded your feed specifically. They know what they're listening to, so what purpose does clock management serve?

It all comes back to what you see for your podcast's future. If you intend to remain in the *podosphere* (the community of podcasters and loyal listeners, a podcast version of the *blogosphere*), it really comes down to your format, your way. No constraints from the FCC. It's just you, the microphone, your listeners, and caution to the wind. However, if you set your sights for taking your passion project to the airwaves — be it AM, FM, or satellite radio — you must format your show to fit the standards.

PODCASTING GOES PRO

Broadcasting networks that present to the airwaves sensational commentators like Sean Hannity, Anderson Cooper, Bill Maher, and Rush (no, not the kickin' rock group from Canada, but the big man of the Right Wing, Rush Limbaugh . . .) often take their shows to the podosphere to market their shows and reach a worldwide audience.

Along with the talk-radio personalities, other major players in broadcasting like NPR, ESPN, Disney, the BBC, and ABC use podcasting to reach audiences that may have missed their original broadcasts. One of Chuck's favorites is a show from "the other ABC," the Australian Broadcasting Corporation, called *Dr. Karl on TripleJ*, while Tee enjoys NPR's *Note to Self* and PBS' *Masterpiece Studio*, both of which were recommended to him by Stitcher. Thanks to podcasting, all of us can learn more about bee stings, double rainbows, and tidal waves on our own schedules.

Think about the possibilities of your podcast and where you see yourself with it several months (or years) down the road. Maybe a bit of management and organization will aid your podcast in jumping to the airwaves.

Concerning Tangents and Their Val — Oh, Look, a Butterfly!

It's hardly surprising that broadcasters who have no experience in broadcasting tend to stray from their topic once the microphone goes hot, and then they lose themselves in the thickets and thorns of tangents. Defensive podcasters claim that's part of the charm of podcasting, but that charm fades as the topic gets closer to serious. If (for example) you launch a podcast intent on addressing the growing concern of television violence and wander into *Sherlock* trivia, don't be surprised if your audience wanders away.

REMEMBER

It's worth repeating: Stay focused on the intent of your podcast. Remaining true to your podcast's subject matter isn't just about staying within your running time; it also makes clear to your listeners that, yes, you have a message and you *will* deliver it. You haven't promised something substantial only to let your mind and commentary wander aimlessly. When people listen, you want them to feel assured that what they will hear is exactly what you've offered.

Read on to find out how you can make tangents work and how to smoothly get back on topic after you've taken your side trip.

"Say, that reminds me of something . . ."

Tangents can also be creative opportunities. You don't necessarily treat tangents as strictly *verboten* in podcasting. If your tangent is directly related to, or benefits your topic, it can be effective and engaging.

Say your commentary begins with "Anyone notice how smartphones are no longer just phones but tiny PDAs that can be easily monitored and hacked into?" You cover that for a bit, and then break off on a tangent about phone etiquette and the lack of manners it brings out of people. This is a tangent that will *keep your listeners engaged* — and that can count as much as staying on topic.

What if your podcast isn't so structured, though? There's nothing wrong with hitting Record and forging ahead into the great unknown of the next 15 or 20 minutes, so long as you have an idea of where you want to go. Tangents are terrific in moderation, but put some reins on 'em and keep them at least (well, yeah) tangentially related to the subject matter of your podcast. If, say, your podcast is about movies but your review of *Doctor Strange* suddenly goes into the decline of the comic book industry (regardless of the onslaught of comic-books-to-film productions), then you still have a sense of focus. However, if your review of *Doctor Strange* wanders off into how your cat is throwing up hairballs every time you podcast or that your car's sunroof chose to stop working, blah, blah, blah, what the heck is going on here? Your audience may grow frustrated enough to stop listening.

"But getting back to what I was saying earlier . . ."

When you're podcasting for 15 or 20 minutes (or longer . . .), it's okay to take the scenic route with your discussion, but make sure that you return to the point you wanted to make in this (weekly, biweekly, or monthly) installment. The listener's delight in podcasts is often the revelation that individuals who (in many cases) have never set foot in a recording studio can produce entertaining, and even informative, shows. Sometimes meandering back to the point is part of that delight.

For instance, a podcast might begin with something read in the headlines — say, a new marketing strategy launched by Apple for the iPhone to reach a wider client base. This can lead to a variety of topics in the discussion, such as the following:

>> Smartphones that begin extending into other functionality like playing games on the PlayStation Network or providing Wi-Fi hotspots

>> Costs for iPhone services from AT&T and other carriers

>> Ways that carriers could bring down the costs of services

>> Continued shortcomings and disappointments from the smartphone industry

But in the last five to ten minutes, a simple segue like "So, to recap our thoughts on this bold marketing strategy from Apple. . ." can successfully steer you, or you and your co-hosts, back to the aim and intent of your podcast. If you return deliberately from a tangent, your listeners arrive back at the point and know the destination as well as the scenery they went through to get there.

THE NAME SAYS IT ALL

Unless you are already an established brand like Bill O'Reilly or Ricky Gervais, your show name is your calling card. For example, *Astronomy Cast* (http://astronomycast. com) — the name tells you right away what the show covers: galaxies, stars, gravity, continental drift, and extra-solar planets. Once you have a topic for your show, it's extremely beneficial that the name conveys the detail the show goes into. That way, when someone asks you "So what's your podcast about?" and you respond with "*Bite Me!*" they will understand it wasn't an insult as you explain "It's a podcast about canines with temperament issues."

But give your show's description a few seconds. Just in case you want to mess with them.

Get your listeners there and back again. Not only will they appreciate it, but they'll tell others about your podcast, and your subscribers will grow in numbers.

We hit on the topic of using a script versus an outline in Chapter 5. When it comes to staying on track, clearly, a script has a distinct advantage over an outline. Regarding interviews (see Chapter 6), having a list of questions is important, but don't be afraid to ask impromptu questions — you can always go back to your prepared list.

Recording!

Whew — there certainly is a lot to think about before you get started. That's what makes a great podcast — someone did some planning. Now it's time to put that planning and practicing into action.

Getting started with GarageBand

When you first start GarageBand, you're presented with an array of choices. How you answer this first question has ramifications on what you can — and in some cases cannot — do in GarageBand: Should you create a new Voice project or a new Empty Project? What's the difference?

The Voice Project is a project already populated with audio tracks that give you a variety of vocal effects, some practical if you are doing dramatic presentations; or comical effects for the fun of it. You can choose to utilize any of these effects, and edit them using the GarageBand interface to cater to your needs. The Empty Project is a clean slate in GarageBand. No filters. No effects. Just an empty project.

For simplicity's sake, choose to create an Empty Project and in the following window select your microphone or audio interface. We also recommend changing a few settings that work better for music composition than they do for podcast recording:

> **Turn off the Count-In feature.** The Count-In sets a tempo and is most often used when recording music, but as you will probably not be concerned with a set tempo, you probably don't need this feature. Turning off the Count-In feature should also turn off the metronome. If you don't turn it off, you'll hear a *click-click-click* while you're speaking — annoying to say the least.

>> **Hide the Library.** By default, a window will be made available on the left-hand side called the Library. The Library is a collection of effects for different kinds of recording. To hide the Library, click the Library icon, located in the top-left corner of the application window.

>> **Show Time in the LCD.** In the top of the GarageBand window is a display. By default, the LCD shows Beats & Measures. For your podcast, time is more appropriate so switch it by clicking on the music note/metronome icon. You will get a drop-down menu that offers the Time option. Select that and your LCD now measures in time.

Now you have a clean slate to start with. There's just one more thing to check before you throw the switch, and that's to confirm GarageBand knows where to get input from. Choose GarageBand ⇨ Preferences and click Audio/Midi at the top of the window that pops up. Check to make sure your Audio Input is selected correctly. The setting varies depending on your actual input (USB microphone, mixer, preamp, and so on). After that's taken care of, close the window.

Return to your project window and click the big red Record button located at the top of the screen, and begin speaking. When you're ready to stop, click the Stop button or the spacebar. Note, clicking the Record button again stops recording, but GarageBand continues playing.

Congratulations, you've made your first recording in GarageBand!

Getting started with Audacity

Audacity was meant to be simple. To record a podcast in Audacity, follow these simple steps:

1. **Set your input.**

   At the top of the screen you can find a drop-down list with several choices — Line In, Microphone, and so on. Your settings depend on your system setup. Audacity is pretty good at detecting what inputs it can use on your system. Go ahead and pick the proper one. Just make sure that your microphone is plugged in before launching Audacity: Otherwise, it won't know your mic exists.

2. **Click the Record button.**

   Audacity creates a new track and begins recording. As you speak your words of wisdom to the world, you should see the meters moving and the waveform being created.

TIP

Audacity comes with a terrific function called *Noise Reduction* which digitally attempts to identify the offending noise and "remove" it from the recording. To do this effectively and efficiently, though, Audacity needs to have a clean sample of the room's natural audio, called an *audio floor* or *noise floor* in professional settings. Record, either at the beginning or at the end of your recording, 5-10 seconds of the space you are recording in. Just leave the mics open but say nothing for a chunk of time, and that is the sample of your *room noise*. That will be your sample to use when, after you record and are working with the audio in post, Audacity's Noise Reduction asks for a sample of the background noise you want to eliminate.

3. **Click the Stop button.**

When you're done, just click Stop.

Congratulations, you've made your first recording using Audacity. Now you know why so many podcasters love it!

Chapter **8**

Cleanup, Podcast Aisle 7!

Although a high-tech activity like podcasting doesn't exactly qualify as quaint, the charm of podcasting is — whether produced by a major studio or by friends with a microphone and a laptop — its inherent, homespun quality. Steve Jobs once described it as the *Wayne's World* of radio. (No kidding, he said that in 2005 at `http://bit.ly/jobs-podcasting` on ABC.) Podcasts, much like *Saturday Night Live*'s classic sketch depicted, are often done on a shoestring budget and recorded in one take, with no editing. All the trip-ups and tangents are captured for posterity and sent to MP3 players everywhere. This is part of the grassroots appeal that podcasting is not only known for, but prides itself on nurturing as new and innovative podcasters enter the podosphere.

Although podcasting purists may harbor animosity toward the editing process, sometimes it makes all the difference between a listenable podcast and an incoherent mess of senseless rambling. For example, you might want to eliminate the sound of a train going by or silence a cough that would otherwise distract your listeners from a brilliant riposte. This chapter shows you how to use editing to shape your podcast while retaining its natural atmosphere, adding depth to that atmosphere with music, and then give the final touch to your podcast's format with an introduction and exit.

A Few Reasons to Consider Editing

Take a serious look at the mood you want to convey with your podcast. From there, you can judge how intense your editing workload will be. The following explains some instances where editing is needed — and (trust us) your podcast will benefit from it:

>> **Professional production quality:** You can't always get everything right on the first take — and sometimes not even on the second or third. Editing makes it sound like you got even hard-to-pronounce names and tricky tongue twisters right on the first try. What's more, you can drop in preproduced clips with just the right amount of space before and after to give it that polished feel.

>> **Removing boring material:** You've probably watched a live show or listened to live audio that doesn't go quite where it is intended. The content gets dull and uninteresting. As a listener, you can fast forward, change the channel, or just turn it off. As a podcaster, you can avoid this situation with editing. But even though it sounds easy to take out the boring bits, be careful that you maintain continuity. If edited improperly, the listeners may find themselves confused because the line of questions changed from space travel to herbs and spices in the matter of a few seconds.

>> **Ambient noise:** As explained in Chapter 7, *ambient noise* is the natural and spontaneously occurring noise you may pick up when recording your podcast. If you're conducting an in-studio interview and suddenly a passing siren or the rumble of a garbage truck makes it into your recording, the noise can disrupt the momentum of the interview and distract the audience. In fiction podcasts, such as *The Raven & The Writing Desk* (http://metamorcity.com) hosted by author Chris Lester, moods and atmospheres must be maintained. For Chris, however, both apply as he breaks up his fiction with interviews. Therefore, control and minimization of ambient noise is a must.

>> **Running times:** You just wrapped your latest podcast with a great interview, and you're confident that you have plenty of material for your 30-minute podcast. And then you check again and realize that you have recorded over *90* minutes' worth of interview. And you love all of it! Now here's where editing works in your favor. Your listeners expect 30 minutes, give or take a segment or two, from your podcast. You could run the whole thing, unedited, but that might test the patience of your audience members (not to mention your own bandwidth and file storage). Or you could split it up into two 45-minute interviews — or even three 30-minute interviews — breaking up the airplay of

the interviews with two smaller podcasts in-between the segments. In this approach to editing, everyone wins.

Editing can easily increase your productivity with podcasts. True, some podcasters define *editing* as cutting and deleting material, but there's more to it. Editing can help you rescue discussions and content that would otherwise be hard to shoehorn into one podcast.

>> **Scripted material:** Some podcasters argue that the true podcast is done in one take, but as podcasting matures as a medium, audiences grow more and more demanding. Expectations for a podcast change when your podcast includes scripted material. Editing is a necessity in these situations. With dramatic readings and productions, moments of "ah" and "um" should be edited out to maintain the clarity of the story, as well as maintain the mood or atmosphere established in your reading.

With the popularity of storytelling in the podosphere, professionalism and performance are the keys to a good product — and usually that means (yep!) editing. Lots of it. If you feel that editing would mar the spontaneity of your podcast — but still want to present literature or other scripted material — ask yourself how good you think *The Lord of the Rings* would have been if Sir Ian McKellen and Viggo Mortensen did everything in one take. Imagine their dialogue sounding like this:

Gandalf: Frodo . . . he, uuummm, grows closer to, you know, the end. I wonder if, um, he's, ahh . . . alive.

Aragorn: Ummm . . . what *sneezes suddenly — sniffle sniffle* . . . what does your heart *ahem* tell you?

Not what we would call riveting drama. With scripted material, editing is a must.

The Art of Editing

Editing out breaks, stammers, and trip-ups may sound easy, but there's a science to it. If you cut off too much from a clip, one word comes right on top of another, and you sound unnatural. If you don't cut off enough, pauses last too long between thoughts.

REMEMBER

When you're editing audio, the key is to review, review, review.

A lot of audio applications are out there, each with its own way to edit stumbles, bumbles, and moments of silence to honor a lost thought. The same principles apply to all those applications:

1. Find the unwanted content.

2. Give your clip a little bit — perhaps a half a second — of silence as leader or *play area* between edits.

3. Review the edit, making sure it sounds smooth and natural; an effective edit doesn't sound like an edit.

But instead of talking about it, how about you do it? In the following sections, we go into basic editing using GarageBand (www.apple.com/mac/garageband) and Audacity (www.audacity.audio) as examples. These are two very common audio-editing software packages in podcasting, and both serve as our benchmarks for how to create podcasts. If you're using some other audio-editing software package, the steps are similar enough for you to apply to your own project.

Editing with GarageBand

You can use GarageBand to edit awkward gaps of silence or eliminate coughs and stammers from your podcast. We assume at this point you just finished recording or opened a GarageBand file with a recorded track already done (see Chapter 7 for instructions on recording with GarageBand). You can also import audio files (perhaps recorded on a portable device) by dragging them from the Finder into GarageBand.

To prepare for editing the silences and splutters, split your audio into smaller segments to isolate the audio that you want to remove. Then follow these steps:

1. **Determine where in the track you want to make the edit by clicking and dragging the playhead to the beginning point of your edit.**

   Use the Time Display readout to see exactly how long the gap of silence runs. The playhead tool is the triangle connected to a vertical line. (See Figure 8-1 for details.) When creating segments, you want to place this line at the beginning and ending points of your edit.

   TIP

   Silence is easy to see when you're looking at a waveform of the audio. Coughs or other noise can be a little trickier to isolate. We suggest watching the waveform while you listen to the audio at the same time. You may want to use the slider in the bottom left to increase your time scale resolution and make it easier to work with smaller bits of information.

2. **Choose Edit ⇨ Split Regions at Playhead to make the first cut.**

   Figure 8-1 shows the first cut.

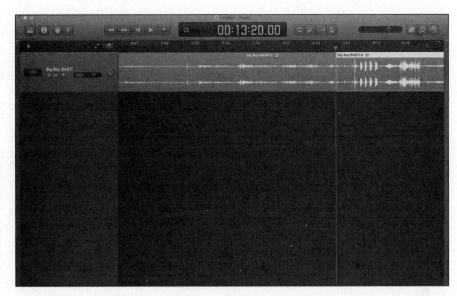

FIGURE 8-1:
Click and drag the
playhead to the
beginning point
of your edit. The
Time Display
gives you an idea
of where you are
in the project's
duration.

3. **Move your playhead to the location where you want the edit to end. Then choose Edit ⇨ Split Regions at Playhead to make your next cut.**

TIP

As you edit, give yourself a second or two of silent play area at the beginning and end of your edits. It makes the editing of two segments sound like one continuous segment, and they'll be a little easier to mix together.

4. **Single-click the segment between your two cuts and then press the Delete key.**

TIP

If you're working with GarageBand for the first time, note that the first track of audio is selected by default. To deselect the segment you're editing, single-click anywhere in the gray area underneath the track(s) you're working on.

5. **To join the two remaining audio segments, click and drag the right segment over the left segment, overlapping the two (as shown in Figure 8-2).**

WARNING

If the selected segment overlaps any part of the unselected segment, it takes priority over the unselected segment, effectively erasing any content there.

You can combine the step of deleting a segment and closing the gap (delete and move) by using the GarageBand key sequence Ctrl+Backspace.

6. **Click and drag the playhead to any point before the edit and click the Play button to review.**

7. **If the edit doesn't sound natural, undo the changes (by choosing Edit ⇨ Undo Drag) and try again.**

Because you're allowed multiple undos in GarageBand, you can step back in your project to begin at the first Split command.

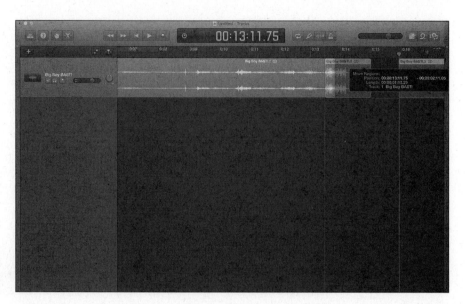

FIGURE 8-2:
To shorten the silence, move one edit over another.

As much as we would love to cover all the neat doodads in GarageBand — and there are a lot of them — we need to stick to the essentials you need to get started podcasting. For more in-depth information on mastering GarageBand, there are plenty of other resources available, including Apple's own Support site at `https://support.apple.com/garageband`.

Editing with Audacity

At this point, we assume you've just finished recording something awesome with Audacity (see Chapter 7 for instructions), or perhaps you've opened a saved project. If you have an audio file from another source, such as a portable recorder, you can import it using File⇨ Import. Now you're ready to follow these steps to make a basic edit:

1. **Find the segment that you want to edit.**

   To view the entire timeline of your project, click the Fit Project in Window tool, shown here in the margin.

   You can easily navigate between the segments of your timelines selected and the project timeline with the Fit Project in Window and Fit Selection in Window tools, located in the top-right section of the project window.

2. **Click the Selection tool — in the upper left (Mac) and upper center (Windows) — and then click and drag across the unwanted segment.**

   The unwanted segment is highlighted, as shown in Figure 8-3.

Right about here would be a good opportunity to use the Fit Selection in Window tool to double-check that the selection border doesn't go into the recorded content you want to keep.

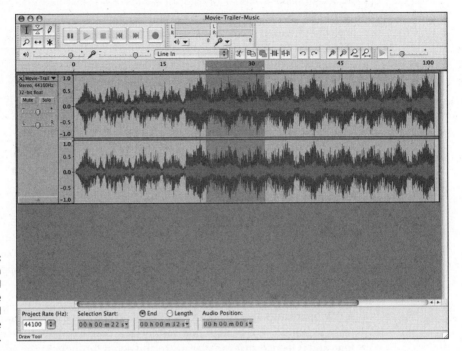

With the Selection tool, click and drag across the unwanted content in the timeline.

3. **Single-click the segment between your two cuts and then press the Delete key (Mac) or the Backspace key (Windows).**

You can also choose Edit ⇨ Cut or press ⌘+X (Mac)/Ctrl+X (Windows) to remove the unwanted segment.

Do not use the Trim command. (HERE'S THE COMMAND NOT TO USE: Edit ⇨ Trim or ⌘+T for Mac/Ctrl+T for Windows.) You may think you are trimming away unwanted content, but this command works differently from the ⌘+T command in GarageBand: Just like when you crop an image, it trims off *unselected* material — leaving you with only the content you wanted to edit out. Ack!

4. **Review the clip.**

5. **If the edit doesn't sound natural to you, undo the changes by choosing Edit ⇨ Undo Change of Position Region or pressing ⌘+Z (Mac) or Ctrl+Z (Windows), and try again.**

You're allowed multiple undos in Audacity, giving you the advantage to go back to the beginning point of your editing just in case you aren't happy with the sound of the edit.

Making Your Musical Bed and Lying in It: Background Music

On listening to podcasts of people in interview situations or in round-table discussions, there can be a strange sense of isolation, especially if the conversation hits a pocket of *dead air* (when conversation or the signal stops), and only silence is recorded or broadcast.

A few podcasters like to add a little bit of atmosphere in their individual podcast with *bed music* — a background soundtrack that's usually two to three minutes long and is looped so it can play again and again throughout the podcast, if desired. Sometimes the bed music lasts only a minute or two into the podcast when the hosts return from the break, whereas other shows keep it going from beginning to end, fading it out if they're bringing in any other sources of audio (voice mail, other podcast promos, ads, and so on).

REMEMBER

Regardless of how long the loop is, you must obtain permission from the artists to use their music and give them audible credit — either at the beginning or end of your podcast. If you're using shareware music, such as from PodShow (http://podshow.com), giving audible credit is one of the conditions you must agree to. Other options include using music loops found in GarageBand, Audition, or Logic Pro.

Finding the right balance

As you add music as a background bed, incorporate sound effects, and bring in prerecorded audio from other sources (such as H4n Pro recordings or a Skype call), the sound of your podcast gets more complex. Balance becomes not only harder, but even more essential. (Note, for example, the various volume levels of the multiple tracks in Figure 8-4.)

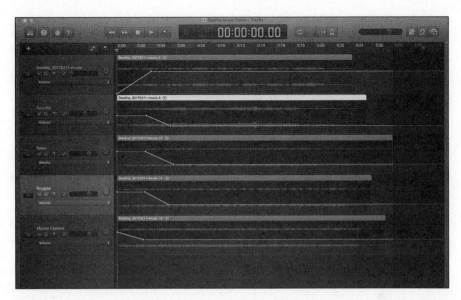

FIGURE 8-4:
Adding multiple
tracks is easy.
Balancing
them can be
challenging.

Bed music should add atmosphere to your podcast. That means finding a proper balance between the talking of the hosts and the soundtrack. The following sections explain why you want to avoid music that's too soft or too loud.

What is that noise?

If your music is too soft, your looped music could be mistaken as unwanted ambient noise of someone listening to music in the next room. Or it could be regarded as technical difficulty such as a stray *signal bleeding* (another wireless audio signal accidentally being picked up by the same frequency as your own wireless audio device) into the podcaster's wireless microphone. Music too indistinct to hear can be a distraction, particularly in quiet moments or pauses in the conversation. Your audience might end up hammering out email after email (asking what's making that annoying noise) or trying to figure out what that faint music in the background is.

Could you speak up? I can't hear you for the music . . .

When bed music is too loud, your voice is lost in the melody. Music, especially classical music and selections that rise and fall in intensity (like any good Queen album) can be tricky to mix into a conversation.

You do want to allow your audience to hear the music in the background, but the music, if you're using it as background music, probably isn't the point of the podcast. It shouldn't be so loud that you have to pump up your own voice track to be heard.

Never sacrifice audio clarity so bed music can be heard and identified clearly. If you want to showcase music, then showcase music properly. Otherwise, your bed music should remain in the background as a setting, not in the forefront of your podcast.

Applying bed music the right way

When you're setting audio levels, you want to find the best blend of music and voice, assuring one doesn't overpower the other. Both tracks should work together and not struggle for dominance.

Always listen to the podcast in headphones and your computer speakers before uploading to the Internet — review, review, review, and find that balance.

To avoid music that's either too soft or too loud, keep the following points in mind as you apply the bed music:

>> **Experiment with levels for the music *before* you record voice.** Watch your decibel level meter and set your music between –11 and –16 dB, depending on the music or sound effects you're using.

>> **When you're comfortable with the bed's level, lay down a voice track and see how your project's overall levels look (as well as sound) on your decibel level meter.** Remember, your aim is to keep your voice in the 0 or red area without overmodulating. With the music bed now behind your voice, it's much easier to hit the red without effort.

>> **Avoid *uneven* music, or music that suddenly dips low and then has moments of sudden intensity.** The best music-bed-friendly loops have an even sound (whether driving and dramatic or laid-back and relaxed) and an even level.

>> **Experiment with putting your music at the beginning and at the end of your podcast instead of throughout.** In these cases, music beds announce upcoming breaks and pauses in your podcast.

Setting volume levels for bed music

Each audio application has its own way to change volume dynamically — but the basic process is the same. In the sections that follow, you find out how to use GarageBand and Audacity to bring music into your podcast at full volume, and then balance it to be just audible enough in the background.

Setting volume levels manually with GarageBand

Follow these steps to set volume levels with GarageBand:

1. **Click the track that *your voice* resides on.**

   All segments in this track only are selected.

2. **Click and drag the playhead to anywhere between five and ten seconds into the project.**

   TIP

   If you look at the Time Display in GarageBand and see a music note in the left corner, single-click it. Doing so accesses the drop-down menu where you can select the Time mode.

3. **Click and drag the beginning of your vocal track (your voice) to the playhead.**

   You now have ten seconds of lead time between the beginning of the timeline and your podcast.

4. **In the Finder, open a window and find the music file you want to use as your bed music. Click and drag the file into GarageBand, just underneath your podcast track, as shown in Figure 8-5. Once the new audio is in place, select the Show/Hide Automation tool (circled in Figure 8-5) to set levels.**

FIGURE 8-5: A simple drag-and-drop from an open window to your GarageBand window not only imports music but also adds a track to your podcast.

TECHNICAL STUFF

When using sound effects or bed music, try to use AIFF or WAV files. An MP3 file is a *compressed* file. Compressed files (film, photo, audio, whatever) are usually far from ideal for editing because there's loss with every compression cycle — you lose a bit of quality. If you have audio bits you want to export for editing, perhaps in another program, we recommend exporting them in a raw format such as AIFF or WAV so you don't lose any quality.

5. **Select the new track of audio you just created, then single-click the Show/Hide Automation tool located above and to the right of the tracks as shown in Figure 8-5.**

   You should see a thin line against your audio tracks. If your audio track is set on the Volume option, the line is your *track volume control.* If your playhead isn't at the ten-second mark, be sure to put it there.

6. **Click at the point where the playhead line and the volume control line intersect.**

   You have now created a *control point* — a place you can click and drag to change volume levels at various times. (See Figure 8-6.)

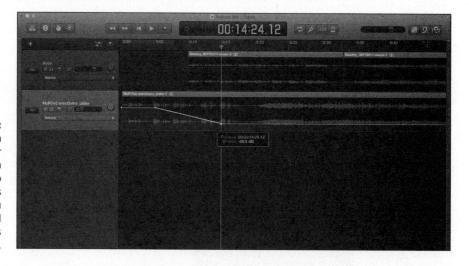

FIGURE 8-6:
Creating a volume curve for a fade-down requires two control points and gives you dynamic control over the track's output.

7. **Move your playhead back two seconds to the eight-second mark. At the eight-second mark, click the volume control to create another control point.**

8. **Return to the first control point you created (in Step 6). Click, hold, and drag the control point halfway between the bottom of the track-volume partition and its current level.**

   You have just created a *volume curve.* Now the sound dips lower, allowing for a voiceover to be heard with music softly playing in the background.

9. **Move your playhead back to the ten-second mark, as shown in Figure 8-6.**

   Doing so completes your *fade-down* (the automatic fading of the music to a subdued volume behind the voiceover).

10. **Select the podcast track and click and drag your podcast segments to where the content begins at the ten-second mark.**

    You now have a bed of music behind your podcast.

11. **Bring the playhead back to the beginning and review your podcast. Change the levels accordingly to set the music at a level you think works best.**

Keeping volume levels in GarageBand after edits

While adding in bed music, sound effects, or additional audio, you might need to make a change — add or delete another edit. Does this mean you go on and manually adjust your various levels? Not if you activate *Move Track Automations with Regions*, located under the Mix menu. This will keep your work up to that point intact while the new audio is positioned in place.

Follow these steps to have GarageBand automatically keep the volume levels in your podcast intact when last-minute audio changes occur:

1. **Find a section in your audio project where you need to add in a segment of audio.**

   Make sure you have levels set in your audio, as shown in Figure 8-7. You will be creating a gap where audio is needed. Make sure you are viewing your Volume Levels, made available by clicking your Show/Hide Automation feature.

2. **Choose Mix ⇨ Move Track Automations with Regions from the menu.**

3. **Select segments you want to move to make room for the new audio, then move the selected audio to the right between five and ten seconds.**

   The changes you made to the volume levels follow the changes of the audio on the project timeline, also shown in Figure 8-7.

Setting volume levels with Audacity

If you're using Audacity, you can set volume levels by following these steps:

1. **Click the Selection tool to activate it and then click at the ten-second mark of your timeline, placing an edit line there.**

2. **Click the Time Shift Tool button on the toolbar, shown in the margin.**

   The Time Shift tool takes an entire track of content and places it elsewhere along the project's timeline.

BEFORE MOVING AUDIO

AFTER MOVING AUDIO

FIGURE 8-7:
By activating
Move Track
Automations with
Regions, your
audio levels
remain intact
when major
changes occur in
your Timeline.

3. **Click and drag your audio to the edit line you created in Step 1.**

4. **Choose File ⇨ Import ⇨ Audio and browse for the music file that you want to use as bed music. Then select the file and click Open to begin the import process.**

   Although you can import MP3 files directly into Audacity when you're editing — be it film, photo, or audio — you shouldn't be working with compressed files. (It's just too easy to lose a bit too much quality along the way.) You can use them in Audacity, but do so at your own risk.

5. **Click the Envelope Tool button on the toolbar.**

   The Envelope Tool allows you to dynamically control the audio levels over a timeline. Clicking at the beginning of the audio track establishes the first volume setting, and the second click (at the ten-second mark) establishes the new volume level.

6. **Select the track of recently imported music by clicking its name on the left side of the project window.**

7. **Click at the beginning of the music and then click at the point where your podcast begins (the ten-second mark).**

   Two sets of points appear in your track of music.

8. **Click and drag the second set of points to the 0.5 dB mark.**

   You now have a fade-down of the music that maintains its subdued volume behind the voiceover.

9. **Activate the Selection tool, click at the beginning of the timeline, and then click Play to review your podcast.**

   Now you can change the levels as needed to set the music at a level you think works best.

Making an Entrance: Intros

Now that your podcast has a solid lead-in and a cue to fade out — or you have a loop throughout your podcast that sets a tone — your podcast is beginning to solidify. It's establishing an identity for itself; be proud of the way this podcast of yours is maturing.

But when the microphone comes on, do you always know what those first words are going to be? For some listeners, you're about to make a first impression. What do you want that first impression to be? Are you looking for something spontaneous every time, or do you want to create a familiar greeting that makes listeners feel like old friends? Your chance to make a first impression with your listeners is with an *intro*, which is the first thing the listener hears, be it with a bit of theme music or a word or two about you and your show.

It's up to you, but think about how strong a first impression and a cool intro can make. Consider the ten simple words that became the signature introductions for George Lucas's *Star Wars* saga:

A long time ago in a galaxy far, far away . . .

This intro leaves an unforgettable first impression. But even if you're not vying to be the next George Lucas, the first impression is always important. No matter who you are, this is a moment that can either establish you as a personality (and a podcast) that people will enjoy and eagerly await from episode to episode, or it will make winning over audiences a little harder. You want the first impression to be fascinating, lasting . . . and positive.

Consistent, iconic intros can serve as a polished touch of preparation or a subtle flair of professionalism. You're announcing to your audience that the show is on the launchpad, you're ready, and the journey is about to begin.

Theme music

How about a catchy theme? Just as television and motion picture themes establish a thumbprint for themselves in pop culture, an opening theme — be it a favorite song (used *with permission!*) or an original composition — can be just the right intro for your podcast. Perhaps you have a friend in the wide world of podcasting who can assist with audio production. Ask — you might be surprised how willing other podcasters are to assist. Earlier-mentioned software applications such as GarageBand, SONAR, Logic Pro, and Audition all offer royalty-free loops that can be easily edited into your own podcast intro. Other great free music sources include Kevin MacLeod's site, Incompetech (https://incompetech.com/music), and the YouTube Audio Library (https://www.youtube.com/audiolibrary/music), which also includes sound effects. If you have a little cash in the coffers, check out memberships with Digital Juice (www.digitaljuice.com) for an *astounding* collection of royalty-free jingles and sound effects.

REMEMBER

Royalty free means you're free to use the audio clip over and over without paying a license fee. You may still need to purchase the audio clips such as Digital Juice. In the case of GarageBand, the loops and clips are included in the price of the package with additional add-on libraries, available in the App Store.

Intro greeting

Some podcasters use quick, snappy intro greetings for their podcasts. For example, Adam Christianson opens every show with a heavy rock riff and the salutation "Hey, Mac Geeks, it's time for *The MacCast,* the show for Mac Geeks by Mac Geeks . . ." that kicks off his podcast, *The MacCast* (www.maccast.com). Others create an imaginative setting; for *Tales from the Archives* (http://ministry ofpeculiaroccurrences.com), the producers have a more complex intro with music, sound effects, and original dialogue. Whether elaborately produced or just a simple welcome, a consistent greeting serves to bring listeners into your corner of the podosphere.

The elements you're looking for in a spoken introduction are

>> The show's name

>> The name(s) of the host(s)

>> Location of the podcast

>> A tagline that identifies your show

Sit down and brainstorm a few ideas on how to introduce your podcast. For example, try these approaches on for size:

>> "Good morning, Planet Earth! You're listening to *My Corner: A Slice of Cyberspace*, and I'm your host, Tee Morris."

>> "From Washington, D.C., welcome to *My Corner: A Slice of Cyberspace*."

>> "With a perspective on politics, technology, and life in general, it's Tee Morris with the *My Corner* podcast."

As you see in these examples, you can mix and match the elements to drop into an intro. Come up with what feels right for you and your podcast, and stick with it. After you've put together your greeting, you can either keep it prerecorded and use it as a *drop-in* (an isolated audio clip that you can use repeatedly, either from podcast to podcast, or within a podcast) at the introduction of your podcast, or you can script it and record it with each session. Whatever method you choose, a greeting is another way of bringing your audience into your 20 to 30 minutes (or 5 minutes to an hour and a half) of time on their preferred media player.

Exit, Stage Left: Outros

Now that you have reached the end of your message or the time limit you have set yourself for a podcast, what do you do? Do you just say "Thanks, everyone, see you next time . . ." or just a basic "Bye," and then it's over? Or do you want to go out with a bit of fanfare? Whatever you decide, an *outro* is much like an intro — as simple or elaborate as you want to make it. Your outro is your final word, closing statement, and grand finale (at least for this episode).

In practical terms, putting together an outro is no different from putting together an intro — same approach, only you're doing it at the end. So review the earlier suggestions for intros and consider what seems a likely direction for an outro.

Some podcasters figure there's little more to think about for an outro than what to say and how to present it. Sure, you could keep it simple — say "Until next time," and switch off, no fuss, no script, just do it, done, and then upload. But other podcasters see the outro as more of an art form. Before taking a shortcut to the end, check out the following sections for some ways to spiff up your outro.

Leave the audience wanting more

Continuing your podcast to its final moments is a gutsy, confident, and exciting outro, carrying your audience all the way to the final second. This is one of the toughest ways to end a podcast, but if it's done right, it can only make your podcast better.

For example, the *Geek Wolfpack Podcast* ends every episode with the segment "ADHDD&D" featuring three families connecting on Roll20 (`www.roll20.net`) to play *Dungeons & Dragons* in between silly tangents. The dungeon crawling usually builds up to a cliffhanger of some description — an upcoming battle, a battle that appears to be turning on the party, or some kind of tension — and then comes an audio cue of a musical sting. The theme kicks in, quickly followed by a (prerecorded) Creative Commons attribution. The D&D cliffhangers offer a quick and easy way to say, "Tune in next week. . ." without doing so.

Catch phrase sign-off

Your outro can be the final word from the host, and it should be your bow during the curtain call. A signature farewell is a classy way of saying "This podcast is a wrap. Thanks for listening."

For example, throughout the years that journalist Walter Cronkite reported the news to America, he always ended with the words, "And that's the way it is . . ." followed by the date. On *Technorama*, Chuck and Kreg have taken a similar approach with their signature sign-off starting with Chuck saying, "And until next time, a binary high five." To which Kreg always responds "1–0–1." It has become such a well-known piece of the show that listeners writing or calling to leave feedback close their pieces with the same tag.

TIP

If you can't think of anything overly clever, a consistent exit such as "This has been my podcast, protected by a Creative Commons license. Thanks for listening . . ." works, too.

Credits roll

Another possibility for your outro could be a scripted list of credits: Websites where past shows can be downloaded, resources can be endorsed, and special thanks can be given to various supporters of your podcast.

REMEMBER

When listing credits, take care that your list of thank-yous and acknowledgments doesn't ramble on for too long after every podcast. Some podcasters reserve a full list of end credits for special podcasts, such as an end-of-the-season or even final episode. By and large, a minute can serve as a good length for ending credits — plenty of time to mention relevant websites, tuck in the obligatory "Tune in next week . . ." statement, and ask for a vote of support on your favorite podcast directory.

Coming soon to a media player near you

Just as television shows drops teasers of what will be coming up next week, podcasters can also give quick hints as to what is planned for future podcasts. The many podcast fiction titles from Mark Jeffrey (`http://markjeffrey.net`) and Scott Sigler (`http://scottsigler.com`) had already been prerecorded for the intent of podcasting. This gave both authors a terrific advantage to edit together montages of audio clips and even record a quick synopsis of what will come in future episodes.

Previews for future podcasts tend to be difficult to plan — mainly because of the spontaneous nature of podcasting that the medium prides itself on. Many podcasters have no idea what will be on the agenda for their next show until the day or even a few hours before recording, and then there are other podcasts that start up the audio equipment and speak with no prep time for their latest installment. However, for those podcasts that can provide glimpses of things to come, this kind of outro serves as a commitment to the audience that there will be more content coming through the RSS feed and that programming is being planned for future installments.

As mentioned with intros, your outro can use one of these approaches or combine them. Find what best fits your podcast and stick with it. The more consistency your podcast can follow, the more professional it sounds — spontaneous but focused, right?

Chapter 9

Roll Camera: Video Podcasting

I n its first year, podcasting established itself as an exciting audio option. It was truly "The People's Radio" for your computer, promising a fresh alternative to cookie-cutter corporate radio. A few potential podcasters took a closer look at the way RSS 2.0 worked and thought, "Wait a second — if we can do this with audio, what about video?" So, a few brave podcasters decided to put moving pictures to their podcasts; while people still search for just the right term (vidcast, vodcast, vodblog, vlogging, and so on), *video podcasting* has come to be and continues to grow.

Once upon a time, professional-quality video production (such as editing, post-production effects, and DVD authoring) on a consumer market was either a pipe dream or a hobbyist's major investment. With the advancements of film technology, advancements in home computing systems, and the ease of video-editing software, producing broadcast-quality video is not only affordable, it's expected. Add to this the popularity of services like YouTube (youtube.com) and Vimeo (vimeo.com), and creative minds both in the amateur and professional circles are now looking at video podcasting as an alternative to distribution.

When to Go Video

Chuck fancies himself as moderately skilled in the ways of live and produced video. He's been working with digital video (DV) at home and work since 2007. However, Tee sports a longer track record with editing video, both in a *linear* (the traditional two video decks tied together to one central deck with a control board offering basic post production effects) and a *nonlinear* (all on a computer, in a digital format) method. Even in those early *Flintstones*-esque days of digital video, Tee found the digital filmmaking art nothing short of amazing. Today, with terabyte drives and gigahertz processors, a lot of things have changed, and Tee's opinion has changed as well.

He now finds editing video on his Mac a cruel, demanding mistress . . . that he finds nothing short of amazing.

Video production is also *not* easy. Some of the downfalls to video podcasting are:

>> **A learning curve:** Despite what the commercials for laptops of all makes insinuate, editing video is not a push-button technology. A lot goes into video, even on the most basic of levels; with video podcasts like *The Joe Rogan Experience* (http://joerogan.net), *Technorama* (www.chuckchat.com/technorama), *Happy Hour from the Tower* (www.happyhourfromthetower.com), and *Universe Today* (www.universetoday.com), the bar to run with the big boys and girls of video podcasting is pretty high.

>> **More production time:** With video, you must contend with more than just ambient noise. Now you need to consider lighting, camera angles, wardrobe, make-up, and so on. Editing also proves more difficult, since you can't just cut a flub out without the host seemingly jumping around. Podcasting audio can prove daunting in its production needs, but video is a step up and demands a great deal of time and attention.

So, with all these daunting challenges, why go video with your podcast? Here are some good reasons to step up to video podcasting:

>> **Your message needs more than sound to get across to your audience.** If you're putting together a show for educational or training purposes, you may want to feature diagrams or procedures that require visual aids. With video, you now can appeal to listeners on a visual as well as an aural level.

OH, YOU TEASE!

Sure, video can take a lot longer to record, edit, upload, and so on than an audio-only counterpart. We don't deny that part. The great thing is that there are ways to make quick, short videos that you can use to promote your podcast be it audio or video! Many podcasters have turned to services like Periscope and Facebook Live to make short vignettes, or teasers to promote a show with larger production. While at your favorite con, expo, or weekend event, you may find yourself gathering interviews or some other footage for your regular show. Take a few minutes to tell your audience what you are working on. Grab your mobile phone and do a quick broadcast. "Hey, this is Chuck coming to you live from Phoenix ComiCon. I just got done talking to The Green Arrow — Stephen Amell! Be sure to listen to the full-length interview on our site when it comes out in a couple weeks." Okay, it's a made-up example and maybe Chuck will get that interview this year.

>> **You want a captive audience.** The ability or temptation to multitask is removed as your subscribers are now applying the visual senses, taking advantage of the video features in mobile phones, computers, and other devices. They can't drive a vehicle, cook a meal, or walk Fluffykins while they watch your video podcast, so you gain greater audience focus. So, make sure the video serves a purpose for your viewers.

>> **You want to create your *definitive* vision.** In travel podcasts (also known as *sound-seeing tours*), where the sounds of a marketplace provide the host with a background, or beer tastings (also called *pubcasts, barcasts,* or *beercasts*), where the flavor of a local bar filters into the show, or podcast novels, where a few sound effects set the scene, the listener's imagination fills in the blanks on what is happening around the podcaster. Now, the subscriber can see and (virtually) experience walking through the marketplace in Athens, take in the sights and sounds of a Western Yorkshire pub, or see the characters as the author intended them to be seen, in the settings he or she imagined.

The Price of Pretty Pictures

You can create video podcasts with any video-editing application running on either Mac or Windows. You can use Apple iMovie, Apple Final Cut Pro, Telestream Screenflow, or Adobe Premiere to create your episode. When it's time to export your movie out of your video-editing software, many of these applications use a format optimized for podcasting.

Of course, you could do the compression by hand, but the question here is *why*. Take advantage of the shortcuts because in this section, we take a closer look at other considerations concerning video podcasting.

That file is how big?!

Provided you follow our Cheat Sheet's compression specs, the standard audio podcast of roughly 80MB will cover anywhere from 90 minutes to two hours — *of audio.* When compared with other podcasts that are far more economical in their running times, 80MB is huge.

To video, this is chump change.

Tee created a 10-second video clip for The Ministry of Peculiar Occurrences that came out to 1MB. Think about that a moment: 10 seconds = 1MB. That is a video at *standard* definition (not high definition, the preferred format for video now) and *without* audio. When video podcasting first came to the hearts and minds of audio podcasters, it was a bit of a shock when they tried to make their 20-to-30-minute audio into a video equivalent. "How do I get my file size smaller?" podcasters asked on various discussion boards. Although the reply might have come across as snarky, it was the only available answer: "Make a shorter podcast." If you have a two-hour podcast and are planning to compress your video down to the same size (or thereabouts) as that 80MB MP3, well . . . that just won't happen.

Maybe you want to make the jump from *standard* (720 × 480) digital-video resolution to high definition (1920 × 1080) resolution. You're going to want to prepare for major demands on both bandwidth and file sizes. Sure, there are compressions that will cut your file sizes by half, but your resolution will not be as sharp as the version before compression. There is always a trade-off with video. You can't have compression, resolution, and small file sizes. For more about the final steps between video editing and compression, consult *Digital SLR Video and Filmmaking For Dummies* by John Carucci (Wiley).

Burn, bandwidth, burn!

Bandwidth is the factor most new podcasters tend to gloss over. That can prove to be costly, especially if your podcast is 50MB or higher per download. If you garner 1,000 listeners, for example, you've gone through 5GB simply for that file transfer. If these 1,000 listeners are going through your archives, your bandwidth needs to increase exponentially.

Now, suppose you decide to produce a video podcast with some length — let's say, 20 minutes. A decent length for a podcast, right? What happens? Your first episode is nearly 900MB compressed in the M4V format at a resolution of 1280 x 720 — a very hefty download.

It's even heftier if your podcast is a runaway success. If you have 2,000 subscribers in your first week, you have burned through 2TB of your monthly bandwidth just for that episode. What about the weeks — and the listeners — to come? What does your web host offer, and can it handle this kind of traffic for your podcast? When you're looking at video podcasting, consider the running time and file size of your episodes, and then look at your web host's bandwidth.

Lock and Load (Your Camera): Planning Your Shooting Schedule

Nonlinear (that is, digital) video applications like iMovie and Premiere have dramatically simplified the process of editing video. However, as we state earlier, the commercials aren't quite accurate when describing the ability to make a movie as quick and easy. It's still far from a push-button technology. We've been talking about the various demands for your video podcast, but perhaps the greatest demand of them all is *time*.

YOU'RE ON TWITCH? NOPE.
STILL NOT PODCASTING.

Maybe you're thinking "Hold on — there's a way we can side-step all these demands. We can set up a recording studio and use *Twitch* (http://twitch.tv) to get our podcast out there!" You could do that, and not have a concern for time, storage space, or bandwidth. Just angle your cameras, get your lighting right, and start streaming.

Sure, you could do that, but you're not podcasting.

Twitch, first introduced in June 2011 and known best for playthroughs of video games and broadcasts of eSports competitions, has branched out to creative content programming from tutorials on Photoshop to live music performances. The content on the site can either be viewed live or on demand, but this is where Twitch is entirely different from podcasting. True, podcasting can also be streamed on demand, but episodes are distributed through RSS, meaning you have the option to have content automatically downloaded. The show is brought to you, not requiring you to go to a site. You can subscribe to a Twitch stream, but the video is not distributed through RSS. It is a streaming website, meaning you can watch it live or watch it on demand, provided you go to Twitch's website or use its app to watch the stream. So, no, you are not podcasting.

That does not mean that hosts of Twitch streams are not working as hard (if not harder) as podcasters. Streamers like OneActual, lulusoccer, Raza528, Frida, and ZGPhoto (pictured here) are known to stream for *hours*, keeping the conversation and the energy up and lively, all while fragging opponents in their favorite video games. Now that's multitasking.

Here's how the process works:

1. Set up the camera, rehearse your podcast (if applicable), and then make time to shoot *from that angle.*

2. Reset for the same shot but from a different angle. Shoot your footage from the new angle unless you're lucky enough to have multiple cameras. If so, combine the preceding step and this one, making sure you do not catch any of your other cameras in frame. (Cinematography speak for catching sight of another camera when shooting.)

3. Review your video footage and *capture* (get the video off the camera media and into the video editor) it onto your computer.

4. Edit your footage together, removing any mistakes, continuity errors, and small trips and tumbles. The result is making the whole project appear seamless and fluid.

5. After all the editing, post-production, and reviewing is done, you must *render* the video, outputting this production in the desired format — be it podcasting, streaming (something we discuss later), full-screen video, or DVD.

Depending on the power of your computer's processors, the length of your video, and what format you're outputting it to, this could take anywhere from a few minutes to a few hours to a full eight-to-nine-hour workday.

The allure of video is intense — and don't mistake us for a moment, we love it! — but make sure you give yourself *time:* time to shoot, time to edit, time to review, and time to render.

TIP

Make that first episode and then give a second episode a shot. Go for three, if you can. Once you have those episodes edited and ready to go, you can decide on what kind of posting schedule you want your podcast to follow.

iTarantino: Creating with iMovie

If you've just purchased a new Macintosh computer, you have *iMovie* (www.apple.com/imovie) within reach. This unassuming application grants you the ability to edit video by dragging and dropping clips where you want them on your project's timeline.

Capturing video with iMovie

You need to get the video off the camera or media it is currently recorded on (SD card, internal hard drive, cassette, and so on) and into your computer. This process is called *capturing.* The video is played back and then captured into the video-editing application in a format that the program can understand.

We're going to make the bold assumption that you have a digital video camera, digital SLR, or some other device that has your video footage ready for importing. Here's how you get your video off the camera and into your computer for editing:

1. **Launch iMovie.**

2. **From the intro window, select Create a New Project by clicking the big plus sign and select Movie.**

3. **Connect your video camera to your computer via USB and set it to playback mode.**

   iMovie detects the camera automatically and brings up the import window shown in Figure 9-1. If it doesn't, you won't have any options available for importing footage. If iMovie doesn't detect your camera, check your camera to make certain it's in playback mode, has power, and is plugged into your computer.

FIGURE 9-1:
Select the clips to import from the Import window.

4. **Select the clips you wish to import and click Import selected, or click Import All to retrieve all clips on your camera.**

Your clips are imported into the My Media Pane, the area on the left in iMovie, as shown in Figure 9-2.

The version of iMovie we are using is iMovie v10. As with most software mentioned in this book, updates happen. Parts of the interface may change between what is shown here and what you get, but the steps should be easily applied to any version.

FIGURE 9-2:
Your video is brought into the My Media Pane in the order of capture.

5. **When your import is concluded, iMovie closes the import window automatically and returns to the main editing window.**

If your video is on your computer as a data file (MOV, M4V, MPEG, and so on), choose File ⇨ Import Media (or press ⌘+I) to import your clips into the My Media Pane.

A walk in the park on a clear Spring day, don't you think? This process is known as *logging*, where you go through and organize your clips as needed.

Always eject your camera like any other USB device before unplugging it from your computer to avoid losing data. You can do this from within iMovie's import screen or from Finder.

Creating your episode with iMovie

When you have your video imported and organized in iMovie, you're ready to edit it into a video podcast. Follow these steps:

1. **Click and drag your opening clip from the My Media Pane into the Timeline along the bottom of the iMovie interface.**

   The *Timeline* in your iMovie interface is where you assemble and edit your clips. Simply drag and drop clips in the order you want them to appear. By default, you're viewing video in the Timeline as clips (View Clip mode).

2. **Repeat Step 1 for the remaining clips in your My Media Pane until you have your clips in the order you want. See Figure 9-3.**

   What you have now is commonly referred to as a *rough cut*. This is your video podcast without transitions, set volume level, or any detailed editing. It gives you an idea of what the video will look like when it's done.

FIGURE 9-3: After you move your clips from the My Media Pane to the Timeline, you have completed your rough cut.

The amount of editing your video podcast needs depends on the amount of footage you shoot and how detailed you want your production to be. When you have a rough cut, here are some editing tricks to try:

>> **Navigate throughout your video.** A scroll bar across the bottom of the Timeline will allow you to move from the beginning to the end of clips, going back and forth as needed.

>> **Zoom in and out.** Underneath the preview window is a Zoom slider that allows you to view the project from beginning to end, or zoom in on specific edit points.

>> **Scrub through video.** With your playhead, you can *scrub* through the video. *Scrubbing* is the process of viewing audio at a user-designated speed. You scan through segments, find what you're looking for, and make edits. With the left and right arrows, you can also advance through a clip frame by frame.

>> **Make a cut.** Move your playhead in the Timeline to where you want to make an edit. Choose Modify ⇨ Split Clip at Playhead (or press ⌘+B).

>> **Delete a segment.** Click the segment you want to remove and press Delete to remove the unwanted video.

>> **Create a cutaway.** Sometimes, you want video that breaks the monotony of a single shot, more commonly known as a *cutaway*.

>> **Drop in a transition.** Click Transitions just above the My Media Pane and select a transition. A *transition* is a cool way to get from one clip to the next (a crossfade, wipe, or some interesting bridge), unlike a *cutaway* or *jump cut* where one video source switches to another. Click and drag the desired transition between two clips to apply it.

TIP

To see a preview of a transition, move your cursor over from left to right.

>> **Place a title at the beginning of your podcast.** Click Titles (on the same row as My Media and Transitions) to bring up the Title Pane. Choose a title and drag it to the timeline just above the first clip. Once you place your title on the clip, edit the text in the preview window (see Figure 9-4). The *Titles Pane* is the feature of iMovie where you can place animated or static text at the beginning, middle, or end of your movie, giving your podcast a polished Hollywood touch.

TIP

Click the T icon above the preview window to bring up more styling options for your title, including font size, color, position, and more.

iMovie renders the title and then incorporates it into the project. If your title needs to change, return to the clip with the attached title, select the title, and click the T to edit it. When you are done, click the T again.

FIGURE 9-4:
FIGURE 9-4:
With iMovie
Titles, you can
come up with
sharp titles for
your video
podcast.

When you have your video how you want it, follow these steps to finish your podcast:

1. **Choose File ⇨ Share ⇨ iTunes.**

2. **After reviewing the dialog box that appears, click Share.**

   Your video is now available in iTunes.

3. **In iTunes, use the drop down in the upper left to select Movies.**

   You can find your video from iMovie in the Home Videos section, located on the left.

4. **Select your video and then choose Edit ⇨ Get Info or press ⌘+I. Fill in the descriptive information about your video. These are the ID3 tags (see Figure 9-5). When your tags are complete, click OK.**

   For more on ID3 tags and why these are important to your podcast, see Chapter 10.

5. **Choose File ⇨ Show in Finder to quickly locate your file on your hard drive.**

FIGURE 9-5:
ID3 tags are just as easy (and as important) with video podcasts as with audio podcasts.

Congratulations, you have just edited and output your first video podcast.

TIP

iMovie is not only designed to be easy, it's designed for you to have fun with video. Remember to go exploring with its various features. For example, you can take your finished episode, export it, then use it (or footage from the original shoot) to create a Hollywood-style *trailer* or a preview of what's coming soon.

It's just that easy! With upgrades to Mac OS X and various incarnations of iMovie, your interface and your results may vary. You may also find iMovie has a lot of features we haven't even touched. That's because we're keeping it quick and easy, fast and furious, and above all, to the basics. If you want to find out more about editing with iMovie, there are many books on the market that will take you deeper into the power of this application. You may also pick up a few cool tips from John Carucci's *Digital SLR Video and Filmmaking for Dummies* (Wiley).

So what happens when you want to go beyond iMovie's features and you're ready to do more? Then consider the step above iMovie, *Final Cut Pro X* (https://www.apple.com/final-cut-pro), a standard in the video production industry.

DV on the PC: Podcasting with Adobe Premiere

Remember Windows Movie Maker? It was considered the iMovie for the PC . . . only a lot less easy. In 2017, with all the various options out there for PCs, both for free and for sale, Microsoft decided there was no longer a need or demand for its built-in, free video editor for Windows, and Windows Movie Maker was discontinued. The PC market is now awash with so many freeware alternatives available. Finding the right editor for Windows that can meet all the various demands and features needed in filmmaking and DV editing has become something of a risky business. What's the best option for you out there?

For podcasters, we focus on two Adobe products that have not only been tried and tested, but are considered trusted and reliable by editors of all backgrounds. *Premiere Elements* (www.adobe.com/products/premiere-elements.html) is Adobe's professional grade video editing suite made available and affordable to consumers. There will be a slight learning curve in finding the workflow that suits you, but the user interface is accessible to newcomers to video editing. It does have a price tag around $70, but that should fit within most podcasters' budgets. If, however, you are looking for something with more options, also available is Elements' "big brother" *Adobe Premiere Pro* (www.adobe.com/products/premiere.html) for the more advanced producer.

Capturing video with Adobe Premiere Elements

For this example, we're going to assume your video clips are on a digital camcorder (one with a hard drive, SD card, or some other high-speed storage). If you are transferring from a camcorder that uses tape, the instructions are a bit different and we encourage you to review the Premiere Elements documentation.

1. **Make sure your video camera, phone, or DV playback device is connected to your PC. Then launch Premiere Elements.**

2. **From the Add Media drop-down box, click Videos from Cameras & Devices (see Figure 9-6).**

3. **In the Video Importer window that appears, check clips you want to import, or rather, uncheck the ones you don't want to import since all clips are checked by default.**

    Don't forget to check out the other options available on the import window, such as naming your clips, deleting them after import (to reclaim space on your camera), and where the video clips are being stored on your hard drive.

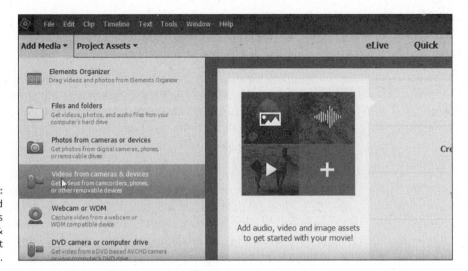

TIP

By default, Premiere Elements will add all your videos to the timeline. If you'd rather have them saved as project assets that you can pick and choose later, uncheck the Add To Timeline checkbox.

4. **Click Get Media to import the selected clips.**

WARNING

If you're capturing on tape, you will be importing your footage in real time. For every second you shoot, it takes a second to import. Also, check your battery level or plug your camera in to AC power. There are few things more frustrating than hitting the Import button, coming back an hour later only to find out your battery on the camera has died partway through the import!

5. **Once your clips are imported, use the Project Assets drop-down to copy the clips you want to the timeline (see Figure 9-7).**

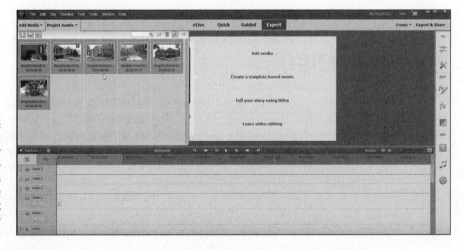

SCREENCASTING: WHAT'S ON YOUR DESKTOP?

Screencasting is a delivery method of an established teaching tool: recording actions of your desktop. In a screencast, a podcaster is usually showing off features of a computer application (like Evernote, Final Cut Pro, Word, and so on); but instead of using screen captures that show drop-down menus already deployed or attempting to film your monitor and sacrificing clarity of image, a third-party application like Camtasia (https://www.techsmith.com/camtasia.html) or Telestream's Screenflow (telestream.net/screenflow/) captures all actions taken on your desktop in a live recording and then allows you to edit with basic editing functions such as copy/paste, titles, transitions, callouts, layering, chroma-key, audio tracks, and popular features found in most video editing software packages. Subscribers can follow along with the video, cursor, menus, and actions all happening clearly and vividly on your media player. You also have the additional option of outputting the raw video from your screencasting and importing it into any of the video editors we spotlight in this chapter.

WARNING

Although programs like iMovie and Premiere have simplified video editing dramatically, as mentioned earlier, this isn't a quick-and-easy process. When the video is done, it must be processed, and that can take anywhere from a few minutes to a few hours, depending on the length of your episode, the dimension of your video, and the compression format. Give yourself that time to edit and time to process the video you're creating. Before announcing your video podcast, try to find out how those first few episodes will progress in production and finally what the processing time will be for a single episode. You may find that a missed mistake can cost you hours. Always preview and then preview again before processing.

And We're Live! — Video Podcasting in the Moment

Quick reminder — podcasting is a means to deliver your content, right? So why not look at some of the other things the cool kids are doing these days, like Facebook Live, YouTube Live, and Periscope? Instead of recording (and hopefully editing), then uploading, posting, and waiting, why not just push a button and go online now?! The truth is, you can do both — and you might choose to depending on whom you want to speak to and when.

Live events are great for on-the-spot broadcasts such as a car show, parade, or a conference floor. You start broadcasting, people can ask you questions immediately, and you can provide them feedback as well. The downside is, if people missed it, they missed it. Sure, people can go to your Facebook page, YouTube channel, or Periscope page (where your content disappears after 24 hours), but that's a different experience from podcasting, which is delivered to their device automatically to watch when they are ready. Are we clear on this yet?

However . . .

These services do offer you the option to download the segment you just shot. This means you can always download the clip, edit for an opening and closing segment and ID3 tags, and then place it into your RSS feed, distributing the video as your next podcast episode. Just like that.

Up Periscope!

Periscope (`https://www.periscope.tv`), owned by Twitter, allows you to take your Android or iOS smartphone, click a button on the app, and start broadcasting anywhere and anytime. As mentioned, once the broadcast is over, others can watch it for up to 24 hours on Periscope's website, as shown in Figure 9-8. As well as broadcasting, the app is also good for watching videos from others who are spouting their message. Like other social networks, you can follow people and be notified when they are broadcasting, as well as be followed. You can also answer and respond to your viewers in real-time, making the connection with your audience even more personal.

FIGURE 9-8: Periscope's website offers your audience, comprised of Periscope and Twitter users, to catch your live streams up to a day after you log off from your live episode.

Here is how to run Periscope:

1. **Download and launch the Periscope app on your smartphone.**

   The Periscope app is available for both Android and iPhone, and automatically syncs up with Twitter once you validate a Twitter account.

2. **From the Options menu along the bottom of the app, tap the Video Camera icon found at the center of the menu.**

   You can also access Periscope through the LIVE option offered in the Twitter app when you are composing a tweet.

TIP

3. **Your interface now features a live picture, a keyboard, Audience options, and a field for you to title your Periscope video. Enter your video's topic here.**

   At any time, you can tap the "X" in the upper-right corner to cancel this video and exit this mode. Your Periscope video can be shot either in a *Portrait* (vertical) perspective or a *Landscape* (horizontal) perspective.

4. **After you title your episode, tap the red Go LIVE option to begin your Periscope video.**

5. **At the end of your Periscope video, the app will offer an option to save your video to your Camera Roll. Doing this will save your video episode on your smartphone.**

   With your episode on your smartphone, you can then transfer it to your video editor of choice and work with it to prepare to send out on your podcast feed.

WARNING

When shooting your video, especially if you are doing a video of yourself on location, make sure you are aware of your surroundings. It is far too easy to lose your footing, bump into someone, or find yourself in a rather precarious (if not dangerous) situation. Be careful!

YouTube Live

What more can you say about YouTube? It's brought us everything from instructional videos how to fold fitted sheets to people jumping off roofs to teach us all that gravity is more than just a theory — it's the law. Most of these videos are recorded on one device and uploaded afterwards. YouTube also offers a live feature (formerly called Hangouts On Air until 2016). These can be scheduled ahead of time, allowing you to embed a video in to a site with a countdown, or you can start streaming immediately. Chuck uses YouTube Live a lot in his day job where he does presentations and software demonstrations. Unlike Periscope, YouTube Live videos are available on your channel forever — or at least until you remove them.

Additionally, YouTube Live events can be broadcast from a mobile device as well as your desktop or laptop with a webcam. If you have more advanced software like Wirecast Pro from Telestream (`https://www.telestream.net`), you can broadcast directly from your studio to YouTube Live.

1. **Point your browser to YouTube** (`https://youtube.com`).

2. **Click your Google Profile icon, located in the upper right of your browser window.**

   Your Google Profile icon should be the image associated with your account. A drop-down menu appears.

3. **Click the Creator Studio button.**

4. **From the menu on the left, click Live Streaming and choose Events.**

   Even if you want to start streaming immediately, use Events rather than Stream Now.

5. **Give your show a name, set the time (Today/Now is good for an immediate broadcast), provide a description and keywords. See Figure 9-9.**

FIGURE 9-9:
With a few details filled in, you'll be live on YouTube.

6. **Click the Go live now button.**

   You are presented with one final pop-up informing you that you will be brought to a Google Hangout On Air to do your live streaming. You're still not LIVE yet. . . . This is a good time to check your camera and audio settings, share your desktop if you plan to do a presentation or software demo, and invite any guests you may want to bring in to the conversation.

7. **Click the Start Broadcast button.**

Now you are live . . . until you hit Stop Broadcast.

REMEMBER

If you have guests on your live broadcast, YouTube automatically switches to display the person who is talking. This is great if you are having a face-to-face conversation but not so great if one of you is doing a screenshare. When the others talk, the viewer is pulled out of the screenshare and one of the other cameras is displayed. Be sure (as the person running the broadcast) that you click the avatar in the lower right of the person you want to lock as the presenter while doing screenshares to avoid the flip-flop effect of auto-switching for the viewer — very annoying to watch! You will know it's locked because a white border appears around that avatar. When you are done with the screensharing, click the avatar again to remove the white border and return to auto-switching.

Don't forget, YouTube is a social network — that's why all the content creators are constantly begging you to subscribe. When you do subscribe to a YouTube channel, you'll get notifications when your favorite creator is broadcasting live so you won't miss a beat.

Facebook Live

Not to be outdone by Twitter or Google, Facebook has gotten in to the act of live broadcasts from your mobile device with *Facebook Live*. Facebook incorporated features Periscope users would recognize, like immediate broadcast capability, back and forth engagement until the broadcast is done. Facebook Live also allows for desktop broadcasts as well, feeding video directly from software like Wirecast Pro (https://www.telestream.net/wirecast/overview.htm). This is how Chuck and Kreg do their live stream on *Technorama* (see Figure 9-10.) When the live stream starts up, sharing happens, followers are alerted, discussions start, and happiness ensues. Afterwards, the video can be downloaded and distributed to your podcast subscribers.

WARNING

Facebook Live has exclusive live broadcast rights. As Chuck found out after upgrading Wirecast Pro in 2016, the software states "if you have the bandwidth, you can simultaneously broadcast to multiple destinations." Terrific! You can do YouTube Live and Facebook Live at the same time, right? Wrong! Telestream had to write Wirecast in such a way that if you are broadcasting to Facebook, you cannot broadcast to YouTube at the same time. Instead, Chuck and Kreg record a local MP4 video file and upload that to YouTube later. The moral of the story is, you may have to make choices when you broadcast live. The best bet, go where your people are!

657 people reached   Boost Post

173 Views

👍 Like   💬 Comment   ↗ Share

🔵 Weber Baker, Chuck Tomasi and 2 others   Realtime Comments ▾

3 shares

FIGURE 9-10:
Technorama
on Facebook
Live using
Wirecast Pro.

To do a Facebook Live event, follow these steps:

1. Launch the Facebook app on your smartphone.

The Facebook app is available for both Android and iPhone. Also available is Facebook's *Pages* app. Both Facebook and Pages can shoot Facebook Live segments.

2. From the status update's options, tap the Live icon, shown in Figure 9-11.

3. Your interface now features a live picture. Tap Describe your live video . . . and type in your video's topic here.

At any time, you can tap the X in the upper-left corner to cancel this video and exit this mode. Your Facebook Live can be shot either in a portrait or landscape perspective.

4. After you title your episode, tap the blue Go Live option to begin your Facebook Live. Once the countdown is done, you are broadcasting video over Facebook.

5. At the end of your Facebook Live video, the app will offer you analytics. After a few minutes, Facebook will post the video for replay. People will still be able to comment on your video, just not in real time as when you are live.

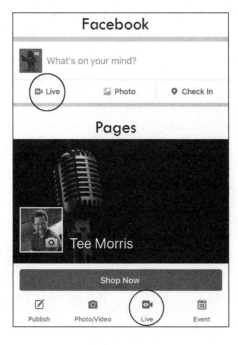

6. **When you replay your video on your Facebook, you can download the video, as shown in Figure 9-12.**

With your episode on your computer, you can now import it into your video editor of choice and work with it to prepare to send out on your podcast feed.

SERIOUSLY? A SELFIE-STICK?

The much-maligned *Selfie-Stick* has been either a source of ridicule or, for those really lost in their own narcissism, a source of horrifying (if not comical) death; but when it comes to video podcasting and using Facebook Live, Periscope, or YouTube on your smartphone, a Selfie-Stick saves your arm from a lot of cramping and offers your video a bit of stability. With the right angle and the right leverage, your Selfie-Stick works as a collapsible steady cam and can allow you better options in capturing more people in the moment and even more activity in your shot. Just remember, as we warn earlier in the Periscope segment, to be aware — well aware — of your surroundings. Getting the best shot for your podcast will not matter one bit if you are dead or recovering in a hospital.

And yes, Tee was being very careful with a vintage steamtrain slowly advancing behind him.

3

So You've Got This Great Recording of Your Voice: Now What?

Get the skinny on audio quality through bitrates and sample rates.

Let people know what they are listening to with ID3 tags and album art.

Upload your content and share it with the world.

Provide additional details of what's in your episode with detailed show notes.

Chapter **10**

Shrink That Puppy and Slap a Label on It

You've finished your final edit (and if you think we're skirting blasphemy whenever we use the *E* word, trust us — creativity sometimes demands a sacrifice). At last you're ready to compress your mondo-super-sized AIFF or WAV file down to the format that inspires terror and indigestion in RIAA representatives everywhere: *MP3*.

The MP3 format was designed to reduce the amount of data (via compression) required for digitized audio while still retaining the quality of the original recording. MP3 files are the best way to keep the audio small enough in size to make it a quick-and-easy download, and it's this format that podcasting uses to get content efficiently from podcaster to podcatching client. Although creating MP3s is a simple enough process, you do need to make some tradeoffs between quality and compression.

A Kilobit of Me, and a Whole Lot of You: Understanding Kbps

The compression process begins with proper *bitrate* settings, measured in Kbps (kilobits per second). Bitrate is a method of measuring data transmission from one point to the next. The higher the Kbps value, the more data being transferred between two points. The more data being transferred per second, the better the quality of information. With each rate of data transfer offered by recording applications, you can digitally reproduce the various qualities of audio:

>> **8 Kbps,** matching the vocal quality of a telephone conversation

>> **32 Kbps,** yielding audio quality similar to AM radio

>> **96 Kbps,** yielding audio quality similar to FM radio

>> **128 Kbps,** matching audio CD quality, and the most common Kbps used for MP3 compression of music

>> **192 Kbps,** a "Higher Quality" setting Kbps used for MP3 compression of music; better audio sound, but larger data files

You aren't married to this listing of Kbps by any stretch of the imagination. Figure 10-1 shows that Audacity offers in its Preferences plenty of variations from the five common settings. Tweak until you find the Kbps best suited for your podcast.

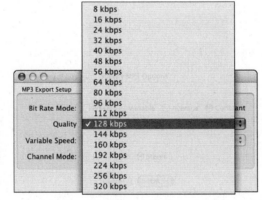

FIGURE 10-1: You find a wide variety of bitrates for compressing your podcast to MP3 with Audacity.

REMEMBER

It's a tradeoff: The higher the bitrate, the larger your file size is — but the smaller your bitrate, the lower your audio quality is. A good idea is to experiment: Compress your podcast using one bitrate, save it that way, and then change your bitrate to something higher (or lower), save it, and play back each clip to compare how they load and how they sound. Note any changes in sound quality and file size. When you find that happy medium between quality and compression, stick with that number for your current and future podcasts.

Setting bitrates in Audacity

Changing bitrates in Audacity is a multistep process. The first step is to get your editor all set for creating MP3 files:

1. **Choose Audacity ⇨ Preferences (Mac OS) or choose Edit ⇨ Preferences (Windows).**

   The Preferences window opens.

2. **Choose the File Formats option in the left column (see Figure 10-2).**

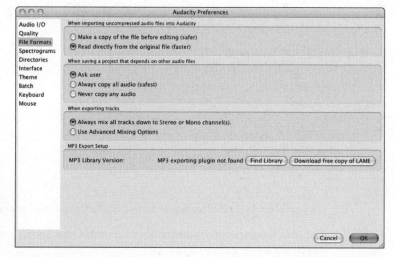

FIGURE 10-2:
Before setting bitrates in Audacity, you need to download a LAME file.

3. **Click the Download Free Copy of LAME button in the MP3 Export Setup section.**

4. **Follow the steps for your OS as outlined on the web page to download the proper files.**

5. **Open the archive file (no need to worry — it's a safe download) and drop it into your Audacity folder.**

6. **Return to Audacity and click the Find Library button.**

7. **Choose Applications ⇨ Audacity (Mac) or My Computer ⇨ (Main Drive) ⇨ Program Files ⇨ Audacity (Windows) to navigate to the** `libmp3lame` **file.**

8. **Select the** `libmp3lame` **file and click Open.**

This step in setting up the LAME Library is a one-time thing. You won't have to repeat this process again unless you move the library to another location.

Now you've come to the point where you set the bitrate. When you have a file, follow these steps to export it as an MP3 file:

1. **Choose File ⇨ Export.**

2. **From the Format menu, select MP3 Files.**

3. **Next to the Format: MP3 Files menu, click Options.**

   The Specify MP3 Options dialog box opens, as shown in Figure 10-3.

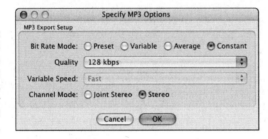

FIGURE 10-3:
Under the MP3 options, you can set bitrates and other variables for your compressed audio.

4. **Choose your desired bitrate from the Quality drop-down menu.**

   If you're following our recommendation from the Cheat Sheet for this book, you would set the bitrate to 128.

TECHNICAL
STUFF

You can also set up your Bit Rate Mode (Constant) and your Channel Mode (Joint Stereo). Constant bitrate ensures the bits are output at a steady (constant) rate despite the audio that is being used (including silence). Variable bitrate attempts to do a bit of compression — for example, the bitrate of a complex music sample would take more space than that of the same length of time in a spoken piece with several pauses. Although variable length audio sounds good on the surface, it can present problems to the listener — actual playback times may not be correct, causing problems when people pause a long podcast. Joint Stereo refers to a technique that saves some space when your recording includes mono channels or tracks. Rather than using the space of a stereo track (left and right) to save that information, joint stereo techniques recognize it and save space by only using half the space.

5. **Click OK to return to the Export window.**

6. **Name your file and then click OK.**

7. **You will be prompted to fill out your ID3 tags (see the ID3 tag section of this chapter).**

After you set the bitrate for this one file, your settings are automatically applied to other MP3 files created from this point. Only when you go into the Options for MP3 files will you change bitrates.

Changing bitrates in iTunes

It doesn't matter how your audio files get into iTunes, be it from Audacity, GarageBand, or anywhere else. When you get the files in to iTunes, you can easily convert them to a different bitrate, change the file format, or make any number of other changes to the file.

WARNING

You can't get better quality out of a file by changing it from a lower bitrate to a higher bitrate. For example, once a file has been saved at 32 Kbps, converting it to 128 Kbps won't make it sound any better.

To set the bitrate in iTunes and create an MP3, follow these steps:

1. **Choose iTunes ⇨ Preferences (Mac OS) or choose Edit ⇨ Preferences (Windows).**

   The Preferences window opens.

2. **In the Preferences window, click the Import Settings button.**

3. **From the Import Using drop-down menu, select MP3 Encoder.**

   The MP3 Encoder dialog box opens.

4. **From the Settings drop-down menu, select your desired bitrate (shown in Figure 10-4).**

5. **Import your podcast episode (currently in an uncompressed format) in iTunes by double-clicking on the file.**

6. **Click the audio in iTunes and then go to File ⇨ Convert ⇨ Create MP3 Version.**

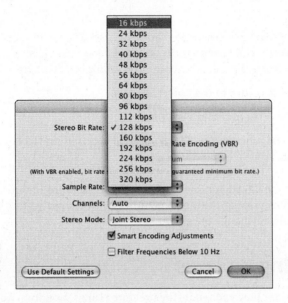

FIGURE 10-4:
The iTunes
options for
sampling rates.

Care for a Sample, Sir?
(Audio Sample Rates)

When you have a grasp of bitrates, you're ready to move on to *sample rates*. This may strike you as a tad redundant, particularly when you see the list of common audio-sample rates. A strange *déjà vu* makes you wonder whether you're in the real world or exist merely as part of The Matrix. No biggie — sometimes technology *is* redundant.

As we discuss in the preceding section, bitrate is a measurement of how much audio data is transferred between two points, such as the computer and your headset. The *sampling rate* is a measurement of audio samples taken from a *continuous signal* (a signal of a varying quantity, defined over a period of time) in order to create a *discrete signal* (a signal made up of samples from a continuous signal).

Very simply, the sample rate determines the maximum sound frequency that can be reproduced — the value you set is twice the frequency value. For example, a 44.1 kHz sample rate can reproduce sounds up to 22.05 kHz, which is slightly above the range of human hearing.

The most common audio sampling rates found in MP3 encoders are

>> 8,000 Hz / 8 kHz, telephone-quality recording or lo-fi

>> 22,050 Hz / 22 kHz, equal to AM radio transmission

>> 32,000 Hz / 32 kHz, equal to FM radio transmission, minimum sound quality on a digital video camcorder

>> 44,100 Hz / 44 kHz, audio-CD quality

>> 48,000 Hz / 48 kHz, digital TV, DVD, films, maximum sound quality on digital video camcorder, and professional-grade audio recording

As with your audio-recording applications, you have a range of bitrates available — and you can type in your own custom sampling rates.

REMEMBER

Using different sample rates in compressed audio files does not affect the file size — only the bitrate and duration affect file size. A high sample rate at a low bitrate can result in poor signal representation and thus poor quality, but if you're using at least 64 Kbps (bitrate), there's no good reason to ever use anything except 44.1 kHz as the sample rate.

WARNING

Be careful when using a sample rate other than a multiple of 11. Choosing a sample rate other than 11.025 kHz, 22.5 kHz, or 44.1 kHz can produce an effect similar to the voices of Alvin and the Chipmunks. It might be funny at first, but most listeners won't stick around to hear your entire message.

Changing sample rates in Audacity

Sample rates are located in the Preferences window and extremely simple to either change or customize to your podcast's personal needs. Follow these steps to customize sample rates in Audacity:

1. **Choose Audacity ⇨ Preferences (Mac OS) or File ⇨ Preferences (Windows).**

   The Preferences window appears.

2. **Click the Quality option in the left column.**

3. **Select your desired bitrate from the Default Sample Rate drop-down menu (as shown in Figure 10-5), or enter your own custom sampling rate by selecting the Other option and entering a number.**

   REMEMBER

   If you're entering a custom sampling rate, make sure you enter the rate in *hertz* (Hz) and not *kilohertz* (kHz). For example, if you decide your sampling rate is 44.1 kHz, you must enter **44100**, not 44.

4. **Click OK.**

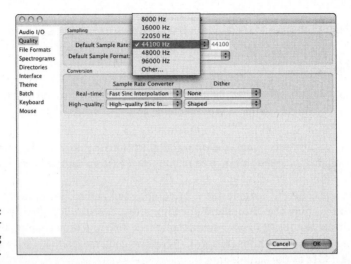

FIGURE 10-5:
Changing your audio sampling rate in Audacity.

Changing sample rates in iTunes

iTunes makes the process of changing the sample rate easy — what else would you expect from Apple?

TIP

To get an idea of what a good sampling rate is, look at the podcasts your aggregator is pulling down and check the settings. Press ⌘+I (Mac) or Ctrl+I (Windows) to see the MP3 Summaries. Settings may vary from file to file. As you work out the final technical details of your podcast, make sure that one of them is the setting that best suits your needs and (of course) your ear.

Follow these steps to change the sample rate in iTunes:

1. **Choose iTunes ⇨ Preferences (Mac OS X) or Edit ⇨ Preferences (Windows).**

   The Preferences window appears.

2. **In the Preferences window, click the Import Settings button.**

3. **From the Setting drop-down menu, select the Custom option.**

   The iTunes MP3 Encoder dialog box opens.

4. **Select your desired sampling rate from the Sample Rate menu.**

REMEMBER

Apple loves to make things easy for its users, and we love that. However, Apple sometimes takes out the *"I did it MY WAY!"* alternative and does not allow for custom settings. Here, iTunes keeps this sampling to the common settings, so you're given no leeway.

ROCKING THE PODCAST JOINT WITH JOINT STEREO

We haven't discussed the difference between stereo and joint stereo output in this chapter, for one reason: It all depends on the method you use for recording — and on how you're listening:

- **Stereo:** By default, many applications that export to MP3 also export as Stereo. Stereo encoding takes the left and right audio separately and divides the selected bitrate for each. The drawback to (plain) stereo is that the channels are equal width, so a 128 Kbps encoding of a mono signal is really two identical 64 Kbps channels, resulting in a 50 percent inefficiency.

- **Joint Stereo:** With this option, one channel carries sound that is identical in both the left and right stereo tracks, and the other channel carries the difference. Both channels are only as big as they need to be, so if your podcast is mostly mono — with just one microphone — you'll get more out of your bitrate than you would with a plain stereo file, but without the reliability issues of a mono file.

When working with a consistent sound for your podcast, working in one stereo output is something you should consider. Setting standards for yourself and your podcasts lays solid groundwork for success. For the writers, their own experiences have them using Joint Stereo as the go-to podcast format.

TECHNICAL STUFF

Note that iTunes offers your sampling rates at kilohertz (kHz), a more common, recognizable presentation of a sampling rate. Again, this is Apple looking out for you, keeping it to the basics.

5. **Click OK.**

You return to the Import Settings window. The default settings for your MP3 compressions are now visible in the Details area.

ID3 Tags: The 411 of Podcasting

Is it soup yet? Not *quite* yet. Adding ID3 tags is the final step before you can upload the podcast to your website. This is the final detail (okay, batch of details) that not only tells other podcasters who you are, but also tells listeners what your podcast is all about, and which episode they're listening to.

Because this is a final detail, we find that some podcasters either skip it or just don't care how they tag their podcasts. And there goes any hope for their listeners to effectively organize podcasts in a computer's media player or remind drivers of what they are listening to while on their commute. Maybe some podcasters are unaware of where or how to identify their podcasts — or want to get their content out to the fans ASAP without taking the time to implement these tags.

Whatever the case, we entreat you: Stop the madness, stop the insanity, and stop the monkeys. Proclaim your true self for the sake of media players everywhere — implement your ID3 tags!

Tell me about yourself: All about ID3 tags

First created in 1996, *ID3 tags* were designed to be added to audio files in order to have the artist, album, and track title displayed in a computer's MP3 player when the file is played back. The current ID3 tags now include composer, bitrate, album art, and even genre.

Of course, another question that comes to mind is *why* would a podcaster want to even bother with ID3 tags?

Look at a podcast you're listening to, regardless of whether you are old schooling it on a portable MP3 player or listening through your desktop computer. Your podcatching client probably organizes your various feeds by the date downloaded, either with the most recent show at the bottom or at the top of your playlist, depending on the player's preferences. Each individual podcast has an episode title, an artist, and a podcast (show) title. If the podcaster working with the ID3 tags is particularly savvy, artwork associated with your show is also displayed.

Now hop from podcast to podcast in your MP3 player, and you can tell which people care — or don't — about identifying their shows. Some podcasts simply use obscure numbers that could be a date, but when you hear two episodes of the podcast back to back, you find out the number and the date read at the intro of the show (provided there is one) don't match up (confusing). With ID3 tags in place, you can now look at your player and get an idea of exactly what you're listening to.

When you add ID3 tags to your podcast, you set apart individual podcasts from one another, making each one unique but keeping it grouped with your podcast show.

IDentity crisis: Making ID3 tags work for podcasting

Some ID3 tags really don't work for podcasting. Album? Track number? Composer? You're podcasting, not producing music. Your responsibility (as a podcaster) is to redefine the following tags we have found useful for the podcasting medium:

>> **Song or Name:** This should be the name or number of your episode. Examples are Show #19, Episode 3: One of Those Faces, BOOK THREE: Chapters 39 & 40.

>> **Artist:** This one is pretty self-explanatory. You're the artist behind this podcast, so let people know who you and your group are. Put in your name (or at least the pseudonym you're using as a podcaster) or the name of your podcasting team. For example, Philippa Ballantine, August Grappin, and Dr. Kelli Dunlap and Josué Cardona.

>> **Album:** Here is the name of your show, your show's website, or your network if you are part of a podcast network. Good examples are The Shared Desk, Destiny Community Podcast, and Podrunner.

>> **Album Artist:** Often left blank, this tag can be a bit tricky for users. You can use it to refer to the show artwork artist, the production studio, or the creator of the podcast. Examples are Imagine That! Studios and Geek Therapy Podcast Network.

>> **Composer:** This tag can be used to feature the name of your producer or head editor. You can enter your engineer's name, or the studio where the show is produced. For example, *The Shared Desk* artists is listed as Imagine That! Studios but the composers are Tee Morris & Pip Ballantine as the show is co-produced and co-hosted.

>> **Grouping:** This tag may remain blank until you're affiliated with a network or distribution hub of some kind. Good examples are QuickAndDirtyTips.com and Geek to Geek Podcast Network.

>> **Genre:** The genre "Podcast" wasn't offered in drop-down menus of MP3 creators, but with the growing popularity of the medium, it's becoming more and more common.

>> **Year:** The year this podcast episode was produced.

>> **Track Number:** Purely optional, this ID3 tag allows you to make sure your podcasts remain in some kind of sequential order. For podcast novelists, the track numbers coincide with the chapter numbers. If podcasts follow a season of multiple episodes, the Track Number coincides with the episode in that season.

>> **BPM:** If you are into staying fit and are listening to or producing a workout podcast, you want to fill in this ID3 tag as BPM is for Beats Per Minute. BPM is also good if your podcast is a house music-dance mix podcast. A good example of a podcast showing off BPM is any one mixed by D.J. Steve boy (Pod runner).

If you're using iTunes and don't see the **Podcast** genre, you can manually type **Podcast** into the field.

>> **Comments:** As with comments you leave in XML, you can give a quick two or three lines of show notes for your podcasts. It's also a great place to put in any Creative Commons notices, websites for more information of the show and its hosts, and special dedications.

There may be other tags offered, but for what we do in podcasting, the tags going unnamed can remain blank.

Reminiscent of John Cleese's aside in a *Monty Python* robbery sketch ("Adapt, and improve. That's the motto of the Round Table"), we podcasters must adapt these ID3 tags to our podcasts to improve how they appear in our players. On playback, the ID3 tags appear on the listeners' interfaces, offering a quick glance at the content of the podcast (as shown in Figure 10-6).

FIGURE 10-6:
How a properly tagged podcast appears on a car's stereo system.

WARNING

A peril in working with ID3 tags is spelling errors. There is no spell check in Audacity, iTunes, or any other tag editor. Because many directories, search engines, and players rely on the ID3 tags to organize and properly display your show, make sure to double-check the spelling of your show title, names of people involved, and any other text you're putting in place. Also, some editors like iTunes create "quick fill" databases that help you fill in your File Info quickly. This database also includes the misspellings. So, when filling in your ID3 tags, take your time and check your spelling.

Creating and editing ID3 tags in Audacity

Unlike iTunes where you tag individual files after they are created, Audacity lets you set up a template for the ID3 tags that gets applied when MP3 files are created. To create this template, open Audacity and follow these steps:

1. Choose File ➪ Open Metadata Editor.

The Edit ID3 Tags (for MP3 Exporting) window opens (shown in Figure 10-7). The ID3v2 option is already selected by default.

FIGURE 10-7: The Edit ID3 Tags (for MP3 Exporting) window in Audacity.

2. Fill in these fields:

- *Title:* The episode name and/or number
- *Artist:* The podcaster or name of the podcasting crew
- *Album:* The show's name or website

- *Track Number:* Optional, unless numerical order is a priority in your podcast

- *Year:* The podcast publication's year

3. **From the Genres drop-down menu, select the option best suited to your podcast.**

Click the More button to add a customized tag (refer to Figure 10-7). You can also add additional ID3 tags and save your tags as a template.

4. **Give a brief description of your podcast in the Comments field.**

Don't make your comments a long, detailed description of your podcast's content. Keep it simple and brief. For example, if the creators of *The Average Geek Show* (http://www.averagegeekshow.com) were to write comments for Show #88, it wouldn't say "On this show we share the mic with Kenny Rotter of the *Dumbells & Dragons* podcast, chat about *Star Wars*, Joss Whedon directing Batgirl, and how Chris Evans is looking at the future of reprising his role as Captain America." Instead, the podcast would boil down this description to "Show #88 — Geek News with Dumbells & Dragons host, Kenny Rotter."

5. **Click Done.**

And that's it! When Audacity generates your MP3, your show is tagged and ready for uploading.

Audacity's ID3 tagger does have its limitations. It cannot embed artwork into your audio metadata. For that extra touch, use an ID3 Tag editor such as IDTE (https://sourceforge.net/projects/idteid3tagedito) or iTunes, as we discuss later.

Creating and editing ID3 tags in iTunes

Using iTunes to tag your files offers more flexibility in customizing genres and even incorporating artwork than Audacity does. Apple's media player, encoder, and podcatcher also make adding and editing ID3 tags extremely easy. Follow these steps:

1. **Single click your newly created MP3 in iTunes. Choose Edit ⇨ Get Info or press ⌘+I (Mac) or Ctrl+I (Windows).**

The Info window appears, which gives you a summary of your MP3 file.

2. **Fill in the following fields:**

- *Song:* The episode name or number.

- *Artist:* The name of the podcaster or podcasting crew.

- *Album:* The show's name or website.

- *Album Artist:* This would be a good spot to give credit to the artwork artist or show producer.

- *Composer:* Fill in this field if you have a separate sound engineer, a tech guru handling the editing, or if you're doing the work yourself.

- *Grouping:* If you're part of a group or network like Farpoint Media, or FriendsInTech, give credit here.

- *Genre:* Select one of the offered genres from the drop-down menu, or you can select the genre in the field and type **Podcast** (or whatever genre you want to use to classify your work).

- *Year:* The podcast publication's year.

- *Track Number:* This is optional, unless numerical order is a priority in your podcast.

- *BPM:* If you're doing an exercise show or a music podcast featuring original house mixes, give your Beats Per Minute here. Listeners will dig that.

TECHNICAL STUFF

One of the cool bonuses of iTunes is how you can create custom genres. Choose Edit ⇨ Get Info ⇨ Info and enter your own genre here. Or go to the song in your iTunes Library and click in the Genre column and edit the genre name. When you return to the Info window later, you can see your custom genre offered as an option on the Genre drop-down menu.

- *Comments:* A brief version of show notes.

3. **Take a last look at your ID3 tags to make sure everything is spelled properly and listed the way you want it, and then click OK.**

Album Art: Getting Graphic with Your Podcast

A big piece of successful podcasting is marketing — and a big part of marketing is branding. Your podcast logo (or album art) is very important to help set you apart. Although not all media players will offer this feature, don't discount its importance. A large percentage of podcast listeners use iTunes and listen at their computers — where the album art may be prominently displayed. Also, Apple is now requiring Album Art as part of registering your podcast with its directory.

Once you have your album artwork designed, and you have your tagged MP3 ready to go, incorporating artwork into your podcast episode takes only a handful of shortcuts and clicks:

1. **Import your MP3 file into iTunes if you have not already.**

    Your ID3 tags should be present in this file.

2. **Single-click the podcast episode and then choose Edit ⇨ Get Info or press ⌘+I (Mac) or Ctrl+I (Windows).**

3. **In the Info window, single-click the Artwork tab and then click the Add Artwork button to locate your show art.**

4. **Click OK to import your show art.**

    If you have a Finder window open to where your artwork resides, you can also click and drag your show art into the Album Artwork window.

5. **Take a last look at your ID3 tags to make sure everything is spelled properly and listed the way you want it, and then click OK.**

    If your logo is in a format that iTunes recognizes, it appears in the Artwork field, as shown in Figure 10-8. See the sidebar "Art for art's sake" to make sure your logo has the appropriate format.

FIGURE 10-8: Show Art is a podcaster's way to brand a show, and give your episode a slick final touch when played back on various media devices.

ART FOR ART'S SAKE

Album artwork, commonly seen in many media players, is a nice option for podcasters who want to brand a podcast with a logo. Mur Lafferty's Parsec-winning *I Should Be Writing* logo is a classic broadcast microphone with a sticky note slapped on it and a pencil, sharpened and ready for use. Then you have *The Onion Radio News*'s trademark onion with a globe ghosted behind it, the stamp of quality journalism at its funniest. These are icons associated with their shows, and this kind of branding is becoming more and more common in podcasting.

But what is the best way to make sure iTunes (and for that matter, the iTunes Store's Podcast Directory) recognizes your artwork? Just make sure that your logo fits the following parameters:

- 3,000 x 3,000 pixels, both in width and height. The image is large as some listeners/viewers are now enjoying podcasts through Apple TV. This is a requirement and considered a standard.

- JPEG (.jpg) format

Keep in mind that when you compress your artwork, overcompression can distort and deteriorate its visual quality. Some JPEG settings work in numbers 1–10 or 0–100. As a rule, if you compress your logos no more than 50, your artwork should retain visual quality.

Chapter **11**

Move It on Up (To Your Web Server)

Y ou've managed to figure out what it is you want to say (or show), you've gone through the trials and tribulations of the editing process (or not), and you've faithfully employed correct ID3 tagging (nonnegotiable). That's great, but no one is going to hear your contribution to the podcasting world until you put your files up on the web.

In Chapter 1, we cover the hosting provider selection process. In this chapter, we take an extensive look at the mechanics of the process, including how to appropriately name and organize your files.

Podcasters have a variety of options when it comes to uploading files. Although the methods are all different, they all help you accomplish the same job: copying files from your personal computer to their new home online. Many hosting providers have easy-to-use browser-based drag-and-drop file transfer utilities built into their service. In many cases, this may be all you need to get your files onto your server for others to consume. In this chapter, we dig a little deeper to ensure you not only know how to use the simple "Fisher-Price" way of doing things but that you understand other options to make it easier in cases where you need to maintain files for multiple shows or multiple hosting providers.

Adopting an Effective Filenaming Convention

In Chapter 10, we talk about the importance of the little things, such as ID3 tags. Equally important is how you decide to name your podcast media files. In this section, we illustrate the importance, not only to you as a podcaster, but also to your listening audience. Although no hard and fast rules for naming files exist, following some common conventions allows everyone to easily find your podcasts.

A good naming convention of a podcast accomplishes the following:

>> **Easy sequential ordering:** Files should not appear at random in your directory. They should line up — first, second, third, and so on.

>> **At-a-glance recognition for your listeners:** Calling a podcast media file `my media file` doesn't help very much. Calling it `Bob's Fencing Podcast` certainly does.

Here's an example of a well-named podcast media file, if we do say so ourselves:

```
Tech_Ep500_170301.mp3
```

Although the structure may not be obvious, this filename adheres to both rules and even adds one more:

>> **Tech:** This abbreviation stands for *Technorama*. Starting the filename with these four letters organizes the files together in the media folder. For listeners who can see only the filename on their MP3 players or computers, they can quickly recognize that files starting with these four letters belong to his show. Pretty much everyone listens to podcasts through some podcatching client these days, but don't discount that small segment of people who like to download files to their hard drive and listen.

>> **Ep500:** This is Episode 500 of the show. Referring to each show with a sequential number is a good idea, giving you and your fans a common reference point that is easier than "Remember when you did that one show with that one guy who said that funny thing? Man, that was great!" Having the episode number right after the name also ensures that the files stack up right in the media folder, as well as in your listeners' MP3 players. You may want to consider adding some leading zeroes to the number so episode 3 (003) comes before 500. Add more zeroes if you plan on doing more than 999 shows.

>> **170301:** The date Chuck posted the file. The order he uses here is year-month-day. He uses 03 instead of 3 so that dates from October (10), November (11), and December (12) don't intermingle with January (which would happen if he used 1 instead of 01). True, in this case the files were already sorted by episode number, but you may choose to go with the date first.

Between each element, he adds an underscore (_) simply to provide a clear distinction of each part for his eye, or anyone else's eye looking at the filename.

WARNING

Don't use any spaces or special characters in your filenames. Stick with A–Z, 0–9, dashes, and underscores. Slashes (/, \), octothorpes (#), ampersands (&), and others can and do cause problems when creating RSS 2.0 files or when clients are handling the file. Also, leaving a space in the filename might mess up a URL, so if you want to space things out, use underscores or dashes (for example, use `My_Podcast.mp3` instead of `My Podcast.mp3`).

The following examples are from well-respected podcasters who all follow the guidelines we set forth earlier:

>> `NMS-2017-04-01.mp3`

>> `scienceontriplej20170406.mp3`

>> `AC_EPISODE_021.mp3`

>> `TSD-075.mp3`

Note how each of them identifies the name of the podcast and provides a sequential way of ordering the files. If you leave out the episode number, as in the case of the Science on Triple J file, the year of the podcast ahead of month and day also ensures that 2017 files are always grouped together. If the podcaster had used the month first, as people traditionally think of dates in the United States, files would be mixed based on the month they were released, regardless of the year.

If thinking about the date that way seems a little too strange for you, do what Chuck does — stick a sequential episode number in front of your date, and don't worry about it.

Understanding How FTP Works

FTP (File Transfer Protocol) is the method by which you can transfer files from one destination to another over the Internet. You likely transfer files every day, from your desktop to your documents folder, from an email to your desktop, or even MP3 files from your podcatching client to your MP3 player.

Transferring your podcast files to and from the Internet isn't much different, at least on the surface and even at any depth necessary for podcasters to ply their trade. Lucky for you, specialty software exists to make this process even more simple. FTPing files has become as simple as dragging and dropping.

TIP

Some podcast hosting services such as Liberated Syndication (http://libsyn. com) make this simple process even simpler by providing a web form to handle the uploading of podcast files, as described later in the chapter in the "Uploading to a Podcast-Specific Host" section. Browser-based systems certainly remove the complexity for many, but it doesn't hurt to understand the processes outlined in this chapter. Many experienced podcasters need more flexibility than the limited functionality a browser-based upload process allows.

Regardless of what software, forms, or other assistance you use to move files around, the concept of FTP is the same.

FTP has been around for quite a while now. As such, archaic and seemingly non-intuitive names abound from the start — such as the following two computer systems involved:

>> **Local host:** The local host is the computer you are sitting in front of and initiating the file transfer from. If you're using a laptop to connect to your web server, your laptop is the local host. If you're at work and logged in from a workstation, your office computer is the local host.

The *local directory* or *local path* is the folder on your local host that contains the files you want to transfer. You can change local directories at will, but most FTP programs have a default starting place. Feel free to move around after that.

>> **Remote host:** The remote host is the computer or web server to which you've connected. It's likely the spot where you're trying to get your MP3 files to go to allow others to download them.

Not surprisingly, the remote host has its own *remote directory* (the folder on the remote system where you drop your files). Again, you can change or navigate through remote directories just as you can change the file folders on your computer.

Making Your Connection with an FTP Application

You need three pieces of information to initiate an FTP connection:

» The IP address or hostname of your remote host

» Login name

» Password

Your hosting company should have provided this information to you. If you don't have it handy, find it. You're not going any further without it.

All FTP programs do the same job but have slightly different methods of going about it. After you grasp the concept, using just about any FTP client is a simple process. Here are the general steps you follow to set up a connection in any FTP client:

1. Launch your FTP client and create a new connection.

Because this step is what FTP clients are designed to do, they usually make this process very simple.

2. Enter the hostname of your web server, username, and password.

This step identifies the remote system and shows you have access to the files and folders it contains.

3. Connect using either a button or a menu option.

Depending on the speed of your connection, the connection is established in a matter of seconds.

The following sections show you how to use Cyberduck (http://cyberduck.io), a free and handy FTP program for the Macintosh system, and FileZilla (http://filezilla-project.org), a similar program for the PC. You can find many FTP programs as freeware, shareware, and shrink-wrapped software, for every brand of modern day operating system. We picked these two for their ease of use and streamlined approach to getting the job done, but you can use the FTP program of your choice.

Step by step (or quack by quack) setup for Cyberduck

After you download the Cyberduck program from `http://cyberduck.io` onto your Mac, you can follow these steps to set up an FTP connection in Cyberduck:

1. **Click the New Connection button in the upper-left corner.**

The Connect dialog box appears, as shown in Figure 11-1.

2. **In the Server text box, enter the name of your server.**

Depending on the requirements of your ISP, this name can be in the format of `ftp.mydomainname.com` or perhaps simply `my_domain_name.com`. And of course, you need to be sure and use the name or IP address of your web server. Chances are good that you don't really own the domain `my_domain_name.com`, right?

3. **Enter your Username and Password in the text boxes.**

The hosting company should have provided this information. If your hosting company is the same company that is supplying your connection to the Internet, it might be the same information you use to check your email. But if you toss some additional money each week at a hosting provider, it's likely something completely different.

TIP

Select the Add to Keychain option to store your username and password for the next time you connect.

4. **Click the Connect button in the lower-right corner.**

If you entered things properly, you now see the file folders on your remote web server. If you didn't, you get an error message or a login failed dialog box. Correct what's wrong and try it again.

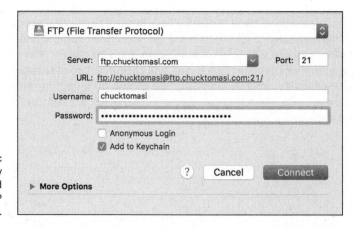

FIGURE 11-1:
A properly configured Cyberduck FTP connection.

TIP

When your connection is established, choose Bookmarks ⇨ New Bookmark. Give your newly created connection a catchy name and simply double-click the given name the next time you need to connect.

Step by step setup for FileZilla

FileZilla (`http://filezilla-project.org`) operates much the same as Windows Explorer, allowing you to drag and drop files between your PC and your FTP server. When you've downloaded the FileZilla program, follow these steps:

1. On the Login toolbar (shown in Figure 11-2), enter your server name, username, and password.

Leave the port blank. (It defaults to 21.)

2. Click the Quickconnect button.

If you did things right, you see a lot of text scroll by in the upper-most window and content from your web server appears in the right windows, labeled Remote Site.

Congratulations; you're now connected to your web server. If you entered something wrong, you get an error message in red text in the upper window. Correct your mistakes and try again.

Login toolbar

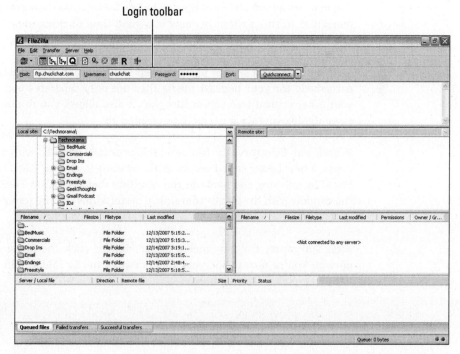

FIGURE 11-2: A properly configured FileZilla connection.

From here, you can navigate through the folders on your web server much as you do on your computer's hard drive. You can move up or down the file system, finding the spot where you want to drop your podcast files.

A place on your web server for your stuff

Logging in to your web server for the first time can be an intimidating process. In this section, we show you how to place your files in a location so you can easily create links to your podcast files.

Don't be intimidated by the odd directory names on your web server. The only one you really need to know is Public_html. Other hosts may call it www or simply html. If you don't have one of those three, poke around until you find one that has a bunch of files in it that end in .html.

WARNING

Look, but don't touch. Going into folders doesn't hurt anything, but doing silly things such as deleting, renaming, and moving files you know nothing about is a bad idea. All those strangely named folders do something, and they're likely necessary to make your website work right. Remember the proverb "'Tis best to leave functioning web servers lie. . . ."

You may see lots of different files and a few folders. We show you how to add even more files to this system, so now is a good time to think about organizing and housekeeping.

Start by creating a special place to keep your podcast files. Making a new folder exclusively for your podcast media files not only separates your podcasts from your other critical web server files, but it also allows you to quickly see what is currently live and what needs to be cleaned up.

In your root directory (the top-level folder usually denoted with a forward slash), create a new folder called media. With Cyberduck, choose File ➪ New Folder, followed by entering the name in the resulting dialog box. On FileZilla, right-click the window with the details (date, size, permissions) on the remote file server and choose Create Directory.

After you create the new media folder, double-click the name of the folder to open it. You're now inside your totally empty media folder, and ready to load it with your podcast media files.

Uploading your files

After you set up a folder for your podcast media files and decide on a filenaming convention, you're ready to move your freshly named files to the web server.

Both Cyberduck and FileZilla support *drag-and-drop* file transfers. If you're new to FTP, the FTP program interface may be easier for you to use.

For Cyberduck, follow these steps:

1. **Choose File ➪ Upload.**
2. **Browse your system to find the podcast media file you want to upload.**
3. **Click the Upload button.**

For FileZilla, here's what you do:

1. **Navigate to the desired folder using the Local Site window on the left.**
2. **Select one or more files and/or folders from the window directly below.**
3. **Drag the selected files to the Remote Site window on the left.**

Depending on the size of your file and the speed of your Internet connection, the file may transfer in a matter of seconds or a matter of minutes. When completed, the file appears in your FTP client and is ready to be linked in your show notes and RSS 2.0 feed.

UPLOADING FILES WITH YOUR BLOGGING SOFTWARE

Many popular blogging tools allow podcasters to upload files without the need for special FTP software, much like the HTTP process.

However, podcast media files often exceed the file size requirements for these services. For this reason, we recommend not using your conventional blogging software to handle your podcast media file uploads.

Consider that blogs are primarily used to communicate text. Although you can easily extend the functionality of a blog to support a podcast, the site management tools are designed for text and images.

WordPress (http://wordpress.org) does allow file uploads, but the file size depends on system parameters that are often set by the web host and can't be changed by the individual. You can upload, but it does take a significant amount of work that exceeds the scope of this book.

Instead, we recommend using blogging software to manage the posting of your content after your file is uploaded to the server. In WordPress, this is easily done with a plug-in called *PowerPress* (https://create.blubrry.com/resources/powerpress).

Uploading to a Podcast-Specific Host

Podcast-specific hosting companies significantly simplify the uploading process; many include web-based forms that take the place of additional computer programs to handle the uploading process. They also take care of archiving, RSS 2.0 creation, and even ID3 tagging.

TIP

Although this web-based uploading process is simple, we prefer the flexibility of using an FTP client — or better yet a command line interface. Or maybe we're old school. . . .

For the purposes of illustration, we use an account with Liberated Syndication (http://libsyn.com) in this section. If you haven't already, you need to sign up with LibSyn and create your own account. Then follow these steps:

1. **Begin at LibSyn's home page. Enter your username and password and press the Login button.**

2. **Click the Content menu option and select Add New Episode.**

   You are taken to the New Content page, as shown in Figure 11-3.

3. **Click the Add Media File button.**

4. **Click Upload File From Hard Drive if your files are on your local hard drive. There are other options available if your file is on another server accessible via FTP or Dropbox.**

   The File Upload dialog box opens.

   Note: *HTTP upload* is another name for form-based transfers.

5. **Find the podcast media file you want to upload and either double-click the file or select it and click Open.**

   TIP

   If you've used proper ID3 tags on your podcast — and you have by this point, right? — you can check the Populate Form with ID3 Data checkbox to save some time. Just be aware that the description may need some additional formatting as the importer doesn't recognize paragraph breaks. Also check your title and description for encoded characters. You may need to do touch-ups like replace & with the & character.

6. **If you did not choose to import the content of the ID3 tags, enter the information for your blog and/or podcast in the form.**

   The blog settings are very simple: things like the name of your blog, your email address, and what category you want it placed in. Nothing here is mission critical, so fill it out however you want to see it listed. You can always come back and change it later.

7. **When you finish, click the Publish button.**

While LibSyn has full hosting capabilities, some may find the blogging feature a bit limited and use LibSyn as a file repository while hosting their blog on their own site, then referencing the files on LibSyn from their blog. To access files stored on LibSyn in your blog (and resulting RSS feed) follow the preceding steps to upload and publish the content. Then follow these steps after your file is published.

1. **Go to the Content menu and select Previously Published.**

2. **Locate the file in the list and click the Link/Embed icon for that episode.**

3. **Copy the URL from the Direct Download URL field and use that as the location of your file in your blog software as needed.**

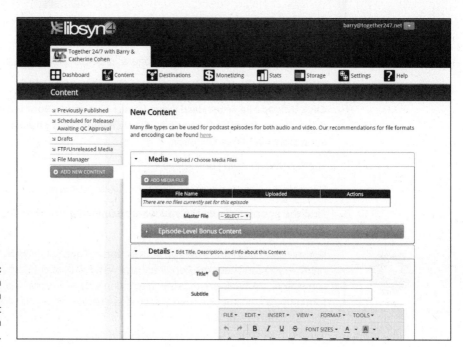

FIGURE 11-3:
Adding media files to a LibSyn account doesn't require an FTP client.

TIP

LibSyn offers an FTP interface if you prefer to use an FTP client or command line interface. Your login and password are the same as through the web interface.

TIP

If you prefer to try it before you buy it, LibSyn offers up to a free month with the promo code *podcast411* allowing you to get a feel for how it works before you fork over your hard-earned cash. Not that the very inexpensive monthly fees will break you or anything, but it's nice to know how your future home might work.

IN THIS CHAPTER

» **Understanding good show note etiquette**

» **Planning your show notes**

» **Deciding on your level of detail**

» **Using images effectively**

» **Posting with searchers in mind**

Chapter **12**

Providing Show Notes

S how notes are brief summaries of each podcast episode. Show notes can take the form of an outline, a detailed bulleted list, or just a few sentences of text. In this chapter, we show you how to effectively use show notes to enhance the listener experience of your show and bring in additional traffic to your podcast through search engines.

And where do you find these show notes? Simply enough, on the podcast's website.

REMEMBER

Getting additional traffic means additional bandwidth consumption, which can cause issues. Flip to Chapter 11 for tips on ways to reduce the load on your servers and for info about optional hosting plans that don't charge for additional bandwidth.

Show Note Etiquette

Several schools of thought exist on how to approach show notes. Some podcasters say you should be very brief, using notes only to hold URLs and other pieces of important offline data that your listeners may not have had time to write down as the show was playing. Others suggest show notes should be filled with information on each concept touched upon in the show. Whether you prefer a more moderate approach or a deeper dive into the format of your show, your personal tastes and style go a long way in determining what is right for you.

Setting aside the length of your prose and the level of detail you want to explain, you need to follow some basic rules of etiquette:

>> **Use intriguing and informative titles.** In general, and to keep things simple, the title of your show notes should match your episode title. Your title is your pitch; you're a huckster competing for the attention of listeners. Some listeners may know all about you; others could be seeing something from you for the first time. Include keywords in your title that accurately and specifically represent the contents of this episode. Your keywords should also generate some excitement and make the episode sound interesting and intriguing to potential listeners.

>> **Include links to resources mentioned in the podcast.** If you're talking about a trip to the local museum, provide a link to the museum's website in your show notes. If you mention another podcast, link to it. If you mention a news story or opinion piece, drop that URL into your show notes. Don't forget about music credits and affiliate or sponsor links too! Good linking brings good karma, and it may provide some interesting and potentially helpful "Hey, you linked to me!" comments (and backlinks) from others.

>> **Concise or complete?** Show notes can be as simple as a bullet list of topics or as detailed as a word-for-word transcript of your show. It's up to you. The advantage to the bullet list is that it's quicker to put together, obviously. If you're already scripting your podcast, it's no extra trouble to post the script, but be aware of the length. A transcript for a 3-minute show is easy for people to read from their browser; however, a 45-minute transcript — yes, there are 45-minute shows that are completely scripted — may be something you don't want the reader to go through.

Figure 12-1 displays how Phil Clark and Mark Naski of *The Brit and Yankee Pubcast* (http://thebritandyankee.com) use show notes. The notes include plenty of backlinks, time marks, and a brief discussion about the topics covered. A thing of beauty, to be sure.

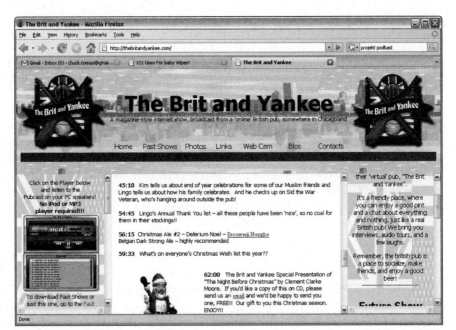

FIGURE 12-1:
Phil and Mark from *The Brit and Yankee Pubcast* properly implement show notes.

Planning the Post

The amount of time you spend planning your show notes is inversely proportional to the amount of time you spend during your show prep (see Chapter 5). If you forgot everything from your high school math class, allow us to paraphrase: The more you prepare for your show, the less time you spend working on the show notes — and vice versa.

Examine the notes you used when you recorded your podcast. Did you talk about any websites? Find the URLs and make sure you spell them right. Test them. Make sure they are headed to the right place. We highly recommend the copy-and-paste technique for URLs, rather than relying on your typing skills, especially for lengthy URLs.

If you recorded and/or edited your show hours or days before you started this notation process, replaying the media file with pen and paper at the ready is a good idea. Look for need-to-know moments and jot them down as the show plays. After it finishes, use a search engine to find additional, relevant URLs you may want to provide to your listeners.

It's all in the details

Now is a good time to figure out what level of detail you're going to employ in your show notes. Several factors can influence your decision, and audience expectation and personal choice are among the more important.

TIP

Here's a good rule: The deeper you dive in to a single topic on your podcast, the less detailed your notes need to be. That may sound counterintuitive, and please keep in mind this is only a general rule and not a law. For example, if your podcast episode features a 20-minute interview with Theoretical Physicist Dr. Michio Kaku on his book *Physics of the Impossible* and how applicable those ideas are to the *Star Wars* Universe, you likely won't have much more than a link to buy the book and/or rent the movie.

Show note details serve two primary purposes:

>> To act as a table of contents for the episode

>> To allow listeners to skip ahead if they so choose

As the podcaster, you can decide how much or how little you embrace these purposes. Here are some approaches that other podcasters have adopted:

>> **Add a time stamp on segment or topic changes.** Some podcasters put the exact time stamp of when they change topics, which can be frequent depending on the show's format and its host. Time stamps can be quite helpful to your listeners if you cover a wide range of topics in each episode and want to assist possible listeners in jumping around.

>> **Write in complete sentences and paragraphs.** Taking cues from the world of blogging, many podcasters, such as Michael J. Riggs' *Steamrollers Adventure Podcast* (http://riggstories.com/the-podcast), write show notes in prose, using complete sentences and paragraphs in place of bullet points and time stamps. This approach feels better to potential readers, giving them a flavor of the show without having to listen. However, we've also heard listeners complain that key elements are difficult to find in this format.

>> **Create a simple one-line summary.** Some podcasters, such as Manoush Zomorodi's podcast *Note to Self* (https://www.wnyc.org/shows/notetoself), take a minimalist approach and post simple one-liners or maybe three sentences that quickly sums up what the show will cover. We suggest new podcasters not follow this lead because it doesn't do much for helping attract new listeners. Many shows that take a quick summary approach enjoy a wider distribution method. In this case, *Note to Self* is also broadcast over WNYC93.9FM.

Detailed show notes improve your search engine rankings, and they enable web surfers to determine the value of an episode before listening. For Tee's *Destiny*-themed podcast, *Happy Hour from the Tower*, he uses a detailed, time-stamped bullet approach to what he, Nick Kelly, and Brandon Kelly cover in their 30-minute talk show. Show downloads and subscriptions spiked whenever the guys talked about hot topics for the week (the launch of "Age of Triumph" and the announcement of *Destiny 2*'s release, for example) as these keywords appeared in show notes as well as blogpost tags. That's how powerful show notes can be.

A picture is worth a thousand words

Some podcasters include a representative image or two in their show notes. Although random graphics serve only to increase your bandwidth consumption and clutter your page, well-selected images can add flavor and dimension to your show notes. In some cases, these are the same images used as album art in the episode files.

Before you add an image to your post, keep in mind these three considerations:

>> **Is the image protected by copyright?** Posting someone else's creative work without first securing permission (which may include royalties and fees) is stealing, pure and simple, and can land even the most well-meaning podcaster in a heap of legal trouble.

>> **Can you link directly to the image, or do you need to copy it to your server?** Some sites, such as Amazon.com, allow you to link directly to images as they sit on the website. These sites have a huge technology infrastructure and can handle remote hosting images that appear on other sites. But many smaller and personal sites can't handle the load a popular podcast can put on their systems if they allowed direct linking to their stored images. In these cases, copy the image to your own server before adding it to your page. If you're going to do this, it's good karma to provide an *image courtesy of . . .* link to the original site. Again, this assumes you've received the appropriate permissions to copy the file. When in doubt, don't.

>> **Does the image fit on your page?** Images too small or too large aren't doing your listeners any favors. Make sure the image you select is the right size. You can add `width="x"` `height="x"` declarations to your image tags to control the size or use your blog engine's editing presets to resize the image (better to go larger-to-smaller than the opposite direction), but keep in mind that this might distort the image. Previewing your post with resized images is a must. If your HTML is a little rusty, check out *Coding For Dummies,* by Nikhil Abraham (Wiley), for additional help.

Posting Your Show Notes

If you've planned and prepared, posting your show notes is easy. And if you've decided for the quick-and-dirty approach or don't really care to use show notes, this process can go quickly as well because there's nothing to do, right?

In this section, we show you how to enter your show notes by using WordPress and LibSyn as examples. If you use another tool to make your posts, or if you create your notes by hand, you still get value out of these examples as we show you things to consider along the way.

Posting in WordPress

WordPress is free, easy-to-use blogging software that also works well for podcasters. Follow these steps to post show notes in WordPress (`https://www.wordpress.org`):

1. **Log in to your website's site administration page.**

   By default, you typically can find a Login link on WordPress pages. If you've already provided credentials, the link may say Site Admin. In most instances, the URL looks something like: `www.your_domain_here.com/wp-admin`.

2. **Choose Posts ⇨ Add New from the menu along the left of your browser window, as shown in Figure 12-2, to start a new posting.**

   You can also select +New from the menu across the top of your browser window. A new posting page opens. Here's where you fill in the details of your new posting. Although this screen displays a lot of items, you don't need to use them all to get started.

3. **Select the appropriate category for your podcast from the Categories section.**

   Though not critical, categories help keep things more organized. It's not uncommon to have one category for text/blog entries and another for podcasts.

4. **Enter the title of your podcast in the Title text box.**

   Label your show with a short descriptive tag, *Classic Car Auction,* for example. For more titling help, see the "Loading up your titles" section, later in this chapter. To make the reader's life easier, we recommend using the same title on your show and your show notes.

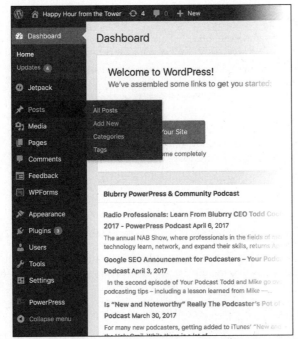

FIGURE 12-2:
Once you log into the WordPress interface, you can begin a new post either be going to the +New option from the top menu or the Posts option from the left-hand menu.

5. **In the large text area below, enter your show notes.**

   Follow a chronological order and list the various topics covered in your show, one on each line.

6. **Be sure to add URLs to any websites you mention (see Figure 12-3).**

   To create a link, highlight the text you want to link and then click the Link button (the chain link icon in the WordPress interface). Copy and paste the full URL — including the `http://` part and then either click the blue Enter icon or press Return. Make sure to set them to open in a new tab, so listeners keep your page open and can easily return to visit your other show note links.

7. **Connect your podcast file to the blog.**

   Before entering in your show notes, you will want to install a *plug-in*. Pictured here is Blubrry's PowerPress interface, but there are others out there you can install into your WordPress. Your media file should be on your server, so use that pathname from your server and the plug-in will detect your file.

REMEMBER

What if you wanted to feature a podcast you were on? What is the best way to share that experience with your audience? Well, this is when you *syndicate* an episode. The episode is reaching your feed, but the statistics go back to the podcast creator. Podcast plug-ins make syndication incredible easy. Instead of the media hosted on your server, it appears on another server, or a *remote* server. Go to your plug-in and use the entire URL in your podcast plug-in — for example, `http://theotherpodcast/episodes/path_to_yourinterview.mp3`.

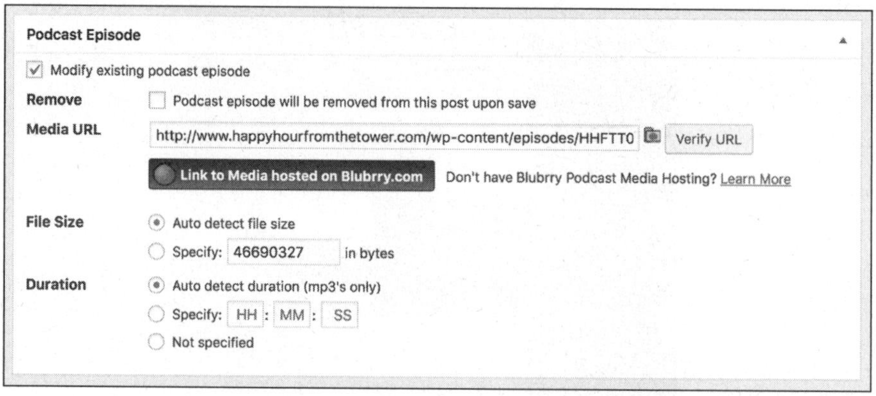

Podcast Episode

☑ Modify existing podcast episode

Remove ☐ Podcast episode will be removed from this post upon save

Media URL http://www.happyhourfromthetower.com/wp-content/episodes/HHFTT0 [icon] Verify URL

[Link to Media hosted on Blubrry.com] Don't have Blubrry Podcast Media Hosting? Learn More

File Size ◉ Auto detect file size
         ○ Specify: 46690327 in bytes

Duration ◉ Auto detect duration (mp3's only)
         ○ Specify: HH : MM : SS
         ○ Not specified

FIGURE 12-3:
Each plug-in will
have its own
interface, but
what is essential
in distributing
your media is
making sure you
know where your
episode is on
your server.

8. **When you're done entering your show notes, click the Save Draft button.**

You can see a preview of your posting by clicking the Preview button — it's not a bad idea to verify the format and ensure links will work before releasing it to the public.

9. **After clicking Preview, scroll through your post to proof it.**

Make sure links work properly — including your podcast file. Few things are more embarrassing than releasing that long-awaited podcast only to find that a link in your show notes doesn't work. When you're just starting out, you likely won't have a lot of people letting you know of technical issues. It's up to you to test as much as you can before releasing a new episode.

10. **Return to your post editor and make any adjustments necessary.**

If you notice links that don't work or typos, you still have an opportunity to fix them by scrolling back up, making the edits, saving your work, and repeating Step 9 until you're satisfied.

11. **When you're satisfied with your show notes, click Publish.**

You can also choose the Schedule option and enter in a date later in the week to cue shows for automatic posting.

12. **Click the View Site link at the top of the page to see how your entry looks.**

Visiting your web page is a good idea to make sure everything looks as you expected it to. If it doesn't, simply edit the post and save your changes.

TIP

Many podcasters with detailed show notes use the ‹More› tag in their WordPress postings, as shown in Figure 12-4. Any text above the More link is displayed on the main page. Those with interest to view the detailed content can click the link. If you have lots of show notes to include in your post, this is a good way to keep your front page tidy with a few bullet items for each show, and then you can hide the longer list.

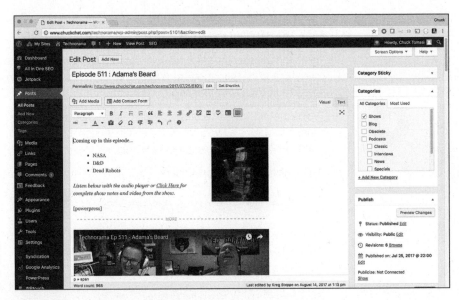

FIGURE 12-4:
A completed
WordPress screen
with show notes.

Posting on LibSyn

Because LibSyn (www.libsyn.com) is a dedicated podcast hosting provider, the steps are quite intuitive and a bit different than those used by folks who work with blogging software.

Follow these steps to post your show notes on LibSyn:

1. **To create a new post, click the Publish tab or the link of the same name from the main page.**

2. **Click the New Post option button.**

   LibSyn also allows text-only posts to the site, which is great for times when you want to post some text without a media file, such as to say, "I'm on vacation for the next two weeks."

3. **Enter a title for this episode.**

   We cover some titling tips later in this section. For now, simply enter a basic description of what this episode is about — "Classic Car Auction," for example.

4. **Choose a category for your podcast from the Category drop-down list.**

   Categories on LibSyn work like they do with most blogging applications. To keep this simple, choose Podcast from the list.

5. **Skip the Post Image drop-down list for now.**

   Yes, you can put something in there if you must. But it's not required. See our earlier comments on using images in this chapter if you decide you can't live without one (but you probably could).

6. **Enter the detailed show notes in the Show Notes text box.**

This is the appropriate place for your detailed show notes. Follow a chronological order and list the various topics covered in your show, one on each line. Be sure to add URLs to any websites you mention.

TIP

Typing the URL in this section isn't quite as effective as providing a true hyperlink. Making a hyperlink isn't difficult, though it may look that way if you aren't familiar with the mysteries of HTML.

Hyperlinks follow this convention:

```
<a href="link/to/website/or/web/page">Name of link</a>
```

Basically, you fill out what's between the quotes, replace the name of the link, and you're done. Here are a few real-world examples:

```
<a href="http://www.chuckchat.com/gmail">Gmail Podcast</a>
<a href="http://morevi.net">Morevi podcast</a>
<a href="http://marsrovers.nasa.gov/gallery/images.html" target="_
    blank">Pictures from Mars</a>
```

Take note of the target="_blank" part of the last link. By including that in the HTML tag, you are telling the link to open in a new browser tab.

7. **Choose your podcast media file from the drop-down list.**

If you haven't uploaded the show yet, LibSyn makes it easy. Simply click the Browse button and navigate to the appropriate file in your media folder (which we show how to set up in Chapter 11).

TIP

Because LibSyn doesn't allow you to preview your post first, we highly recommend checking your spelling and double-checking your links before you proceed. An ounce of prevention and all that.

Figure 12-5 shows how your post looks on LibSyn before it is posted.

8. **Click the Publish button.**

LibSyn makes it hard to screw up, requiring you to fill out the appropriate fields before allowing you to continue. If you're successful, you see a green check box next to your new post.

9. **Check your page.**

Click the link to your show name and see how it looks in the real world. Check your links, spelling, and layout. If it's not the way you want, close the window and click the name of your post to edit it.

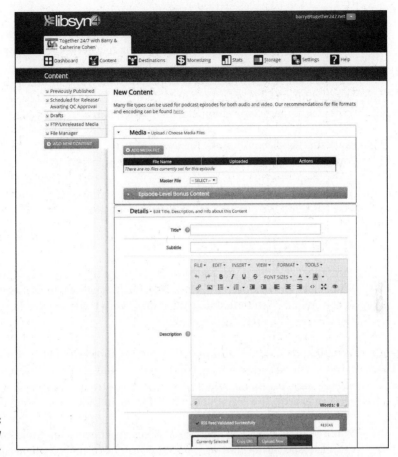

TIP

It never hurts to mention that you have show notes. You can do so as part of the running dialog — for example, in the middle of your show dialog say "... We found a great deal on those at Frobozco. We'll have a link in the show notes on our website ..." or mention it at the end of the show with contact information, as in "Don't forget to stop by our website, where you'll find links to everything we mentioned in the show notes, information on how to contact us, and much more at *www*...."

Using a wiki for your show notes

A *wiki* is a website that allows your listeners to contribute to your show notes. This may sound rather scary — "let others modify MY website? Are you crazy?" Before you dismiss the idea, consider sites like Wikipedia (www.wikipedia.org), one of the foremost reference sites built entirely by volunteer public efforts. Now imagine the power of your listener community helping you build and maintain your show notes. By giving your listeners access to show notes, details you might miss can be provided by those consuming your media. Keep in mind, you are not handing over the keys to your castle to your listenership. Any changes listeners provide are suggestions. In the end, you make the final approval to what is contributed and what is not.

One method of using the wiki is to post a framework, or bullet list for your show notes, and let the users contribute. Another way is to just start writing and let the user community come along and do the cleanup.

Note that wikis won't work for every podcast. It takes a certain level of listener loyalty — something the podosphere has no shortage of.

You can employ a wiki in two basic ways: Build one yourself or use a wiki someone else has built. We discuss each way in this section.

Using MediaWiki

MediaWiki (`https://www.mediawiki.org`) is the software that runs the popular Wikipedia. The software is freely available to anyone who wants to set up a wiki. It does require you to maintain a database with your web hosting provider. Check the website to install the software.

REMEMBER

Installing MediaWiki is similar to installing WordPress in that it requires you to have a web host that allows you to upload and install software and access to a MySQL database. Some web hosts, such as Dreamhost (`https://www.dreamhost.com`), may provide a One-Click Install option and allow you to run it through them.

When it's installed, you can create pages specifically for show notes. MediaWiki does use special formatting characters to create links, bulleted lists, numbered lists, and more; however, using the wiki formatting characters is simpler than trying to teach yourself HTML. An example of your show notes in a MediaWiki page might look something like this:

```
=Show 15: HP Laptops and me=
* Introduction
* The week in review
* [http://www.microsoft.com Software troubles]
```

In this example, the line flanked with one or more equal signs (=) indicates a section heading. The more equal signs, the further the indent. The lines starting with asterisks (*) are a bulleted list. The last line enclosed with the single square brackets ([ ]) is a link to another site; everything after the site is the text displayed. In this example, the web browser displays a link `Software troubles`, which takes users to the Microsoft home page.

The following steps show you how to create a new page of show notes. We assume the top-level page is at `http://www.mysite.com/wiki`.

1. **Click the Log In/Create Account link in the upper-right corner.**

2. **Log in to your wiki with your username and password.**

   Assuming you set up the wiki, you already have an account. New visitors must use the link Create an Account.

3. **Click the Edit tab.**

   The page will change to Edit mode, allowing you to enter text in a large text area.

4. **Create a page link.**

   Enter the formatting code `[[Some Text]]`, where *Some Text* is the name of your page. For example, **[[April 30, 2017]]**.

5. **Click the Save Page button.**

   MediaWiki goes back to Browse mode. You now see a link with the text of your new page link. Note that the link is in red, which means there's no actual page for this link — yet.

6. **Click the newly created link.**

   You're taken to the same page editor as before, but there's no content. This is where you enter your show notes using the formatting codes for headers, bullet lists, and so on.

7. **Click the Save Page button.**

   Congratulations! You've created your first set of show notes using MediaWiki.

In very little time, you can create fairly extensive show notes and then link to them from your blog post. Other listeners can then come along (and set up accounts if necessary) and make changes.

TIP

You can use the wiki for more than show notes. You can create almost any web content to support your show from listener show suggestions to results to a contest — there's practically no limit to the ideas.

REMEMBER

Most wikis feature revision control — meaning you can roll back changes in the event something goes wrong. With multiple people editing the same information, it happens from time to time.

Using Wikifoundry

If you don't have the ability to install software on your hosting server (which MediaWiki requires), or setting up your own wiki just isn't your thing, you can still take advantage of a wiki's features with a site like Wikifoundry (http://www.wikifoundry.com). Figure 12-6 shows a sample of show notes from *Technorama* using Wikifoundry.

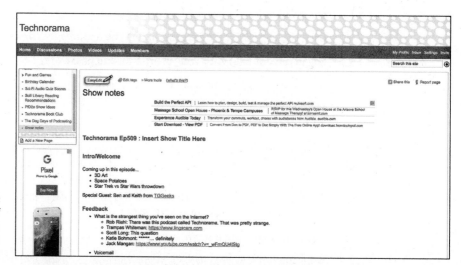

FIGURE 12-6:
A sample of show notes from Technorama using Wikifoundry.

Wikifoundry is a free site to manage wikis. Begin by going to the site and creating a login ID. You can create a personalized wiki and give it your own hostname — for example, `http://technorama.wikifoundry.com`.

Updating your wiki is as simple as running a word processor. Just click the Easy Edit button at the top of any page. The graphical toolbar makes it easy to create headings, bulleted lists, and even insert widgets like an RSS feed so visitors to your wiki know your recent postings to your web page. And the best part for you is that no HTML is required!

REMEMBER

You can use the same wiki for other crowd-sourced information. Chuck and Kreg ask listeners to put in their birthdays and give them a shout out on the show when their time of year comes around.

Boosting Search Engine Rankings with Good Show Notes

One tangible benefit of quality show notes is the impact they can have on your listings within search engines. Traditional search engines cannot (yet) scan and index the contents of your podcast media files. As such, you need to provide text for search engines to examine and evaluate for index inclusion.

Podcasters can pick up a lot of tips and tricks from bloggers and other website owners on how to boost search engine rankings. Many include page-level changes to positioning of elements, correct usage of headings, meta and image tags, and back-linking techniques. That conversation is far beyond the scope of this book, so grab a copy of *SEO For Dummies* by Peter Kent (published by Wiley) if you want to make a bigger splash.

In the following sections, we show you some best practices you can implement right away that can make your notes (and podcast) more accessible to search engines — and ultimately search engine users.

Loading up your titles

Search engines (and searchers) pay close attention to titles. You should consider the title of your individual podcast episodes every bit as important as the title of a given web page.

Important as they are, most podcasters struggle with effective titles. The biggest problem comes from confusing titles with descriptions. If your title starts with "In this episode," stop right there. You're writing the description, not the title. A title is a string of well-chosen and crafted words that has no room for superfluous baggage.

We find that the best titles come from a reexamination of your show notes. If you haven't made your notes yet, you may find coming up with a solid title quite tough. Here's the process we suggest:

1. **Read your show notes and pull out the key elements, thoughts, or themes covered on the show.**

   Let's say you have a podcast on a Classic Car Auction. In your show notes, you have covered:

   - Sleeping in the Seattle airport while the flight was delayed

   - Interesting discussion during the flight with an 80-year-old man who is a car restorer

   - Under the hood of the 1965 Ford Mustang

   - Custom headers and exhaust systems

   - A short interview with the owner of a 1972 Chevy Nova

   - Taking a 1957 Chevy Belair for a cruise

   - Listener feedback request: What's your favorite classic car

2. **Boil down each element to a single word or phrase, if possible.**

Think about the people who might be interested in the contents of your show and pick common words they're likely to search for.

Potential show titles from your bullet list above:

- Sleepless in the Seattle

- The Old Man and the Chevy

- Two Decades of Drive

- Making a Classic Your Own

These all make solid titles, giving searchers a good tease about what they can expect. It all depends on what kind of title you want for your show. A sense of humor? Alliteration? Something more literal? Whether your audience is more casual or, in the case of our Classic Car Auction podcast, more serious collectors and restorators, you select the key points from your show notes and condense them to what works.

REMEMBER

Notice how the title doesn't cover everything, and it shouldn't try. That's the job of the description where you can go into even greater detail, plus the many other things you talk about on the show.

Titles also carry good keywords likely to be of interest to your audience. Chances are good that you know your audience much better than we do. Think about how people are likely to search and write your titles for that. Keep them short, don't try to cover everything, and employ more detailed descriptions to carry the rest of your story.

Soliciting backlinks

Backlinks are the Holy Grail of search engine optimization. A *backlink* is simply a link from someone else's website to yours — whereas a regular link is from your site to another. Sites that have a lot of backlinks pointing to them are considered more important to the computers that control where your site shows up on a search engine. To get backlinks from others, you must create links to their websites in your show notes.

TIP

When you're soliciting backlinks from sources, make each email personal, provide the exact link you want them to use, and tell them why you think it's important for them to link it.

Before you post your show, contact other podcasters, bloggers, and perhaps notable websites to see whether they're interested in linking to you (and you to them) to generate interest in your podcast, rather than a specific show. Many sites have a section somewhere for related sites. This can be a very effective tool for drawing people to your site and your podcast. Then you can also find folks who might want to backlink to particular episodes.

You've posted your show and got your show notes online. It's time to start soliciting backlinks to individual episodes:

>> **Company backlinks:** Write to the companies that manufacture the custom headers to tell them you're posting a review of one of their products. Getting big companies to link to you doesn't always happen, but sometimes it does. And getting backlinks from big popular sites is very beneficial to your rankings.

>> **Courtesy backlinks:** If someone helped you with a part of your podcast and you mention it in your episode, let that source know. Send an email to the agency you booked the trip with and maybe even the hotel.

>> **Backlinks from fellow podcasters:** If other podcasters cover topics related to your episode, let them know about it because they might be willing to spare you a backlink. Notify various car bloggers and podcasters about the new episode. It takes only a few moments of your time and is information they would or should welcome.

WARNING

A fine line exists between asking for backlinks and spamming someone. If you can't think of a good reason why that site should link to you, then you don't ask for it; otherwise, just mention what your show is and what you've covered that might be of interest and let those site owners decide whether they want to provide a backlink.

4

Start Spreadin' the News about Your Podcast

IN THIS PART . . .

Build a community around your show with a blog, forums, social media, voicemail and a wiki.

Let people know your podcast is live!

Promote your podcast through social media, traditional media, and potential sponsors.

Chapter **13**

Speaking Directly to Your Peeps

C ommunication can be defined in a multitude of overly complex ways. For the sake of argument (and not to copy each and every dictionary entry we can find), we define the term this way:

The exchange of information between two points.

Note that last part — *between two points.* To us, this implies a bidirectional flow of information, to and from both parties.

If you've had the pleasure (note how well we can say that with a straight face) of attending any productivity or team-building seminars, the presenters really drive the message home: Effective communication is not a one-way street.

Over the past few years, podcasting has evolved as a more effective communication than traditional media (such as radio or television). We all have the same tools to communicate at our disposal — email, websites, phone lines — so why do podcast listeners seem to get more involved with podcasting? Two simple reasons:

» There seems to be a closer bond between podcast consumer and podcast producer. The simple fact that anyone can do this makes the producer seem more like a real person than a personality and easier to relate to.

> » The podcasters are asking for the feedback — and getting it. Audience size doesn't matter. We've seen some instances of shows with a couple hundred loyal followers where the podcaster has to spin off a second show just to handle the listener feedback.

In this chapter, we show you some real-world examples of how to foster communication between you and your audience, touching on a variety of methods and venues you probably haven't considered.

Gathering Listener Feedback

It must be a natural human reaction to fear the opinions of others. Perhaps it's insecurity, but we think it has more to do with our culture's constant reinforcement of the "How are you?" — "I'm fine. You?" — "Fine." meaningless chatter that precedes most of our conversations.

That cultural crutch, however, is left next to Tiny Tim's seat when it comes to podcasting. Listeners, for whatever reason, are compelled to give real and meaningful criticism. And podcasters, for the most part, take to heart those responses.

Of course, we're speaking in general terms. Yes, there are flamers and trolls out there with less than helpful opinions at the ready. Podcasting can't change basic human nature for the ill-evolved, unfortunately.

You can foster good communication with your listening audience in a multitude of ways, such as:

> » Allowing and responding to comments on your blog
>
> » Creating and visiting online discussion groups and forums
>
> » Responding to listener email
>
> » Participating in online social networks
>
> » Leveraging voice mail

So, let's get cracking on how we make these methods of reaching out and touching someone work for your podcast.

Fostering Comments on Your Blog

In an ideal world, all communication, feedback, rants, and raves about your show would take place in a neat little box, keeping things nice and tidy for you. But because that won't happen, your best bet is to build a website that both enables and encourages the communication in your own backyard.

In Chapter 12, we demonstrate how much adding show notes can improve reaching new audiences on account of search engine optimization (SEO). Well, here's one more reason show notes are important to your podcast — show notes serve as mechanisms for interaction.

In the world of blogs, this interaction is referred to as *comments*. Visit just about any blog you can find, read a post, and you're likely to find a small Comments link at the bottom. Figure 13-1 shows one example, though the treatment varies widely from site to site.

FIGURE 13-1: Grammar Girl gets quite a few comments on each episode.

REMEMBER

If you're already using a blog, you usually don't have to do anything special to turn on the Comments feature. Most software comes configured to accept comments by default. If you decide comments are not for you or your podcast, turning off that capability is simply a matter of selecting the right option.

Some podcasters get dozens of responses per episode. Some get none. Although there is some relation to the size of your listening audience, the frequency of your podcast, and the number of comments you're likely to receive, it really has more to do with the connection users feel they have with your podcast.

Much like two co-workers chatting about last night's *The Late Show with Stephen Colbert,* two or more listeners using your website to talk to each other about your show speaks to the attachment they feel to what you have to say (or play). From the very first moments of attachment, you can nurture for your podcast its own community. Here are some simple ways we recommend to foster your following:

>> Mention that you have comments on the blog either as a standard practice as part of the show — part of the intro, outro, or break perhaps.

>> Include a one-line promotion of your podcast in your email signature.

>> Ask questions during the show and direct listeners to your blog to leave their comments or opinions.

>> Actively respond to received comments.

Communication develops amongst the listening community itself. Rather than talking to you, listeners start talking to each other, and the conversation — and sometimes, the community — takes on a life of its own. If this happens to you, don't fret over it. Encourage it! Podcaster Jack Mangan did just that during the run of *Jack Mangan's Deadpan* (http://jackmangan.com) blog. Comments on *individual show posts* were consistently reaching into the hundreds, and these comments would begin on one show only to break off into a tangent of their own and appear on *another* show. The activity had become so lively when the podcast was live that Jack developed a regular segment where he used a 20-sided die to pick several comments at random to read on the show. Even with his podcast on hiatus since 2015, long-time fans of *Jack Mangan's Deadpan* continue to banter between one another on the show's blog and even schedule yearly "MMMMMeetups" so fans can get in real-time face-time with Jack and one another. This kind of interaction between host and listeners reinforces the value of a community that not only supports your show but meets regularly on your blog to share links, feedback, and random thoughts. Even after your show goes dark.

WARNING

Sometimes, comments that take on lives of their own mutate into hostile take-overs, and the conversation is lost amidst an onslaught of personal attacks either to other posters or to you, the podcast's and blog's host. Neither your community nor you need this kind of conversation. You may want to consider *moderating* blog comments. Moderating still allows people to post comments, but you get to approve those comments for public consumption. When someone posts a comment, you get an email. With a couple mouse clicks, you can choose whether to approve it. You have to do a little more work, but moderating ensures all comments meet your quality standards.

You may find your name or podcast mentioned other places on the Internet via search engines (discussed both in this chapter and Chapter 12). We recommend you get engaged with those discussions as well. Be sure to check back in a couple days for additional follow-ups, or if you are responding to a blog comment or forum, check to see if they have an option to alert you to replies.

Focusing on Online Forums

An *online forum* allows individuals to post their thoughts and ideas on a variety of topics — at their own choosing. Through a concept known as *threading*, multiple discussions can exist independently of all the others. Topics can get buried quickly in a mailing list like those mentioned in the previous section. Forums work differently, keeping all threads and topics available for clutter-free commenting at any time.

REMEMBER

As easy as it is to create places for these types of conversations to occur, someone else may have already done it. Spend some quality time searching the Internet for your name and your show. Maybe a devoted fan has already done the not-so-heavy lifting for you.

Finding free, hosted forums

Using a hosted forum, like a hosted blog, takes away much of the burden of downloading, installing, and configuring the software. On the other hand, you don't have quite the flexibility with a hosted solution as you would with a package you host yourself. One of the easier hosted forums to use is ProBoards. To get started, just follow these steps:

1. **Browse to** www.proboards.com.

   If you have a ProBoards account, enter your username and password.

   If you don't have an account, click the Sign Up link.

2. **Create a username.**

   Choose carefully. Your username becomes part of the URL that followers will navigate to. We suggest using your show name as the username.

3. Enter the remaining information in the form.

Provide a password, your name, email address, and category for your topic.

4. Click Sign Up.

Information regarding your newly created forum will be displayed including the URL to publish, your administrator account, and password. That's it! You've created a new forum, like the one shown in Figure 13-2.

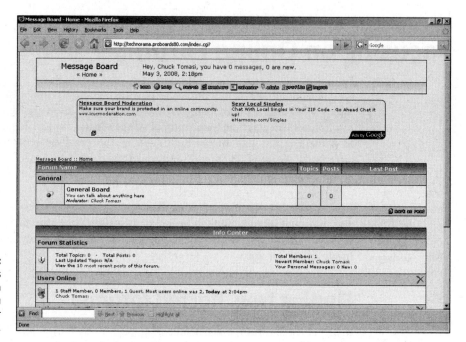

5. Customize the forum.

Click the Admin link at the top of the screen, and you can create new boards, categories, and other customizations to create a framework around which discussions can happen. For example, visitors will find it easier to find information about where to get car parts if that discussion is kept separate from auction values for classic vehicles.

6. Send invitations.

Using the same etiquette as a distribution list, let the world know your forums are available. You can send an email or announce it on your podcast.

REMEMBER

Keep in mind the issue of how some people might see invitations as spam.

That's it! You can now customize your forum, start new posts, and spread the word of your newly created forum. Much like discussion groups, you can promote your forum by

>> Posting the address on your website

>> Adding the address to your email signature line

>> Mentioning the forum on each of your podcast episodes

Other hosted forums are available. You can find plenty of options by entering **hosted forums** into a Google search. Most are supported by web ads or voluntary donations.

REMEMBER

Forums take some time to build steam. Be persistent, post every day, and constantly encourage your listeners to interact with you and your podcast in this manner. But above all, be patient!

Now, although your forum performs admirably — for free — it most likely doesn't have *The Look* (and you know what we mean by *The Look*) of other online forums. Popular podcasts also host forums that sport a spit-polished look, interfaces that make posting and replying easy-peasy, and little details peppered throughout that make you think "Wow, I'd love to have a forum that does that!"

You can . . . but a bit more effort (and investment) is needed. See the following section.

TIP

Remember when we said podcasting has an element of marketing with it? Here's another opportunity to take your name to the people. Developing a public forum means your information becomes available to a lot of potential listeners. They may find your discussion list and become interested in your podcast, rather than the other way around.

Gaining more control of your forum

After a time, you may find yourself wishing for more control of your lively forum. Perhaps you'd like to implement the look and feel *(branding)* of your website on the forum, eliminate the advertisements you get with the free service, or more tightly integrate your forum into your overall web presence. When that happens, it's time to think about installing some forum software on your website.

Here we go with the tech stuff again. We're not going to go into great detail on how to install and configure forum software on your web server. But we give you some things to think about when wrestling with the decision of using free forum software or dropping some cash on one you can purchase.

There's the old saying: Why should I pay for the cow when I get the milk for free? Choosing between a free or paid solution depends on many factors, at the top of which are your level of technical prowess and tolerance for downtime. Like anything in life, there are tradeoffs with each option. Consider this checklist:

>> Are you comfortable editing PHP or Perl scripts?

>> Do you have the ability to create new MySQL databases?

>> Can you change the permissions of files and directories on your web server?

>> Are you willing to continually seek out patches and updates to keep the hackers out?

>> Can you handle having your forum down for days on end while you research problems?

>> Do you want to field "I can't remember my password" questions from your listener base?

>> What is the capital of Assyria?

If you answered *No* to one or more of the preceding questions, you probably aren't ready to tackle installing your own forum software.

If you answered *Yes* to all the preceding questions — except for the last one, and, by the way, the answer is *Aššur* — you don't mind getting your hands dirty. We recommend finding out what forum software your hosting company already has preconfigured on your web server, if any. If your hosting company doesn't have a forum preconfigured for your system, start searching through the multitude of options out there ready for downloading and installing. You can also visit some existing podcast sites that use forums and ask them what they use, what they like (or dislike), and perhaps some of the technical details.

One option for your own forum is to consider open source solutions that many podcasters implement on their sites. For the *Fear the Boot* guys of www.feartheboot.com, their forums as seen in Figure 13-3, are powered by phpBB (www.phpBB.com), a download that needs only your web host to support PHP (a programming language that gives site developers methods of creating dynamic content that interact with databases) and databases in order to work. Although knowing PHP helps you use phpBB to create a better forum, it isn't a prerequisite. With its built-in GUI (graphic user interface), phpBB can do quite a lot for you, even if you know nothing about PHP. It's a bit like working with the WordPress blogging software in that you can use what phpBB provides or go beyond it with a background in PHP.

FIGURE 13-3:
Fear the Boot hosts a forum with sizzle, powered by phpBB.

Moderating a forum takes only three to four hours a week for troubleshooting, answering user requests, and keeping the spammers and forum troublemakers at bay. Four hours is a modest investment considering the return is a strong community of *Fear the Boot* listeners.

Like blog comments, you might find your name or podcast being thrown around other forums. We highly suggest you sign up and participate in the discussion. Respond to the comments — positive or negative. (See the section about not-so-positive comments later in this chapter.)

WARNING

Like many other things on the Internet, the most popular software is often the biggest target of attacks from spam and hacking — that includes phpBB. You might want to choose a "path less traveled" like Simple Machines Forum (www.simplemachines.org) that is very secure and easy to set up.

Social Media

Social Media has become a part of our lives over the past decade and a half. Online communities built around these platforms are made up of profiles, tweets, updates, pages, images, and snaps for people of all ages and backgrounds. They can serve as one-stop shops for when you pay a visit, or combine popular forms of communication into a hybrid that gives you all the best features. Some of these platforms have been online longer than podcasting has been around, but podcasters rely on these platforms as a ways and means of reaching new audiences.

We cover many of the more popular networks out there. Yes, there are more than the ones highlighted here, but these are the ones getting a lot of the attention.

REMEMBER

You can find plenty more social networking sites out there, and many more will probably appear (and disappear) in the time it takes this book to reach your hands. What's important is finding the network or networks that can get the word of your listeners back to you, help you create a better show, and make you a better podcaster.

Facebook

Facebook (www.facebook.com) has evolved from the "alternative to MySpace" (yeah, remember when MySpace was cool?) to a one-stop shop offering a blog, bulletin board, online scrapbook, video streaming, and forum, all on one convenient location. Facebook gives registered users the ability to create online *Groups* where comments can be circulated across others' networks as well as your own. You can also establish a *Page* where you control the message being sent out to the public and boost posts that will appear in Facebook News Feeds around the world. Facebook provides your listeners a quick interface both through your computer and your mobile device to not only offer feedback on what just went live, but also preview what's coming up next on your podcast. You can also use your Groups and Pages to solicit voicemail or offer up polls that serves as instant content for your show.

TIP

Facebook now offers Facebook Live (as we talk about in Chapter 9), a video streaming service where your mobile device's camera captures where you are, what you are doing, and what you are saying. While you are filming, comments and reactions are shared with you and your audience. If you are sharing video in your podcast feed, you can easily download your video and drop it into your feed. If you would prefer not to offer video, then go on and pull the audio from your Facebook LIVE segment, then drop it as a new podcast episode. Facebook LIVE can be used as either a promotional device for your podcast, or provide content for upcoming episodes.

For more information on Facebook, pick up a copy of *Facebook For Dummies* by Carolyn Abram (Wiley).

Twitter

Twitter (www.twitter.com) continues to be a fantastic and instantaneous way of beginning conversations, garnering feedback, and getting word out about your podcast while not becoming a distraction or time-sink from your productivity as Facebook sometimes tends to be. Twitter, either through its website, its mobile app, or a third-party application that is Twitter-enabled, gives you 140 characters to say anything. You can use Twitter to direct people to your blog when a new show posts. Listeners can post (or *tweet*) what they're listening to and comment on it. From various tweets, topics can be created on the blog or forums, resources can be cited, and quick announcements can reach a wide variety of listeners in moments.

Twitter delivers the instant gratification of posting a comment but gives you only 140 characters to do it, preventing you from losing your intent in a drawn-out posting. It's based on the premise of answering the question "What's happening?" If you find people listening to your podcast, ask them for feedback. Good or bad, begin a simple chat and ask for the opinions of others in your Twitter network. Use Twitter to post teasers on upcoming episodes, ask for validation from comments found elsewhere, and tweet relevant links either you or your listeners provide that tie back to your most recent episode's topic.

TIP

Before Facebook LIVE, Twitter developed its own video streaming platform — Periscope (`www.periscope.tv`) — allowing for viewers all over the world the opportunity to comment on what you are sharing. As we discuss in Chapter 9, your video in Periscope can be saved to your phone, and then uploaded either to your feed or your video platform of choice. If you would prefer not to offer video, then go on and pull the audio from your Periscope segment, and drop it as a new podcast episode. Periscope can be used as either a promotional device for your podcast, or provide content for upcoming episodes.

Pinterest

Known more as a haven for D.I.Y. projects or slow cooker recipes, Pinterest (`www.pinterest.com`) is a platform waiting for you and your podcasting street team to take full advantage of. How podcasters should tap into the potential of Pinterest is to understand how Pinterest works. Think of the social network as a visual bulletin board and every time you post a new show, you go to your virtual bulletin board and post an image relevant to your show. That could be your show art, or it could be an image you dropped into your show notes. Your fans go up to this board, click the image you just posted, and they eventually find themselves on your podcast's site. That's how *boards* on Pinterest work.

Set a podcast board for your show, and then, when putting together show notes, incorporate relevant images for whatever you are talking about. When you create a new post — Pinterest calls this a *pin* — Pinterest will ask where to pull images from. Use your latest episode's URL and then pick an image to represent the new content. Others in your Pinterest network can now interact easily with this by either leaving a comment or re-pinning it to their boards, reaching a whole new network.

YouTube? For audio?!

"My podcast is audio-only. What possible use could I have for YouTube?" Yeah, that's what many podcasters think — they couldn't be more wrong. The challenge is that YouTube (www.youtube.com) doesn't allow uploading of MP3 files. Everything has to be a video. It's not a big leap to use something like iMovie, Premiere Elements, or Screenflow to take your audio track, slap in an image, and create a video file you can put on YouTube. You've already done the editing for the audio file (if you're in to that sort of thing). Now it's just a couple additional steps to import and export to upload to YouTube. If you skipped over Chapter 9, this gives you a good opportunity to go back and find some of those useful bits for creating a simple video file.

What's the point of putting your audio-only podcast on YouTube? Simple: You want to be where the people are. Billions of people are on YouTube all looking for content. Suppose your podcast is on Chinese history . . . People are searching for information on Chinese history on YouTube. Sure, it may not be your biggest distribution channel, but like the other sections in this chapter, it's all about making yourself as visible as possible.

One example of a successful podcast published on YouTub is the *TGGeeks* podcast, shown in Figure 13-4.

FIGURE 13-4:
Ben and Keith of *TGGeeks* distribute every episode on YouTube.

Instagram

Instagram (www.instagram.com) may not come to mind as a promotional platform or communication channel for your podcast, but with some ingenious approaches, the image-exclusive platform gives your podcast an exciting new way to let people know that new episodes are live and how to send feedback through voicemail.

So how do you turn an app all about capturing the moment visually into a community platform for your *audio* podcast? It may require a few workarounds, but once you find your workflow, it becomes second nature after a few postings.

Once your latest episode goes live:

1. **Mail your Show Art to your smartphone.**

   At the time of this writing, there are no apps that allow you to upload photos from your computer to your Instagram account. Instagram was always meant for smartphones.

2. **Save the Show Art into your smartphone's Photo app.**

3. **Open your smartphone's browser and find your new episode's URL. Copy the URL to your phone's clipboard.**

4. **Launch Instagram and go to your Instagram profile by tapping your profile icon in the lower-right corner of the app's Options.**

5. **Tap the Edit Profile option.**

6. **Where you can enter in a URL for your Instagram profile (shown in Figure 13-5), paste the new episode's URL into your profile.**

   You can use the main URL for the podcast, but the individual episode's URL will take your audience directly to the new episode.

7. **Tap "Done" to accept and activate the changes.**

8. **Tap the Create Post option (the "+" icon) in the Instagram menu.**

9. **Create a new Instagram post with your Show Art as the featured image. Be sure to include in the post "Follow the URL in my Instagram profile . . ." so people know where to find the new content. (See Figure 13-6.)**

   URLs are not active in Instagram posts.

REMEMBER

WARNING

If you are creating an Instagram profile just for your podcast, you do not want an Instagram account that is nothing but images of your Show Art. You will want to either create "Instagram Show Art" that feature images relevant to your show's content, or post other content that may be in tune to your interests, or even the show's interest. Reporting the same image over and over again could get you reported as SPAM and, in turn, shut down.

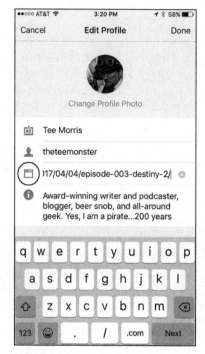

FIGURE 13-5:
Dropping in an individual episode's URL into your Instagram profile gives visitors to your Instagram direct access to new content.

FIGURE 13-6:
Use Instagram to give people a platform to comment on as well as discover what you are up to in the podosphere. (Don't forget your keywords.)

Now that you have your podcast featured on Instagram, how about giving your listeners an easy way to leave you voicemail? They are already on their phones. How can you make that happen?

1. **Launch Instagram and go to your Instagram profile by tapping your profile icon in the lower-right corner of the app's Options.**

2. **Tap the gear icon in the upper-right corner of your screen to access the Account Options menu.**

3. **Scroll down to the Switch to Business Profile option. Tap this option and follow the steps to link this Instagram account to a Facebook account.**

   You will be asked to link your account to a Facebook Profile. Any Pages where this Facebook Profile is listed as an Admin will appear as an option for where you can post.

4. **In the steps featured on switching your Instagram account from Personal to Business, you will be prompted to enter in various contact options. Enter in your email and voicemail line here.**

On finishing this process, you will notice your Instagram profile now comes with a Contact button. By tapping this button, visitors to your Instagram profile can directly reach out to you, as shown in Figure 13-7.

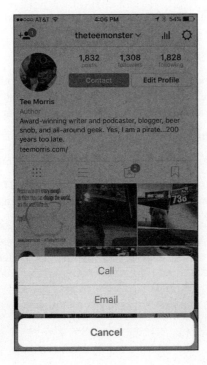

FIGURE 13-7: With a simple tap, listeners of your podcast can now leave you either email or voicemail feedback on your latest show.

Social media offers you these options and a whole lot more. These platforms are a breeze to set up, but you know what else is easy-peasy to set up? Voicemail. If you have a smartphone and if you can navigate through Google, you are only a few clicks away from your own voicemail account.

Using Voicemail

One of the strengths of podcasting is that the content is so portable. That means your listener is quite likely to be away from a computer while listening to your podcast — making the interaction more difficult. Plenty of people, including your authors, listen to podcasts during their commute to work or on road trips. How do you get comments from those listeners? Simple: Have them call in.

Mobile phones are practically ubiquitous. It's a fair assumption that if your listeners have one — they will often listen to your podcast on it. If you want those listeners to give you feedback, give them a number to call. Many podcasters have set up a number through Google Voice (https://voice.google.com). Google Voice lets people call and leave a message.

To set up a "listener line," follow these steps:

1. **Sign up for a free Gmail account (https://mail.google.com) if you do not already have one.**

2. **Go to** https://voice.google.com.

   Notice the message at the bottom of the screen that prompts you to choose a number. In the left menu, seen in Figure 13-8, click the option with three vertical dots (More. . .) and choose Settings from the menu that appears.

3. **Click the Choose Number link.**

4. **Review the Terms of Service and Privacy Policy, then click Continue.**

5. **Enter the city or area code for which you would like to get a free phone number. Note, this does not have to be a number in your area.**

REMEMBER

You can choose the phone number, so find one that is easy for your listeners to use. If you are doing a *Star Trek* podcast, for example a number with 8735 (TREK) somewhere in it makes it easy for your callers to remember.

6. **Click Next to link your Google voice number with your mobile number.**

   Be sure to enable the Do Not Disturb option for your Google Voice number. This will automatically take any calls going to your Google Voice number straight to voicemail.

7. **Google will send you a verification code. Enter this on the screen presented and click Verify.**

8. **When the process is complete, click Finish.**

You can now tell the world about an easy way to leave you a voicemail. When someone leaves you a message, you'll get an email notification!

Okay, Google Voice is fine and dandy if you're calling from the United States, but let's not forget that podcasting can reach anyone anywhere. How do you get in touch with the listeners from Australia, South Africa, or Tierra del Fuego? You can encourage your international audience to leave you a voice memo through Facebook Messenger or take advantage of WhatsApp. Their audio can come from anywhere in the world for free.

You may find yourself with so much voicemail that you'll have to do what several podcasters have done and create a separate show for their listener feedback. Listeners, including your authors, often get a kick out of hearing their comments aired before the world.

DISCORD: IT'S NOT JUST FOR GAMERS ANYMORE!

Jason Citron was looking to design a platform where he and his gamer friends could all gather to chat while gaming. In 2014, Citron and his game development studio Hammer & Chisel conceived the idea of *Discord* (www.discordapp.com) and in 2015 released their first desktop app to the general public. The communications platform, now available as a smartphone app along with the desktop client, gained popularity through eSports and Twitch streamers, and today hosts over nine million daily users and 200 million messages a day. While Discord is more associated with console gaming, podcasters can easily take advantage of the platform in how Discord works. Discord allows you to build a community, either through invitation only or public membership. By establishing a *server* on Discord, you offer one location for your listeners or viewers to meet. Once on your server, you and your audience can keep in touch through *text channels* and *voice channels*, designated by hashtags, as shown here. These channels can be (as you might imagine) text only or real-time audio chat. Discord offers you a unique ability to not only develop and build a community around your podcast but also keep the conversation rolling in real time either through text or as an audio forum. With the right connections and consent from those attending, you can record the Discord gatherings and offer them up as podcasts themselves. Think of these shows as feedback forums.

Discord is still new territory for podcasters. Consider this an opportunity to do some trailblazing.

Seeking Out the Comments of Others

There's an old saying about the best-laid plans of mice and men (and how they often go awry). That adage can be applied quite aptly to when podcasters pick up a walking stick, throw a haversack over their shoulders, and proclaim, "I'm going on an adventure!" You see, it is a certainty that listeners of your show, both fan and foe, will talk about your show to others in a variety of formats and on platforms of which you have absolutely no control.

There are existing forums, chat rooms, and social media threads that deal with your podcasting topic. At some point, those people will find out about your show and start listening. Current research shows these people will post reviews faster than Han Solo's time in the now legendary Kessel Run. In fact, uneducated opinions on the Internet stand as the *only* things faster than the Millennium Falcon's unbroken Kessel Run record.

Welcome to the community of the Internet.

There are a variety of ways to keep your eyes and ears on these groups and to find comments regarding your podcast. Doing so will give you valuable, direct feedback from listeners and let you respond quickly and easily. But before you set off on that journey, consider the warnings passed on to Indiana Jones before setting off on an archaeological quest: Be careful what you unearth.

Whoa. Two Harrison Ford references in one section? Madness, We tell you. Madness.

Trying a general search

Is it just us, or don't most people do a Google search for their own name at least twice a week? Could be just us, but that's a great way to see whether people are talking about you. Google has a gazillion pages in its search database and constantly crawls a good percentage of the web, finding interesting tidbits and adding more data with each pass.

When you search, try various combinations. If your name is a common one, such as *John Smith,* you're probably going to get a lot of hits unrelated to you. Try adding the topic of your show to the search for more relevant results. For example, if your name is John Smith and you're podcasting about underwater basket weaving, type **John Smith underwater basket weaving** in the Google search box. If your show name is unique, or at least uncommon, try using the name of your show as a search term.

TIP

We realize that there are other search engines besides Google. Yahoo! and Bing produce fine results, as do a few others. If you have neither the time nor the inclination to experiment with a dozen search engines, we suggest these three. They syndicate their results to other lesser-known (but equally valid) search engines.

But as we've said countless times before, your mileage may vary. The same techniques we outline work well on just about any search engine you prefer.

Searching within a site, blog, or social media platform

As extensive and cool as search engines are, they can't cover everything on the Net. Not only are there physical limitations as to how wide of an area the spiders and bots can cover, there are also self-imposed limitations set up by website owners that inhibit a good indexing of the site.

Take forums, for example. Some forums are set up in a manner that renders their internal pages invisible to the spiders and bots of even the best engines.

But most forums have an internal search engine that you can use to find the content within the forum — though you may be required to register with the forum to access its search engine. Blogs, forums, and even social media platforms such as Twitter have search features, and the results are easy to track down, as shown in Figure 13-9.

FIGURE 13-9: With the right hashtag associated with your podcast or episode, people can easily search and track Twitter for comments related to your show.

When the Comments Are Less than Good

First, don't panic.

Second, don't respond. Not yet.

Third, let your blood pressure come down to a normal level.

Let's face it. Anytime someone has any critical comments about us, we get an emotional reaction. We call that being human, and it's perfectly understandable and impossible to suppress. Following that impulse of replying right away only leads you to discover the two reasons why it's called a *knee-jerk reaction*: It's a reflex to clashing viewpoints, and you come across like a real jerk when you don't think about your response before riding the emotional roller coaster. (The classic wooden ones like the *Rebel Yell*, *Beast*, or *Grizzly*. Yeah. Roller coasters. Cool.)

When you're calm and feeling a bit more detached, reread the comment and plan your course of action. Here are some suggestions:

1. **Reflect on the comment.**

What does the comment say, really? Does the person make a valid point? Is there an area of improvement you should make? If the comment was specific, relisten to the show in question. Did you say what the person said you did or stumble as bad as the person made it out to be? You may need a different perspective, so feel free to get someone else involved.

2. **When you fully understand the criticism, decide whether you want to respond.**

Obviously, if a comment is in any way libelous, you may want to seek legal counsel before proceeding. If a comment is simply pure vitriol, your best course may be to ignore it and go about your business.

3. **If you decide to reply, consider sending an email.**

If you send an email, count on that email being posted right alongside the negative comment. There's no guarantee the person will keep your correspondence private. In fact, count on the opposite. Whatever you say in a private email should be something you would be willing to say in a more public forum. Keep your rebuttal rational, civil, and, above all, professional.

REMEMBER

Just like any argument, it's best to keep things on a professional level with your words and mannerisms. Although it may be hard to not put it on a personal level, try to refrain. It's not going to help the situation.

AVOID THE BAITING GAME

Tee recalls, after watching a scene in *Bull Durham* where an umpire goads Kevin Costner into insulting him, saying, "That's so Hollywood." His dad, a highly respected umpire in college and semi-pro baseball, said, "Actually, that's not. That's *baiting*. I've played that game too many times." Although you may not think there is a common trait between baseball umpires and podcasters, there is: The Baiting Game.

Fast-forward to 2005 when on Tee's podcast *The Survival Guide to Writing Fantasy*, he posted a tribute to a friend lost to breast cancer. Billed as a "Special Edition" this show was simply to raise awareness. An anonymous poster came on to the show's blog and left a long comment that said in so many words, "We don't care about you. We don't care about your friend dying of cancer. Stick to the content of the show." While Tee did not reply, his community of *Survivalists* did, to which the anonymous poster rebutted with a lot of contempt and very little reason. On his following *Survival Guide,* Tee asked the poster to stop listening if he found the show so distasteful. The anonymous poster returned to say, "You can't make me stop listening . . ." and then listed other writing podcasts he found better than Tee's.

At this point, Tee recognized this for The Baiting Game that it was.

There are people out there who live to pick fights. They are commonly referred to as *Trolls*. Trolls can be listeners of your podcasts or, sometimes, other podcasters looking for a thrill in bucking the community. A way to tell it's The Baiting Game is to look closer at the criticism with (pardon the pun) a critical eye. Usually the feedback from baiting is comprised of personal attacks, misconstruing of facts, flawed reasoning (if there's any reason present), spin control, and a healthy dose of verbal insults akin to punching someone in the ear and then running away. When this happens, don't reply. Ever. By not replying, the words sent to you are a waste of time and effort on the sender's part, not yours. Not replying isn't a guarantee that the baiter will simply disappear. You may need to moderate your blog just to be sure people don't post comments that you deem inappropriate.

And as you may be moderating said comments, you can continue to delete the trolls' comments, and they never see the light of day.

The high road has a better view than the low. In some cases, like The Baiting Game, the best response is none at all.

Negative feedback is never an easy thing to stomach, but look at the positive aspect of this: People are listening. They're listening, and now they're most assuredly talking, blogging, and podcasting about you. We're not saying to rush out and say something completely irrational simply to drum up controversy, but we're saying that people will disagree with you now and then. It should be expected, and you should be ready to face that tough love when it comes your way.

More than anything, grow from the experience. Understand that anything you say in your podcast will be heard by a variety of people, with different backgrounds, experiences, and expectations of the world. We've been on both sides of this and can count many times where the negative comments we received turned out to be some of the best feedback. We think we're better podcasters for it.

Feedback, good or bad, is only as constructive as you make it out to be.

Chapter **14**

Fishing for Listeners

A s of this writing, there are hundreds of thousands of podcasters. By some estimates, the number of subscriptions exceeds one billion. However, that pales in comparison with the potential audience, which is somewhere in the billions of people worldwide with a broadband Internet connection. Although the audience is large, the options for listeners are legion. But how do you attract an audience to your podcast?

In this chapter, we show you a variety of options that you may want to use to help gain a larger listener base. Some cost money; others cost time. But using these options, you can expose your podcast to the right people at the right time.

Getting Your Podcast Ready for Promotion

Whether you plan on spending real money or expending real energy, you need to do some prep work before you start your campaign. You shouldn't rush your promotional campaigns, but take the time to carefully plan and execute them. Failure to do so can not only be a huge waste of time and money, but it may also result in turning off potential listeners to your show, making it many times more difficult to attract them back for a second chance.

Polishing your presentation

Most podcasters need a few episodes under their belts before they hit their stride. If you're on podcast episode number three, you likely haven't fleshed out your show. Granted, you may have been planning your podcast for months on end, or have previous experience behind the mic on another medium, or have nailed it from the beginning. If so, great. But understand you're in the minority. And much like a new TV series with experienced writers, producers, and directors, experienced podcasters launching a new show should consider releasing a few shows until that show is running like a machine.

REMEMBER

Even though each person is different, we suggest giving yourself at least five full episodes to find the sweet spot. Experimentation is part of the format, so play with a few things along the way to see where your strengths as well as your weaknesses are.

Checking your bandwidth

In Chapter 3, we talk about the negative aspects of too large an audience. Each new listener means more of your precious bandwidth being consumed. For podcasters with limited bandwidth, getting more listeners can be an expensive proposition.

REMEMBER

If you're using the services of Liberated Syndication (http://libsyn.com) or another unmetered bandwidth podcast hosting company, you don't have to worry about your bandwidth and can safely skip ahead to the next section. See Chapter 11 for more information about these very affordable services.

Many podcasters start out using the standard web hosting service to host their podcast files and are quickly surprised when they run out of bandwidth. We're more surprised about how poor their math skills are. Suppose that you have 100MB of monthly transfers allowed for your site. On the 10th of July, you log in to your bandwidth stats page and see that you're already at 60MB for the month. Will you make it? Here are the formulas to figure this out:

> Bandwidth consumed / number of days so far this month = Daily bandwidth rate
>
> Daily bandwidth rate × 31 (the total number of days in the month) = Total bandwidth needed

Now you plug in your numbers to find out your daily bandwidth rate:

> 60MB / 10 = 6MB

You're consuming about 6MB per day. Now multiply this number (6MB) by the number of days in the month (31) to get the total bandwidth you need for the month:

$$6MB \times 31 = 186MB$$

It's inevitable; you're not going to stay within your 100MB limit. You will be roughly 86MB over your 100MB plan.

That sounds — and is — simple. As a real-world example, Chuck checked his bandwidth usage on July 18 and found that he had used 256.65GB in the first 17 days.

First, he needs to find out his daily bandwidth:

$$256.65GB / 17 \text{ days} = 15GB \text{ average daily transfer rate for July}$$

Then, he must find out his total bandwidth for the month:

$$15GB \times 31 \text{ days} = 465GB$$

As you can see, he needs 465GB of bandwidth to get through the month, assuming his traffic stays steady and doesn't increase. If his bandwidth ceiling was 500GB, he'd need to think twice before starting an advertising campaign, as he'd likely hit that ceiling, and his hosting provider would likely shut down access to all those brand-new podcast listeners he just worked so hard to get. Not a good way for anyone to spend his or her time.

As a good rule, you need to be using less than 50 percent of your monthly allotment of bandwidth before starting an advertising campaign. If you're using any more than that, you'll run out of room and will have to seek alternative hosting options before proceeding. We cover some of these alternative options in Chapter 11.

Figuring out your USP

USP is a marketing term, and it stands for *unique selling proposition* — a message that sells your podcast to potentials listeners. Although you probably aren't charging money to listen to your podcast, make no mistake that you need to sell it to potential listeners if you're considering advertising.

Why should a potential listener listen to your podcast? And more importantly, how can you, as the podcast advertiser, present a message that makes a potential listener want to listen?

Plenty of books, websites, seminars, and post-graduate degree programs are dedicated to the subtle nuances of marketing and advertising. We're not suggesting you go that far, obviously. But we do suggest you take a good, hard look at what you produce every week and come up with a concise and consistent message with which to promote your show.

For example, when Chuck was looking at advertising for his *Technorama* podcast, he found that the market for another tech podcast was saturated. Several dozen shows repurposed the same news about Microsoft, Google, and Apple. Instead, Chuck chose to spotlight the strange, bizarre, and unusual items that are typically passed via email from geek to geek — the steam-powered Nintendo DS, the motorcycle that folds in to a briefcase, and who can forget the device made of wood that adds binary numbers. Thus, the USP for *Technorama* goes like this:

> *Technorama* takes a light-hearted look at the world of tech, science, sci-fi, and all things geek.

TIP

Sometimes calling in help from the outside can be a good thing. Ask your friends and family, or even your listeners, to come up with some key points of why they listen to your show. We're not talking about a catchy slogan or jingle of the sort a Madison Avenue marketing firm might designate as the perfect thing to attract new listeners, but plain English (or your language of choice) ways to tell interested folks what your show is about and why they should be listening.

We can't give you a step-by-step outline on this one. Spend a few days on it. Try it out on some folks first. When you find a message that fits, you're ready to proceed on your advertising quest.

Exploring Various Advertising Options

In this section, we discuss some of the many ways you can advertise to give your podcast exposure to a larger audience.

Give me a boost, Facebook

With well over two billion users and growing, Facebook continues to dominate the social media space, so it makes sense to consider a modest financial investment to reach a larger group of people with hopes of converting them in to loyal listeners. This is the same reason you see ads for shaving razors, car batteries, or pillows to help you stop snoring on your Facebook timeline. Someone wants you to see what he or she has to offer and somewhere in your massive collection of data, you fit the profile — so why not turn the tables and start reaching people who fit your profile?

IS ADVERTISING RIGHT FOR YOUR PODCAST?

Before launching your advertising campaign, apply some *Jurassic Park* logic. In that movie, Jeff Goldblum's character chastises the dinosaur-resurrecting mogul with "Your scientists were so preoccupied with whether or not they could, they didn't stop to think if they should." Good advice for podcasters and mad scientists alike.

For many, podcasting is a labor of love and not a money-making proposition. As such, spending too much money or time on advertising may make a passion seem a heck of a lot more like a job — and you probably already have one of those.

If you're interested in making money on your podcast, you might also consider the Return on Investment, or ROI — oh, now we're starting to sound like a corporation so bear with us a moment. Simply put, is the money you spend on advertising going to generate you any additional . . . anything? It doesn't make sense to spend $5 or $5,000 if you won't get more . . . something — listeners, advertisers, sponsors, money — in return. Spending money just to spend money doesn't sound like a lot of fun to us.

Some of the podcasts we enjoy the most, such as Dave Slusher's *Evil Genius Chronicles* (www.evilgeniuschronicles.org), are very vocal about not advertising and not working toward a huge listener base. Dave makes a podcast for one person — Dave Slusher. If other folks hear about the podcast and decide to listen, great, so long as they enjoy it and don't expect him to be something he's not. Fame is a double-edged sword — even the moderate fame a popular podcaster can achieve. Before long, emails and voicemails are flying in with ideas, suggestions, and even mandates of how you can make the show better — for the listeners. Don't forget that *fan* is short for *fanatic,* and fanatic people don't always behave rationally.

Choose this path with caution. "Doing it for the love" probably means you can (and should) forgo advertising your podcast. It's not a fast way to get more listeners, but it is a fast way to burn through money without a lot to show for it. We talk more about intangible returns on your investment in Chapter 15.

How it works

Facebook boosts allow you to expose, for a price, your Facebook post on the timelines of people who don't directly follow you or those who may have shared your content. The price is determined by how many people you want to reach.

For the sake of argument, let's assume you've already set up a Facebook page for your podcast as one of the many ways you can stay in touch with your people and your people can stay in touch with you. As you post a new episode, you are mentioning it on your podcast's Facebook page, right? But let's say your Facebook page has 30 followers. It's great that those 30 people know about your new episode, but you want to reach more, so you share it via your personal account to your 500 followers (mostly family, friends, and co-workers) in hopes that some of them share it. How do you reach more people you *haven't* already met to let them know? That's where Facebook helps. It allows you to boost a post for a few dollars and define whom you wish to target.

Boost a post containing your episode, not your page. People will be more interested in hearing your breakthrough research on stopping telomere breakdown to extend a cell's lifespan than just knowing about your science research show.

Using the service

You should have no problem finding your post to boost. Facebook practically pushes it in your face when you view your own timeline. Chuck found it odd at first to see *Technorama* ads with his latest episode on his timeline. This is Facebook's subtle way of increasing the likelihood of him paying for a boost. Very clever! Then Chuck looked closely at the top of the ad and noticed the text `Only you can see this preview until you run this ad` and a blue button at the bottom that says `Boost Post`.

Save your *"boost budget"* for your special shows. Like most podcasters, you are working on a budget and want to save it for when it really matters. If you do a music podcast and just landed a spectacular interview with Alice Cooper, that's a good candidate to boost!

When you click the Boost Post button a window pops up, as shown in Figure 14-1.

Facebook gives you a few ways to choose your target audience for your ad:

>> When you click the option for **People you choose you choose through targeting**, you'll also notice an Edit button that allows you to pick specific genders, age range, locations, and topics of interest. Think of the topics of interest as your way to match keyword searches with people. If you just did an episode with a noted independent horror film director, you might include things like Independent movies, horror movies, movies, and other related items that might capture the interest of Facebook users.

>> The option **People who like your page** doesn't sound like it's going to get you anything more than people who already like your page and are likely to see your content, but thanks to Facebook's magical algorithms, it also targets people who like other pages similar to yours.

FIGURE 14-1:
The Facebook Boost Post feature lets you target Facebook users with interests that align with your show's content.

» **People who like your page and their friends** lets you place your ad not only one the timeline of people who already follow your page, but their friends as well. It's almost like paying everyone to share your link for you — does that make you feel dirty too?

» And the final option: **Create a new audience** is similar to the first option, but you can create groupings of targets to save and use on multiple ads. This is handy if your show has a variety of topics on a regular basis. Let's say you do a science podcast, you might set up one grouping that targets people interested in space exploration, NASA, and Mars, while another ad would be better targeted to DNA, gene sequencing, and genetic mutations. That way when you finish that interview with the rocket technician, you can target the right group and repurpose that group weeks or months later when you air the tour at JPL.

Of course, there's always the subject of money. How many people can you reach and how long do you run the ad? Fortunately, you can choose a budget that works for you starting with just a few dollars and running for as little as a day. The more you spend, the larger potential audience you can reach. The longer you run the ad, the more it will cost you. The pop-up window has a special section that helps you calculate the cost before you commit. No surprises here that will force you in to a second mortgage, thank goodness.

Finally, there's the method of payment. Facebook makes this pretty easy by taking credit or debit cards, PayPal, and online banking accounts. Pretty straightforward.

WARNING

Be sure to read the Facebook Advertising Policy (https://www.facebook.com/policies/ads) before launching your campaign. Yes, it's a lot of text, but it can save you from nasty surprises that get your ad rejected. Chuck discovered this his first time out when he learned that images on boosted posts must not contain more than 20% text (see Figure 14-2).

FIGURE 14-2:
Facebook has
specific rules
around the
format and
content of
your ad.

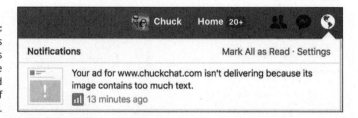

While Facebook is a major player in social media, this may change over time. We encourage you to look in to other avenues for ad campaigns including: Blogads (http://web.blogads.com) and Project Wonderful (http://projectwonderful.com).

Insta-traffic with Instagram

In the Chapter 13, we walk you through the process of switching your Instagram profile from a personal account to a business profile. With a business profile, you can offer your listeners and viewership quick and easy access to your podcast's email and voicemail.

Now we're going to show you exactly how you can do business on your Instagram business profile.

In 2016, Instagram — with a lot of help from its parent company, Facebook — offered to business account holders the option to boost Instagram posts. This meant you could easily take one of your images and turn it into a sponsored post, meaning you could reach beyond your own network and reach Instagrammers that you may not be following who share interests relevant to your podcast.

When you activate your (free) business profile, Instagram connects to either a Facebook account or a Facebook Page that you manage. Along with the option to go to a profile and tap a Contact button, all your posts will offer you the option to promote that post. When you *promote* a post, your Instagram post — the image and its accompanying text — appears in feeds of audiences you target. If this sounds a lot like what happens when boosting Facebook posts, it's because you are working with the same audiences you are building with Facebook.

And promoting a post on Instagram is just as easy as on Facebook:

1. **Launch your Instagram app.**

   Your Instagram business account must be activated to complete these steps. See Chapter 13 for the steps for how to do so.

2. **Create a post pertaining to your podcast, or find a post about your podcast in your Instagram profile.**

3. **Tap the blue Promote button.**

4. **From the options offered, tap Visit your website to set this promotion for a specific episode.**

   This is called an *Action Item*. What do you want your audience to do when they see your ad? Most of the time, you will want your audience to visit a URL.

5. **Tap the Shop Now option associated with the Action Button option. Select Learn More as your button.**

6. **Select your Audience, either from audiences you have built in Facebook, walking through steps to build your own audience, or having Instagram do it for you.**

REMEMBER

   When you have synced your Instagram business account with a Facebook Page, any audiences you have built there that you have previously advertised to will automatically carry over to Instagram.

7. **Scroll down to set your Total Budget and Duration for this ad campaign, then tap Next in the upper-right corner of your Instagram app.**

8. **Tap the Shop Now option associated with the Action Button option. Select Learn More as your button.**

9. **You can now review your order at this screen and enter a payment method. The ad campaign can be previewed here (as shown in Figure 14-3) or submitted for review by tapping Promote in the upper-right corner.**

After you send your Instagram post, your post is reviewed by Instagram (just as Facebook does when you boost a post there), and you are notified when a promotion goes live. Instagram will then keep running analytics on your post, keeping you informed regarding how much traffic you are seeing, what your *CTR (click-through rate)* is, and how much remains in your budget.

TIP

When you set up a boosted Facebook post, you are given an option to also simultaneously run a boosted post on Instagram, provided the post you are boosting is an image that supports the image's resolution. Make sure you use an image that looks good on a laptop as well as a smartphone.

theteemonster
Sponsored   •••

The Shared Desk

with special guest

Two Writers, One Podcast, and Various Points-of-View.

Learn More   ›

♡ ◯ ◁   ▭

theteemonster Look who's back in studio—it's #TheSharedDesk with @pjballantine and me, talking about #SWR2017 with @ktbryski. We drop a lot of names and share stories at the URL in our profile, so give us a listen on #itunes or #stitcher and leave us a

FIGURE 14-3:
Before you submit an Instagram post for review, you are given a chance to review your order before making it live.

Instagram's analytics on a boosted post, you will notice, are kept separate from the analytics you collect on the original post. In other words, you will see that some people liking your boosted Instagram post do not add numbers to the original post. This is Instagram's way of keeping organic traffic separate from paid traffic. Once again, it falls on you to decide, based on your budget, whether the number of people you reach is worthwhile Do you run the ad longer? Do you try a different demographic? Presently, Instagram's budget suggestions for posts are modest, if not humble. Choose a budget that works for you, starting with just a few dollars a day and having it run for a week. As with Facebook, the larger your budget and the longer you run it, the larger your *potential* audience.

TIP

Regardless if you are using the Promote option or simply using Instagram to promote your podcast, consider the accompanying post and your Profile's URL. As we mention earlier, you cannot make active links in Instagram (yet). Before posting your show's art or image related to your episode, go into your Instagram profile and paste the URL of your latest episode into your featured URL field. Once you have the episode's URL in place (see Figure 14-4), compose a post with "Visit the URL in our Instagram's profile . . ." somewhere in there. This way, people can reach your podcast through Instagram easily.

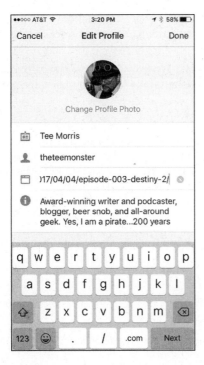

Boosting on Instagram is still a relatively new option for Instagrammers, and at the time of this edition, the hard and fast rule Facebook adheres to that images on boosted posts must not contain more than 20% text does not apply to Instagram posts. This is subject to change but presently show art like the one in Figure 14-3 is more than okay to use, provided it is at a good resolution like 600 x 600, for example.

Writing press releases

Some podcasters have had enormous success attracting new listeners with press releases. When you release a press release, it's available to be picked up by a variety of news sources. On the positive side, you have a lot of room inside a press release to talk about your show. On the negative, you have no guarantee of who — if anyone — will pick up and run your press release.

Writing an effective press release is a true art form. It must appeal both to the managing editor of the publication considering your release, as well as being worthwhile reading to John Q. Public.

Here are some ideas to help you write a good press release:

>> **Hook them early.** This is also known as B.L.U.F. — stating your bottom line up front. Whatever you have to say, be sure to say it first and grab their attention.

>> **Tell a story.** Your press release should convey a condensed version of what it is you want to say. Three or four paragraphs made up of two or three sentences each is a good guideline to follow. Try to answer the most common questions people will have about your announcement. Start with the basics of good journalism — who, what, when, where, and why.

>> **Target the press release.** Write the press release suitable to your target audience. You will likely have to write more than one version — and send your story to those likely to run it. A story about *"hometown boy writes successful book on podcasting"* is more likely to get published in the college alumni school paper than *USA Today*.

>> **Give the tag line.** Use your USP. This is the perfect place to give someone that 30-second pitch about your show.

>> **Give some quotes.** Include a couple lines from the people involved. Keep them positive and upbeat.

>> **Provide appropriate URLs.** Don't forget to provide links to your site(s). This should go without saying, but sometimes you may get so wrapped up in the wording of the press release that you forget the point of the press release — to get people to come to your site and try the content.

TIP

We recommend reading several press releases to get a feeling for the marketing aspect.

If you know people who have written press releases in the past, see if they can lend some help — if not, reach out. Remember that podcasting can be a very helpful network.

PR Newswire

PR Newswire (`http://prnewswire.com`) is the cream of the crop when it comes to online and offline distribution of your press release. PR Newswire can send your press release to thousands of media outlets, ranging from newsprint, radio, websites, television, and more.

The company also provides editorial services for your press release, as well as tips and tricks on how to write an effective release that's more likely to get results. If you're serious about getting the maximum exposure to your show and are thinking about using a press release as part of your strategy, PR Newswire is worth considering.

However, many independent podcasters may find the cost prohibitive (around $300 to start) and the registration process somewhat daunting. In a world where online registration and upfront disclosure is commonplace, PR Newswire follows a more traditional approach. Gaining access requires you to contact your local bureau either via email (information@prnewswire.com) or by telephone.

PRWeb

Considerably less archaic is PRWeb (http://prweb.com). This organization offers paid and donation-based services, and it boasts of a good number of media outlets. The main difference between the two organizations (other than cost and the hassle-factor) is the quality of the distribution. PRWeb works to put your press release in front of thousands of online media outlets. Offline media sources may subscribe as well, but the primary distribution is online.

Not that that is a bad thing. After all, your podcast is an online service, and you're likely most effective reaching an audience who is already online. Both of us have had various write-ups in both online and offline media, and we've always received more traffic and attention to our websites from the online sources.

We don't want to make PRWeb sound somehow inferior to the traditional sources of press release distribution. Far from it. Although the service may not be as full featured, it can still be a great way to get your word out, and one that is quite cost effective.

For $99, PRWeb distributes your press release (among many other things) in search engines and news sites. Additionally, press releases at this level are reviewed by the PRWeb editorial team, providing valuable feedback on ways to make your press release more meaningful and more likely to be picked up by various other news organizations around the Internet.

Promoting Your Podcast

Before you start throwing money toward an advertising campaign, consider all the things you can do to spread the word about your podcast that don't require a financial investment. In fact, you probably should be doing these things even if you plan on tossing out some cash for effect.

Optimizing your site for search engines

In Chapter 12, we give you several tips on how you can make show notes more appealing to search engines. You can employ similar methods to your entire website so that it receives the maximum exposure and visibility to search engines.

For more information on optimizing your site, we highly recommend *SEO For Dummies* by Peter Kent (published by Wiley) and *Search Engine Optimization All-in-One for Dummies* by Bruce Clay (Wiley) Additionally, Cre8asite Forums at http://cre8asiteforums.com is an invaluable discussion board to keep up on the latest techniques on keeping your website search engine friendly.

Submitting promos to other podcasts

Podcasting has been called by some to be a great hall of mirrors, as it seems that many podcasts spend at least some portion of their time talking about . . . other podcasts!

We think this feeling of community adds to the distinctiveness that is podcasting, and something that is, for the most part, accepted by the general podcasting audience. The podcasting landscape isn't shrinking anytime soon, and it's so fractured that many listeners are looking for their favorite podcasters to help steer them toward other podcasts they may find interesting.

REMEMBER

Not all podcasters do this. In fact, most corporate podcasts must see other podcasts as competition and are as likely to talk about another podcast as a traditional broadcaster is to talk about another station across town. Even some of the independent podcasters make a point not to talk about other podcasts, simply because they don't want to add to the hall of mirrors effect.

One of the more widespread ways podcasters talk about other podcasters is with promos. A *promo* is a short (or long) audio clip that describes your show. Other podcasters then insert this clip into their shows — play it on the air so to speak — thereby presenting your message to their subscribed and downloading audiences.

Promos are a great way to let other folks know your podcast exists. Spend some time listening to other podcasts and see whether they're playing promos. When you find one that does, see what the average time for the promotion turns out to be and what type of content is being presented. Is it all serious business, or is more lighthearted humor involved? Query other podcasts and offer up your promo.

In exchange, offer to make a promo for your host podcast. Some podcasters are good at making promos and even offer to make promos for free for other podcasters.

One final note on sending out promos: Ask. Unless the show specifically says, "Submit your promos to us at . . . ," be a good podcasting citizen and send the podcaster a note asking whether she'd like to run your promo. Requests that start off with "I listen to your show every week because you . . ." are likely to get a better response than those starting (and ending) with "Please run my promo." Consider taking a reverse approach, as well. If you listen to a podcast and want to run her promo on your show, ask if she has a promo and offer to play it. Most podcasters are more than happy to contribute.

Recording your promo

Recording your own promo isn't difficult, and we tend to enjoy the ones that come from the voice of the podcaster. You've done the hard work by figuring out what makes your podcast special; now you need to sit down and record your promo. Here are a few tips:

>> **Write your script.** Or don't. Some folks are happy flying off the cuff. But in the interest of time, we highly recommend putting some thoughts down on paper and running through them out loud to see how long it takes. Most promos are under a minute long, unless you have lots of great stuff to say.

>> **Add effects and music from your podcast.** If you use the same music (see Chapter 8) in your show each week or have some special sound effects that brand the show as yours, include them in your promo. Effects are a great way to tie in your promotion to your show, assuring new listeners that they have subscribed to the right place.

>> **Don't forget your website URL!** Too many podcasters provide the link to their podcast feed. Useless, in our opinions. Instead, repeat the URL of your website, where it should be painfully simple to subscribe to the RSS feed for your podcast. Now here's to hoping you picked an easy-to-remember domain name!

>> **Include a link to the promo on your website.** Recording one and sending it out to a few podcasts is great, but what about all the other folks you inspire to make their own podcast? Chances are good that if you put a link to your promo file on your website, others will grab that file and include your promo in their shows. It's also a good repository for when you find another podcast you think might want to run your promo.

>> **Speak clearly and enunciate!** You may know the name of your show very well. Like your own name, you've said it "millions" of times. This means you might say it so quickly, it may not come out as clearly as it should. When you introduce your show to someone who has never heard the show name before, you need to slow down a bit. Say your podcast's title as if you are introducing yourself to someone new. Let him hear the words clearly. While doing research for this book, we listened to several promos where the podcaster said it so fast that it reminded us of those misheard lyrics in a song. Was that Jimmy Hendrix podcast actually called "Kiss this guy dot com"? If it weren't for a printed URL, we would have no idea what the show was called or where to find it.

TIP

When you send other podcasters your promo, save some email bandwidth and send the link that's on your website, rather than the file itself.

Giving interviews

Don't forget that podcasting is the fastest growing medium we've seen . . . ever! If your podcast covers a brand-new area of the world or addresses an underserved market, folks are out there who want to talk with you about it.

Contact the publications, radio shows, websites, and other outlets that cover the industry your podcast falls under. Send them your press release, along with a personalized note telling them about your show and stating that you're happy to do an interview.

Interviews can be done in person, but most today are conducted over the phone or online phone services like Skype. A handful are conducted via email. Preparing for an interview can make the difference between a poor interview that never sees publication or airtime and a well-delivered interview that keeps the audience — as well as the interviewer — engaged and entertained.

Here are a few tips to make your interview go swimmingly:

>> **Eliminate the BS factor.** If you have only a passing interest in the subject for which you're trying to pass yourself off as an expert, you'll quickly be discovered, thrashed repeatedly, and left out for the buzzards. The people who are interviewing you likely are already experts in their fields, so don't try to come off as something you aren't. Be open and honest about your experience and focus on why you're doing the podcast. Even if you're considered a subject matter expert, remember that your listener may not be. You might want to consider simplifying things on behalf of the listeners new to the subject. Of course, this depends on your listeners and the subject being covered.

>> **Mention your website again and again.** Remember that the listeners, readers, or viewers you are being interviewed in front of have no idea who you are and what you are about. This is your chance to sell yourself and your podcast. If your interviewer is good, he'll give you ample opportunity to mention your website and podcast. If not, it's up to you. Look for chances to drop the name and URL if necessary.

>> **Stay positive.** If the interviewer knows anything about podcasting, he'll likely ask questions on the future of podcasting, the death of radio, amateur versus professional, and all sorts of other controversial topics. Unless your podcast is about podcasting, we recommend rising above the din. This conversation doesn't serve you or the listening/reading/viewing audience well. Point out how your podcast addresses the issue and resist the temptation to get into an argument. Unless your podcast is about arguing with interviewers; in that case, go right ahead.

Generating buzz

All the processes we outline in this chapter are geared toward one thing: generating buzz for your podcast. The more folks you can get talking about your show, the better off you are. We don't buy the "any publicity is good publicity" line, but we do think that "Hey have you heard about . . .?" conversations among real people are the best form of advertising you can get.

Sometimes, you need to take the message to the masses. Find a discussion group or an online forum germane to your podcast's area of interest and start posting.

When you post, don't start out with "Hey, I'm new to the group and have this great podcast!" Instead, listen in to the conversation, comment on a few threads, and get folks used to your voice before you hit them with the come-listen-to-my-podcast pitch. In fact, the best way to pitch your podcast is to never utter those words at all. Instead, offer up things like "Last week on my podcast, I covered the very thing you were talking about, Jill." It shows you're paying attention to the conversation and not just looking to spam a newsgroup or mailing list with your podcast URL.

WARNING

A very fine line exists between tasteful self-promotion and outright spamming. Generating buzz isn't the same as advertising. Advertising has its place, but most forums don't welcome it. If you can't decide whether your post contains too much advertising or not, it probably does. Discretion is the better part of valor, in this instance.

5

Pod-sibilities to Consider for Your Show

Chapter **15**

Show Me the Money

Throughout this book, we show you novel and interesting ways to toss significant amount of coinage into the proverbial black hole of podcasting. Throwing money at your podcast can easily become a habit — and it likely should come with a warning from the Surgeon General or perhaps your accountant.

Hosting fees, bandwidth overages, shiny new microphones, music royalties and licensing fees, phone charges, travel expenses . . . the hard and soft costs of this little hobby of yours just might add up quickly.

That's why this chapter shows you some ways to offset a portion (or all) of these costs and perhaps even add a few dollars to your pocket while you explore your newfound passion. In case you anticipate a large following, we cover some ideas you can use to make this your paying gig.

REMEMBER

Being a podcaster is a lot like being an actor, a writer, or a movie star. A few select individuals may make it big, but most folks just get by — and that can be okay. If you're reading this chapter first in hopes of getting a crash course in how to get rich quick with your podcast, you're about to be disappointed. If not, we can talk.

How Much Money Can You Make?

Most podcasters fall into one of three categories in terms of their audience size: small, medium, and large (well, yeah). Because of the very low barrier-to-entry — in effect, almost anyone can create a podcast — the smaller variety of podcaster will likely make up the bulk of the community for the foreseeable future.

Here's a closer look at the moneymaking opportunities for these three podcast categories:

REMEMBER

>> **Small:** Roughly, a small podcast has under 1,000 listeners. Having a small audience size doesn't exclude you from drawing a revenue stream from your podcast. It likely limits the size of your potential revenues, but it doesn't mean you can't bring in at least some income.

Small is a relative term, and we're not about to start tossing out audience-size statistics to draw a clear demarcation between small and medium. Small is also not a derogatory term; many podcasters enjoy the idea of keeping their community intimate. There's a certain comfort in the small podcasts, a charm that some would say is diminished as the size of the podcast's audience increases. Small can be an asset — some podcasts are so niche that they draw a small, but extremely loyal following. To a potential advertiser, you have a target audience.

>> **Medium:** When you have more than a handful of dedicated listeners (in the four-digit bracket with over 1,000 listeners), you find yourself in the medium category. This category affords you additional opportunities. For instance, corporations and advertisers may be more willing to consider placing ads or providing sponsorships.

However, you also find yourself in a more competitive marketplace, as other podcasters start fishing for monies to help offset their costs. Stepping upward in the ranks also means stepping up your game, and you may find yourself in an unfamiliar place — trying to develop a media kit that boosts your podcast above the din raised by all the other podcasts chasing the very same advertisers.

TIP

Creating an effective media kit, especially for a newly discovered marketplace such as podcasting, is a pretty important task. (For more about the why, what, and how-to, see "Developing a media kit," later in this chapter.) We highly recommend Paul Cooligan's *The Podcast Report* (http://thepodcastreport. com) to anyone looking for ideas and ways to make your podcast into a money-making venture along with making your podcast more visible through SEO and promotional strategies.

>> **Large:** Breaking the barrier at the far end of the size spectrum is an elite set of podcasters who occupy the *large* category and are in the five-digit bracket

with over 10,000 listeners. When it comes to making money with your podcast, size really does matter. With a huge audience base, you'll likely find advertisers a lot easier to approach; you can present listener numbers that are more like what the advertisers are used to seeing in their more traditional media buys.

Outside the mainstream media (like NPR, CNN, and ESPN), there aren't that many large podcasts out there — yet — so thus far the playing field is still fairly open. Still, it's no picnic for large podcasters; after all, they're still targeting a very narrow audience on typically one topic (or show), and they probably won't rake in as much as a nationally syndicated radio program. Don't be surprised, however, if you see that paradigm change. Podcasters have much more flexibility than broadcasters and arguably a closer relationship with the audience.

DOES YOUR PODCAST NEED TO PAY FOR ITSELF?

"You spent *how much* on a new microphone?" You'll soon be hearing that or a question just like it with a different gizmo attached to the question mark. Your non-podcasting friends, colleagues, and perhaps even family will gaze in wonder at your apparent lack of good judgment as you seemingly spend money as if it grew on trees — *trees we say!* — adding just one more piece to your previously professed "perfect" podcasting setup.

How can you, in good conscience, justify this outlay of cash without the financial backing of someone else? Surely if no one is willing to pay you to do this podcasting thing, you shouldn't be doing it at all, right?

In a word, wrong.

Let's take a hypothetical, yet not atypical, household scenario — the family that likes camping. They've got their initial investment of tents, stove, sleeping bags, perhaps RV or pop-up trailer, maybe an ATV or two. For those of us who prefer podcasting, even a high-end, mic, mixer, mic boom, pop-filter, and some cables are a lot cheaper! Then there's the ongoing expenses. The camping family has campsite fees, vehicle maintenance — those ATVs don't fix themselves — food, fuel, park permits, and if we did more camping we could come up with a few others. The podcaster has hosting fees which we're pretty sure are a lot easier on the budget than vehicle maintenance. Don't even get us started about how much space it takes to store a canoe compared to an iPad! We're sure you can think of several other hobbies/passions to do this little exercise.

(continued)

(continued)

Now back to the camping-loving family . . . ask them, "Have you ever thought about getting sponsorship to help pay for your love of the great outdoors?" The look on their faces would be priceless — you might want to have your camera ready. Just because you love to podcast doesn't mean you *need* a sponsor.

Think of the amount of money you spend eating out each week. Or for movie tickets, theater presentations, concerts, and/or bar tabs. These are things you love and enjoy, not things you're trying to find others to pay for. Most podcasters will spend no more than a hundred bucks a month on their show — average over time — and that's stretching it. And for such a small investment that has such a high personal payoff . . . do you *need* to be paid off in cold hard cash to do it?

Convincing Advertisers to Give You Money

If the idea of begging for money sounds rather repulsive, good. If you have to resort to begging, you shouldn't be asking at all. People will only part with their cash if you give them a compelling reason. "Because I'm a poor podcaster" is not a compelling reason.

Whether your goal is to gain sponsors or sell advertising spots, you must answer a very important question: What's in it for them? Why should someone else make a financial contribution to your show? There are a multitude of good reasons that you'll need to uncover, understand, and be able to explain if you hope to be successful in asking for funds to support your podcast.

Contrary to popular belief, there aren't nearly enough corporations so bursting-at-the-seams with unused advertising dollars that they'll welcome you with open arms when you approach them and ask, "Hey! Wanna advertise on my podcast?"

Most corporations have an advertising *budget* (as in, a limit on what they can spend). In nearly all circumstances, this budget is significantly smaller than the range of potential places they might be advertising — so they're looking for the most bang for their buck. As one of the would-be venues for their ads, you're competing with other forms of media — including outlets that already have well-established pitches and presentations at the ready.

Before you start cold-calling possible advertisers, do a little homework. Spend some time, energy, and money developing something your potential advertisers can touch and see: a media kit and a rate sheet, which we describe in the next sections.

REMEMBER

Sometimes all you can do is put your best foot forward and make your pitch. Talk to the advertiser about your dedicated audience, and how loyal it is to your show. Breaking down the costs into per-listener numbers might help as well. Whatever your approach, don't try to compare your numbers with those of traditional outlets the advertiser is already working with. Instead, talk about how *adding* podcast advertising to the mix can enhance its current efforts, allowing the company to reach an audience that has turned away from traditional media sources in favor of this new medium.

Developing a media kit

A *media kit* is, in effect, a collection of marketing tools designed to awaken potential advertisers to their crying need to shell out big bucks to support your product or service (in this case, your podcast). The size of your media kit depends on many factors, among which are how much you want to spend and how much important stuff you think you have to say. It's not size you're striving for here; it's a compelling argument that you can present to your potential advertisers.

Media kits are most certainly not one size fits all. Your media kit should be representative of the actual feeling you try to produce on your podcast — competent and real, not over-the-top glitzy. Consider it like a job interview: It's okay to comb your hair and put on a fresh shirt, but you wouldn't send your good-looking-but-ignorant roommate as a stand-in, would you? Know how to clearly communicate what your podcast is all about and how it would benefit a potential sponsor.

REMEMBER

The big fish are very well armed in this pond. Large media outlets tend to have large media kits that were developed with the assistance of large advertising agencies that charged large sums of money for their expertise. The small- to mid-size podcaster need not go this far. You need something more than just a burned CD of your latest episode.

So, here's a practical list of dos and don'ts to keep in mind when considering what to put in your media kit.

First off, the "Yes, go for it" list:

>> **Include accurate listener statistics.** Well, as accurate as you can, anyway. Include the total number of subscribers to your podcast feed; estimate how many direct downloads an episode of your show attracts. If your podcast is seeing great growth, include a chart that shows the increasing numbers. (For more about listener statistics, see the handy nearby sidebar, "Can you ever really know the size of your audience?")

>> **Display your show schedule.** If you update your podcast several times a week or once a month, include a calendar or schedule of when your updates happen. If your show has no set schedule, be prepared to explain your methodology of updates. Many advertisers expect some sort of consistency (read: reliable exposure) from the places their ads are running.

>> **Provide demographic information.** Some advertisers want to know the general make-up of your audience. The more detailed you can get, the better. At a minimum, show a breakdown of gender, age range, and household income level. These statistics can be difficult to gather, but doing so increases your chances with many advertisers. Consider asking listeners to take a voluntary survey. If you ask your listeners to take a survey, it never hurts to offer them an incentive. Perhaps one lucky random survey taker wins a $50 Amazon gift card. There are many sites like http://surveymonkey.com that cost a few dollars — remember sometimes you have to spend money to make money.

>> **Showcase your popularity.** If you get 50 comments on each of your show note entries, talk about it. Technorati (http://technorati.com) and Google (www.google.com) can support any claims for the popularity of your site. Print any great testimonials showing your knowledge and expertise in the field. Favorable comments from other known experts go a long way, too!

>> **Provide a sample CD or USB flash drive of your show.** You can, in your kit's literature, provide a link where people can sample the "Best of . . ." reel, but do not count on that initiative. With a press kit, you do want to make the best impression you can. That means you take initiative and offer media that already has your show burned on it. CDs are the easiest media to do this with, but as many computers are side-stepping the need for a CD player, consider USB flash drives as part of your kit. As these are podcasts and only a few

episodes sampled (no more than five in their entirety), you do not necessarily need flash drives larger than 1GB. This means money in your budget to get these drives branded with your show title and URL, if possible.

And in the "No, no, a thousand times no" corner, we have . . .

>> **Don't artificially inflate your statistics.** Grandmother always used to say that lies just cause you to make bigger lies. Eventually you find yourself with an advertiser who wants you to explain how you came up with your numbers. Make sure you can support your claims.

>> **Don't use terminology without really understanding what you're talking about.** Marketing and advertising professionals have a vocabulary all their own. ROI. Conversions. CTR. Maybe you do know what these mean; but if you don't, peppering your media kit with these terms is dangerous. For example, say you look at your numbers in Google Analytics and discover that an episode you promoted received over 10,000 impressions. You then proclaim, "My podcast has earned over 10,000 impressions!" to potential advertisers. An impressive stat, but what does that mean? It means that someone has clicked on a link to watch or listen to your podcast, and that Google was able to look at the network of where that click originated from and calculate how many people *potentially* saw or heard your episode. In other words, ten people with 1,000 followers each clicked on the link leading to your episode. That's 10,000 *impressions*. Welcome to the Doublespeak of Digital Marketing.

>> **Don't offer reduced pricing.** Unless you have been podcasting for a couple years, and you likely haven't had time to put things on sale yet. Pick a price you're comfortable with and justify why it's worth it. If you're not sure of a starting price, ask other podcasters. Avoid discounting right off the bat; it implies that you're over-valuing your product. You can always negotiate the price, but don't try that in a media kit. We talk about putting together a rate sheet in the following section.

>> **Don't include a copy of your entire podcast season on CD, USB flash drive, or online.** People like to know what they're getting themselves into. You have a great opportunity to offer that courtesy to potential advertisers — to let them listen enough to sample the wares. Remember, however, that their time is limited. You may include entire episodes if you like, but as mentioned earlier you may find better success by stitching together a "Best of" reel from your show instead of a full season of your podcast. Select shows, or even highlights from your favorite episodes, take less time to consume.

>> **Don't make a halfhearted effort.** Okay, you don't have to create a full-blown presentation that would make the mavens of Madison Avenue envious of your skill set. But we're not talking Elmer's glue and crayons here, either. Treat it like a business; invest the right kind of time and money to make your media kit look (and sound) as professional as you can.

When you have your content figured out, go buy a nice, pretty binder. Or better yet, order some custom ones online that feature your podcast logo, slogan, and website address. You can get them online from VistaPrint (www.vistaprint.com) if you want large quantities. For smaller runs, see what your local office-supply or copy center can provide.

Establishing a rate sheet

A *rate sheet* is simply a table of what you charge for ads and other services — this could include things like audio or graphic production. And you thought you were headed into uncharted waters by just creating a podcast? How about figuring out a fair price to charge for running advertising? That's by no means a science. Heck, it's not even an art form at this stage! It's total guesswork — picking a number, throwing it out there, and seeing what sticks.

CAN YOU EVER REALLY KNOW THE SIZE OF YOUR AUDIENCE?

Tracking down listener statistics is elusive — and that's quite an understatement. Although many of the podcasting pundits will tell you how important understanding your audience size is (especially when you're trying to attract advertisers and sponsors), it's difficult for them to agree on the best way to snag those numbers.

Web server analysis tools are wholly unreliable in this regard; after all, they weren't designed for this purpose. They can tell you how many times your podcast episodes were requested, but not how many of those requests were successful, and if successful, how many of those downloads were listened to. They can tell you how many times your RSS 2.0 file was accessed, but they provide no tool to filter out requests made every five minutes by the same obsessed podcatcher.

The most widely used model of determining audience size is the *bandwidth-division method*. This requires you, the podcaster, to know two pieces of data: the average size of your podcast media files and the total amount of data transferred in each month. For example, suppose your ISP reported that you transferred 350GB of data in the month of May. Convert that to MB by multiplying by 1,024 (the numbers of megabytes in a giga-byte) to get 358,400MB of data transfer.

Okay, suppose that during that month, you put up four podcasts, each with a size of 10MB. Divide the total number of transfers (358,400) by the average size of your file (10MB) to get the total number of accesses to that file — in this case 35,840. Finally, divide that number by the total number of podcast media files released (4, in this case). The answer (in theory, at least): You have approximately 8,960 listeners to your show.

This number, however, does not consider the data transferred by your web server simply to run your website — say, images and text. Nor is it helpful when your podcast media files vary widely in size. And it still doesn't factor in those folks who downloaded 90 percent of your show before the connection broke.

That is not to say developers are not trying to come up with a better system. At the time of writing and editing this edition of *Podcasting For Dummies*, Apple is offering a new Podcasts app for the upcoming iOS 11 for iPhone and iPad. Along with a complete overhaul of how podcasts are organized and consumed by the subscriber, the Podcasts app now offers for content creators Podcast Analytics. This new feature will include total hours listened to a specific episode, average minutes per listener, where listeners stopped listening (and never returned to the episode), and the average number of listeners that finish an episode from beginning to end. This iOS 11 Podcasts app sounds fantastic, but we have yet to see it in action. This is why we have *Podcasting For Dummies: The Companion Podcast* (http://podcastingfordummies.com), where we will review and discuss the new app in depth.

Our advice on this matter: Find a method that seems to work for you and stick with it. It's the best you can do . . . for now.

You can start by reviewing rates of other podcasts — hopefully podcasts with similar topics or audience sizes. Ask them for their media kits and rate sheets — if they are separate items.

A rate sheet can be as simple as a fixed price for a given ad segment — we like to think podcasting is more flexible than that. Can you offer cheaper prices for shorter ads? Can you offer prices for different placement within the show, keeping in mind that the closer to the top of the show, the more valuable the ad placement? You can offer decreasing rates based on how many shows carry an ad. How about giving better pricing if there's an ad in your show along with a link on your website? Are you capable of offering production services for an audio or video ad? These options can be combined in a variety of ways to complement each other.

Getting a Sponsor

Sponsorship and *advertising* are often used as interchangeable terms, but they're distinct approaches with different requirements. For the purposes of this discussion, we consider sponsorship as a relationship you (the podcaster) have worked out with an organization that regularly funds — and has a vested interest in the success of — your show. (Obviously, you can't say that about all advertisers.)

Sponsorships were popular — almost to the point of exclusivity — in the old days of radio in the early 20th century. During that time, corporations would create the various radio programs as an advertising vehicle — they could even censor content if (for example) some writer goofed and had the villain using the sponsor's product. Modern-day advertising deals, which allow a station or program to drop a 30-second ad into its already-established programming, came into play much later; these days, such deals dominate the scene.

Traditional media sponsorships have all but disappeared, and their last bastion can be found in the world of daytime television: They have morphed into . . . the dreaded infomercial. We're not suggesting that you turn your podcast into an infomercial. However, if you're catering to a niche audience and a corporate entity can service the needs of your audience, that angle may be worth considering.

REMEMBER

Understand that obtaining a true sponsor for your show likely means you give up some creative control. Instead of paying you a few dollars to run a preproduced ad, your sponsoring corporation underwrites your entire show, or at least a significant portion of it. Rather than getting you to take a break from your content while you talk about its product for a few moments, your content becomes *dedicated to* talking about its product.

Examples of sponsored podcasts include Mike Rowe's *The Way I Heard It* podcast (`http://mikerowe.com/podcast`) and WNYC's *Note to Self* (`www.wnyc.org/shows/notetoself`) sponsored by such companies as Blue Apron, Squarespace, and Zip Recruiter.

If you're thinking about approaching a corporation to underwrite your show, you need to provide much of the same information necessary for securing advertisers, as discussed earlier. In addition, however, you need to demonstrate how your show can help bolster the success metrics of the corporation. "It's a cool show that your customers will love" probably won't cut it.

There's no secret sauce that irresistibly attracts corporate sponsorship. Each corporation has distinct goals and objectives. Any podcaster trying to solicit sponsorship would be well served to understand these goals and objectives inside and out, and be prepared to clearly demonstrate how sponsoring a podcast can help the company achieve those goals.

MORE VALUABLE THAN MONEY

Tee and Chuck haven't gotten rich off podcasting. They do it for the love (see Chapter 17). The return on investment they have gotten from picking up a microphone and hitting record has gone far beyond cold hard cash. We know, this is starting to sound a little hippy-dippy love fest, but hang with us. Sure, we aspired at one time to get a nice source of funding and perhaps a fleeting moment to quit our day jobs and turn our hobby (or should we say *another* hobby) in to a full-time paid gig, but the fates had other things in store for us.

Looking back on it, though, your humble authors were not expecting the pile of indirect benefits podcasting has led them to, and through. Thanks to podcasting, both Chuck and Tee have found some great career opportunities. As his gateway to social media, Tee not only wrote other books on social media but is a full-time professional in social media, managing social media platforms and devising strategies that resonate with audiences around the world. Podcasting made Chuck a better presenter, which led to promotions at his day job, and even prepared him for an unexpected job transition in 2010. Podcasting helped Chuck quickly transition to a new role at a new company in just three weeks. As for Tee, his own understanding of podcasting and social media sent him coast-to-coast and around the world, leading workshops and seminars on the subject. Finally, let's not forget the awesome network of people and amazing friendships both Chuck and Tee have forged over a decade of firing up microphones and sharing their views through RSS feeds.

They cannot promise everyone future success such as what they have been blessed with, but keep this in mind: When the people in your life question you for buying some (more) electronic gear, start recording your voice, and publish it to the world, tell them you're doing it for more than money.

Asking Your Listeners for Money

There is one group of potential financial backers out there who couldn't care less about your fancy media kit: your listeners. They couldn't give a hoot about your anticipated growth curve in subscribers or your ratio of direct downloaders to feed–based audience. They do have a vested interest in your continuing to produce the very best possible show, each episode — and they are (usually) content to let you take the show in the direction you feel it should go.

Sometimes your show is important enough to them that they're willing to pony up. That's why the following section discusses some novel ways you can go about soliciting your listeners for funds to help offset some of the costs of creating a podcast.

Please don't turn your podcast into a weekly telethon. Most people tolerate the time when NPR goes into pledge-drive mode, but no one looks forward to it. If you're going to ask your audience for money, do it tactfully and as rarely as possible. Please.

Gathering listener donations with PayPal

Some of your audience will so love your show that they'll happily hand over some of their hard-earned money — if you'll only ask.

Asking for listeners' support is a two-step process: First you ask for the money, and then you provide an easy and convenient way for your listeners to send you money. PayPal (www.paypal.com) has been handling small and large web-based transactions for years. A PayPal donation link can be fully integrated into your website with minimum hassle. Here's how:

1. **Log in to PayPal.**

   If you don't have a PayPal account, click the Sign Up link and follow the simple instructions. You need a valid credit card to sign up.

   PayPal, like much of the web, is subject to change. The flow of these steps might be slightly different at the time you're reading this. Regardless, the steps you need to follow will basically be the same.

2. **From your Account Overview page, click the Details in the Selling Tools section on the left side.**

   The Merchant Services page allows you to set up a variety of ways people can send you money.

3. **Click the Create payment buttons for your website link on the right side of the page.**

   You are taken to the My Saved Buttons.

4. **In the Related items box, click Create New Button.**

   You are taken to the Create PayPal Payment Button page, as shown in Figure 15-1.

5. **Enter a donation name and donation ID in the appropriate text boxes.**

   We recommend using the show name, and perhaps a suffix - *Donations* to help you identify your donations if you have other types of income to your PayPal account.

You can also use the ID field to denote multiple types of donations or donations for different shows in the event you produce more than one podcast. You can put anything you want in this field, but keep in mind that it will be visible to those making donations — so make sure it isn't something confusing.

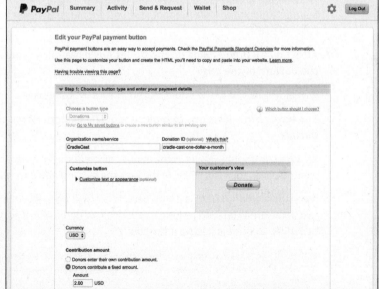

FIGURE 15-1:
PayPal makes accepting donations as easy as filling out a few fields.

6. **Enter a set donation amount if you want in the Amount text box. Also, change the designated country if you'd like your currency to be something other than U.S. dollars.**

If you want your listeners to donate a set amount, choose that amount now. If you leave the Amount field blank, your users will have to enter an amount before they donate. You decide which is best for you.

TIP

If you're familiar with using HTML forms, you can later add a suggested donation amount, and allow your listeners to change the amount if they desire. Get a copy of *Coding For Dummies* (Wiley) by Nikhil Abraham if you need help with editing forms.

7. **Select the style of Donation button you would like to use from the Customize Button section.**

If you have a custom button, here's the place to change it. If you don't have one, don't worry. The default button works just fine on your website, and you can always change it later if you want.

8. **Under Merchant Account ID, choose Use My Secure Merchant Account ID.**

Using your merchant account ID links your account to your email address and protects you from spammers.

At this point you can optionally review the information the collapsed sections labeled Step 2: Save your buttons (optional) and Step 3: Customize advanced features (optional). While not required, you should get familiar with what's covered there.

9. **After you fill in the fields on the Donations page, click Create Button at the bottom of the page.**

PayPal whisks you to the Add a Button to Your Website page.

10. **You have some decisions to make about the custom HTML code for your button:**

If you're comfortable doing some minor editing of the HTML that makes your website work, copy the HTML in the Website tab and add it to your page.

If you think editing HTML is a little beyond you just now, then simply copy the text in the Email tab and include it in your show notes. You'll want to make it a hyperlink, so don't just leave it like this:

```
https://www.paypal.com/cgi-bin/webscr?cmd=_xclick&business=chuck%40chuckch
    at%2ecom&no_shipping=0&no_note=1&tax=0&currency_code=USD&charset=UTF%2d
    8&charset=UTF%2d8
```

Instead, you want to enclose it with an `<a href="">` `</a>` tag and include some descriptive text, like this:

```
<a href="https://www.paypal.com/cgi-bin/webscr?cmd=_xclick&business=chuck%
    40chuckchat%2ecom&no_shipping=0&no_note=1&tax=0&currency_code=USD&chars
    et=UTF%2d8&charset=UTF%2d8">Donate to my show</a>
```

That should do it for the donation link.

Building patrons with Patreon

Another alternative that many podcasters and creative artists are exploring is called Patreon (`https://patreon.com`). Patreon offers a couple ways for you to get paid for your content. Like PayPal, you can set up a monthly billing system to charge your loyal followers at the beginning of each month. However, you can also set it up to tap your patrons' wallets on a *per creation* method. For the podcaster, this means the harder you work, the more you can potentially get paid. For the patron, it means if the podcaster starts to get complacent and doesn't produce any new content, you don't have to pay.

Many podcasters will set up *tiered patronage,* much like the different levels public radio can set you up with only on a per episode basis rather than per year. For example, for $1 per episode, you get a special episode, show notes, or a postcard once a year. For $2 per episode, you get your name read on the show and a T-shirt. You see how it goes? If you support the show, you get goodies. Each show has its own take on what it charges and what it offers.

But how effective can Patreon be? For writers Chris Lester (`www.patreon.com/authorchrislester`) and Phil Rossi (`www.patreon.com/philrossi`), Patreon has proven to be quite the motivator in turning out new fiction. Chris Lester, host of the award-winning *Metamor City* podcast, had stepped away from storytelling for quite some time before returning with *The Raven and the Writing Desk,* his own author interview show that also journals his own return to writing fiction. His accompanying Patreon was solid enough to keep him writing, even when finding himself unexpectedly in-between jobs after moving from the West Coast to the Midwest. For Phil Rossi, author and podcaster behind *Crescent, Eden, and Harvey,* his greatest challenge for writing fiction was time. His Patreon income allows him to invest less in lucrative performance gigs as a musician so he can continue producing more fiction. Both Lester and Rossi offer their Patreon investors exclusive fiction both in audio and digital formats, and additional incentives when print versions of their podcasts are released (see Figure 15-2).

FIGURE 15-2:
Authors Chris
Lester (left) and
Phil Rossi (right)
turn to Patreon
backers for
funding, and in
return backers
receive exclusive
content made
available only
to them.

To get started on Patreon, first have a plan. Think about what you can offer the potential contributors to make them want to sign up. Once you have your plan, create an account on Patreon by following these steps:

1. **Click your icon in the upper right and select Become a Creator.**

2. **Click the big blue button Create Your Page.**

3. **Enter your name and click OK.**

4. **When prompted for what you are creating, enter your podcast name and click OK.**

5. **Pick the category that your podcast best fits.**

   Lucky for us, there's a category called Podcasts!

6. **Answer the question about the material content by clicking the appropriate option.**

7. **Watch the short video from the CEO of Patreon. It's informative and perhaps a bit inspiring. Click Continue.**

8. **On the Settings page, review the various bits of information.**

   Some information, like your name and what you are creating, was entered earlier whereas some, like cover picture and appropriate social media links, are new. You can even set a custom link at patreon.com if you fancy yourself a vanity URL.

9. **Visit the other links across the top of the page and review the information for each. When you are done with each section click the big red Save Changes button.**

The About page lets you describe who you are and what your show is about. The Rewards page is where you define the different patron levels and what they can expect in return for their fantastic contribution to your artistic work (see Figure 15-3). If you have certain goals you would like to meet, you can specify them in the Goals page. The Payment page determines whether you will charge monthly or per episode. The Thanks page allows you to send a note (or video link) to your supporters — always a nice touch.

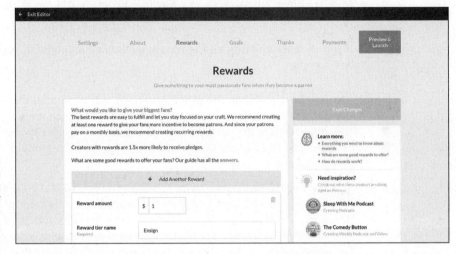

FIGURE 15-3:
Patreon allows you to set different levels of rewards for different donations.

REMEMBER

Don't forget to set your Payout Preferences if you want to get paid! Visit your accounts settings by clicking on your icon in the upper right and choosing Account Settings. Click Payout Preferences on the right. Complete the form and click Save Preferences.

10. **When you are done reviewing and saving all the other pages, click Preview & Launch in the upper right.**

Look at your sample page. Make sure it looks the way you want and has accurate information. If you need to make changes, go back to any of the other pages and save.

11. **Finally, hit the green Go Live button.**

Now you can put a link or button on your website guiding your audience to your Patreon page, announce it on your show, or any other way to let people know how they can help you. Once a month, it automatically withdraws money from their account and deposits it in yours.

REMEMBER

Patreon takes a service fee for hosting and managing your content. Typically, this is 5%. However, be sure to review the payment processing fees to understand how much you can expect from your donors.

Selling stuff

Some podcasters offer merchandise for sale to support their show financially — T-shirts, hats, mugs, CDs, autographed pictures, you name it. If it's sellable, chances are good that some podcaster out there is selling it.

If you're contemplating selling merchandise via your podcast, you fall into one of two groups:

>> **You have merchandise to sell.** Musicians, authors, artists, and craftspeople fall into this category. For these podcasters, offering CDs, books, prints, or other items to the listening audience can bring in significant revenue. (Down the road, there's no reason why it shouldn't be possible to make a living via podcasting.)

Once again, PayPal (www.paypal.com) can be very helpful in taking away the technical hurdles for selling items online and integrating them into your podcast and website. If you can master the process for setting up online donations, you aren't far from having PayPal work as your entire online shopping cart. But this book is about podcasting, not about PayPal. Luckily for you, Victoria Rosenberg and Marsha Collier wrote *PayPal For Dummies* (Wiley).

>> **You need merchandise to sell.** If you need stuff to sell, CafePress (www.cafepress.com) is more than happy to step in and offer its assistance. Remember the T-shirts and other stuff mentioned earlier? You can go to the trouble of making those yourself, carrying an inventory, and shipping the orders out as they trickle in — or you can let CafePress take care of all of that for you.

Setting up a CafePress storefront is a breeze, though it's a highly configurable task, and how you set it up depends on what you want to sell. A basic shop is free to set up and to use. Your listeners buy the T-shirts and coffee mugs (or whatever), with your logo or design on them, from the CafePress store, and CafePress pays you a commission. It's very simple and requires only some quick setup information from you to get started. It takes about five minutes to set this up; CafePress takes care of the rest.

REMEMBER

Don't expect to make tons of cash via CafePress. Unless you can convince a large group of your listeners that they simply *must* have an $18 T-shirt with your logo on it, we wouldn't recommend quitting your day job just yet.

Handling Fee-Based Subscriptions

Getting your listeners to donate a couple of bucks to you or buy your latest CD is one thing, but getting them to *shell out money for the privilege of listening to your show* is another matter altogether.

WARNING

If you don't have a preestablished following, a fee-based subscription approach likely won't help you. If you do have a following but have never required anyone to give you money, you may find yourself with less of a following afterwards. Use this option sparingly — and only if you really think others are willing to give money to listen to your podcast. You'll need to come to the decision whether you want x listeners for free, or $1/10$ x listeners to pay — okay, we made that number up, but it will definitely be far less than your current listener base.

TIP

One way to get your listeners interested in parting with their money would be to give them a sample of what to expect. Offer the first episode or two for free download and in them, mention how to get the rest. (We knew podcasting was addicting, but this is ridiculous.) Another method is to offer the opening 15-20 minutes of your podcast for free, then offer the rest of the episode for a fee, provided your show has the content to follow it up with.

Securing your feed

Okay, we're sure you're wondering just how you prevent giving away your podcast to anyone who cares to download it, not just to those who pay for it. The answer is to create a secure RSS feed with logins and passwords.

It's time to be blunt — setting up and maintaining a secure feed is a little ugly. The good news is this is a *For Dummies* title, so we don't expose all the technical warts and scars here. We keep the process simple but still manage to get you in touch with the inner code monkey that lurks in everyone.

To start, there's nothing special about a secure feed. The web server handles prompting for the login and password. You are responsible for setting up the feed and a configuration file. If you're using a web server based on Apache — which a lot of hosting providers are — the high-level technical bits look something like this:

>> Create a separate RSS feed for your protected content in a separate directory — we'll call it members.

>> In the new members directory, create a file called .htaccess with some special instructions. These instructions tell the web server where to look for accounts and groups allowed access to this directory.

The authentication process works like this:

1. The Apache web server receives an instruction from the podcatching client to download the new feed file. It peeks inside the .htaccess file to find the logins and passwords.

2. The podcatching client presents a prompt for a login and password.

3. The user types his or her information.

4. The podcatching client sends the info back to the web server. It checks to see whether a) the information provided is correct, and b) that the account is in a group with permissions to the directory.

5. If both of those are correct, the feed is downloaded and processed by the podcatching client like any other feed.

A sample .htaccess file looks like this:

```
AuthType Basic
AuthName "Members Only"
AuthUserFile /www/users/chucktomasi/html/security/passwd
AuthGroupFile /www/users/chucktomasi/html/security/group
Require group members
```

The first line (AuthType) tells the server what type of authentication to use — for now, stick with what it says. The second line (AuthName) is the text that appears when the login/password prompt appears. The AuthUserFile line points to a file with login names and passwords. The AuthGroupFile file is a simple list of accounts associated with a group name. It's important that the files indicated in AuthUserFile and AuthGroupFile are placed where the file says they are or this doesn't work.

The contents of the .htaccess file are case-sensitive — except for the text between quotes. It's extremely important you get the case right for this to work. One of your authors spent many hours trying to figure out why things didn't work because he had Group instead of group.

A sample line from the AuthUserFile file looks like this:

```
chuck.tomasi:2nyp44rex
```

In this example, the login name is chuck.tomasi, and the password is encrypted, so nobody can download your file and find out all the passwords. You, the podcaster, are responsible for creating and maintaining the AuthUserFile (and AuthGroupFile). For a small list of user accounts, it's fairly easy to maintain the password file by hand, using a command-line utility called htpasswd — commonly provided as part of the Apache web server.

Not all hosting accounts provide access to a command-line interface. You should check with your web hosting provider to see whether you have this capability. If not, you may have to resort to creating and maintaining these files on another system and uploading the files. For Mac OS X users, you already have Apache installed and can access these tools from the Terminal window. Windows users have to download Apache (http://apache.org) to install them.

If you find yourself with a runaway hit podcast on your hands with lots of accounts, managing them can be a bit of a pain. In such a case, look at a product like aMember at www.amember.com, which is a PHP web interface that runs on your web server. Make sure your hosting account allows you to upload and run PHP programs beforehand, though.

A typical line from an AuthGroupFile file might look like this:

```
members:tee.morris,chuck.tomasi,kreg.steppe
```

The format is pretty straightforward — first is the group name (members), then a colon (:), then a list of comma-separated names from the AuthUserFile file. You can name the group anything you like — as long as it corresponds to the Require group line in the .htaccess file. The AuthGroupFile can also manage multiple groups with each line following the same format described earlier.

The path less traveled

When you have your AuthUserFile and AuthGroupFile files set up, you must designate the *physical path* to them. You get the physical path to your password and group files from your hosting tech support.

REMEMBER Be sure to ask for the physical path and not the virtual path. A *virtual path* is a shortcut that the web server gets from the browser on the other end in a URL to get to your files — for example, `/security/passwd`. The *physical* is how the operating system on the web server gets to the same information — for example, `/www/users/chucktomasi/html/security/passwd`. Most modern podcatchers and RSS readers support basic authentication. If you would like more information on configuring an Apache file, refer to the Apache web page (`www.apache.org`).

If all else fails, seek out an experienced web geek and offer pizza, extra cheese, and a six-pack of Red Bull!

A great example of a pay-for-podcasting is Bill O'Reilly (`https://www.billoreilly.com`). The former Fox News channel host has taken his cadre of loyal listeners and charges about $50 for a premium membership to his audio and video content (which includes a free gift.)

Chapter **16**

Podcasting for Publicity

T rue podcasters bristle at the growing commercialization of podcasting. With many corporate podcasts dominating iTunes and Stitcher, independent podcasters have voiced many concerns that boil down to one: A *true* podcast is done for passion, not for profit. The movement towards podcasting as a moneymaking venture goes against the grain of a true podcast. The words, opinions, and emotions should all be aimed for the listeners' hearts and minds, not their wallets.

Well, yeah, that's all fine and dandy — but before we cheer on the sentiments of the purist, indie podcaster, sheer love of the medium does not pay the bills. Also, when juggernaut organizations like NPR create runaway hits with millions of listeners, you won't hear their producers or creators thump their chests and proclaim proudly, "No, you go on and keep your commercial revenue and corporate bankrolls. We're going to keep on podcasting with our USB mic and preamp."

Truth be told, podcasting has proven itself a great way to reach the consumer. It's economical, unobtrusive, and can be a great way to build a potential audience.

With blogging, social networks, and the still-mysterious podcasts all struggling to find their place in the corporate world, all these platforms are finding themselves becoming integrated as part of a business marketing and promotion machine; and with the right directors, strategists, and content producers in place, these platforms are gaining traction. Podcasting has come a long way since the first edition of this book, but for larger corporations (such as Coca-Cola, Nike, and many others), podcasting remains an unproven medium. Because podcasting is audio-on-demand, there's still no easy way to measure numbers, feedback, and response in the same way radio and television advertisements are tracked. However, statistics from WordPress plug-ins like JetPack, online services like Google Analytics, and service providers like LibSyn continue to develop new methods to do so.

This doesn't mean the change is taking its time. With iTunes and its podcast subscriptions going from zero to 1 million in *two days* — match those numbers, J.K. Rowling! (oh, wait, you did. . .) — the corporate world is wanting to know more about podcasting, realizing that some independent podcasts are discovering new audiences for their products (and broadening their existing audience) one MP3 at a time. If the end goal of your podcast is publicity, this chapter is for you. We go through several examples of where podcasting has paid off — maybe not in dollars and cents, but in good word-of-mouth buzz.

Podcasting and Politics

In the political arena, innovation can be a political candidate's best strategic option in winning an office. The podcasting fad that some of Capitol Hill's old guard snickered and scoffed at is now part of its own outreach initiatives. Individuals interested in holding office — be it local, state, or national — are side-stepping conventional media and adding to their platform the people who listen in the podosphere.

REMEMBER

What we're defining in this section as a *political podcast* is a podcast hosted by a political figure or an individual seeking a political office. (We're *not* talking about podcasts where a host discusses current affairs, rants about the state of the world, or cracks jokes about the latest scandal.)

So, what can a podcast do for you, the tech-savvy politician?

>> Podcasting (and its companion blog, if you use a blog as part of your delivery) connects you directly with your constituencies.

>> Podcasting can reach young voters, the elusive demographic that can easily make or break a victory at the polls.

>> Podcasting avoids the bias that creeps up in media outlets, allowing you as a candidate to present agendas and intentions uninterrupted.

When going political with a podcast, whether you're running for the U.S. Senate or podcasting your term as School Board representative, here are a few things to keep in mind:

>> **Keep your podcast on a consistent *weekly* schedule.** Monthly podcasts don't cut it; the tide of politics is in constant flux. Daily updates are less than practical, but weekly podcasts work well for ongoing political issues, and you can shape their content to remain timely enough to fit the podcasting medium. Set a day for delivering your weekly message and stick to that schedule.

>> **Focus on the issues, not the opinions.** A political podcaster will always walk a fine line between public servant and political commentator. You need to stay focused on the issues. If you suddenly start hammering away with opinion and commentary, you'd become more like Hannity, Beck, or Maddow. If you want politics as your podcast's subject matter, ask yourself whether you're looking to help listeners understand the issues accurately and take meaningful action, or whether you're just ranting and venting to entertain people who want their opinions reinforced.

>> **Give your listeners a plan for action.** When you cover the issues in your podcast, provide possible solutions to the pressing matters of your community and your constituents. Whether you're detailing blood drives or fundraisers, or launching an awareness campaign for cancer research, increase that divide between *political figure* and *political commentator* by offering listeners ways they can get involved in the community and make a difference.

WARNING

Podcasting is definitely an avenue to explore if you're venturing into the political area, but this is not your sole means in reaching out to voters. You will need to campaign, of course. Get out on the road, shake hands, kiss babies, and the like. Unless you are recording said baby-kissing and hand-shaking, campaigning will mean your podcast goes on the occasional break. Make sure to communicate to your listeners that changes in the posting schedule are upcoming. When you can, give a podcast from the road to keep the communication lines open.

Anytime a podcast goes public on the issues, its creator walks a fine line between public servant and political commentator. The podcasters described in the following paragraph all keep their content focused on the issues and less on what they feel about the issues.

The first politician to host a political podcast of this nature was North Carolina Senator John Edwards with the *One America Committee Podcast with John Edwards*, covering poverty, Internet law, and environmental issues. His wife, Elizabeth Edwards, was also featured, raising awareness on breast cancer. The success of the *One America* podcast caught the attention of the govern-ator himself,

Arnold Schwarzenegger, who podcasts his weekly radio address. Then, direct from the Oval Office, George W. Bush and Barack Obama hosted podcasts on a weekly basis, much in the same manner as FDR's Fireside Chats only this time happening on your mobile devices. And at the time of writing this, Senator Bernie Sanders podcasts from the left side of the aisle at `https://www.sanders.senate.gov/bernies-podcast` (shown in Figure 16-1) while Senator Ron Paul offers from `www.stitcher.com/podcast/ron-paul-liberty-report` a look at the issues from the right.

FIGURE 16-1: Senator Bernie Sanders has embraced podcasting as a viable platform for making constituents aware of issues through *The Bernie Sanders Show*.

REMEMBER

If you're a politician and you want to get in touch with the people (to respond when voters complain about poor communication with their representatives or the candidates running for office), why not invite them into your kitchen, offer them a cup of virtual coffee, and ask them to relax a bit? Instead of dishing up prepared statements from professional speechwriters, you can offer voters (and worldwide listeners) impromptu, candid, sincere opinions on issues facing the country and the world.

Telling the World a Story, One Podcast at a Time

The whole point behind promotion — be it for books, film, or other forms of entertainment — is to win prospective target audiences (or build on existing ones) with something new or to give a different take on a familiar commodity. For a fraction of the cost of print advertisements and broadcast-media commercials, podcasting opens markets for your creative work — and can even start to get your name into an international market. If you're an established presence in the writing market, or any entertainment field, the fans you have nurtured, with time, will not only eagerly support your podcast, but also introduce your MP3s to reader groups, friends, and enthusiasts of the subjects you're writing about.

Podcasting can introduce your writings or your music to audiences worldwide. For artists in more visual arts such as film, dance, painting, or sculpture, podcasting — audio or video — can serve as a journal leading up to the premiere of your work or a behind-the-scenes look at how works go from idea to fruition. It's an instant connection with your audience, and a great way to build an audience by getting them to know you on however intimate a level works best for you and your work. Planning a strategy for this kind of promotion only helps your agenda:

>> **When podcasting even in a visual media, briefly describe the action for the audience.** In *Masterpiece Studio*'s podcast (www.pbs.org/wgbh/masterpiece/podcasts), both hosts and guests add into their interview details about scenes and moments that accompany audio clips from productions being discussed. It is never taken for granted that people have seen the episode or special event this companion podcast is showcasing. (Many times, the host will give a quick spoiler warning.) In only a few words and a few seconds, *Masterpiece Studio* sets the scene for what's happening and why it is talking about it for the sake of listeners who are currently watching the latest PBS offering.

If you're documenting your visual art, it will take only a moment to describe what you're doing. For the painter: "I am using green with just a hint of black so we can make the eyes appear more unearthly, unnatural." For a dancer, "In reconstructing the Australian Aboriginal dance, you must remain grounded and deep in your squats, more so than what is normally seen in modern dance." Commentary like this, especially in a voiceover with video, does not need to go into every minute detail; but a few words are needed to create or complete a picture.

>> **For writers and musicians: Edit, edit, edit.** Awkward pauses, stammers, and stumbled words are obstacles for a writer introducing his work to the podosphere: They've gotta go! The approach is no different from that of an independent musician who podcasts a rehearsal session or a recording: You don't want off-key instruments and vocalists missing the high notes. Your podcasts need to sound sharp and clean.

Musicians, no matter if it takes 5 takes or 50 takes, should have their instruments in tune, lyrics clearly pronounced, and all notes sung on key. Writers should enunciate, speak clearly, and (most importantly) enjoy the manuscript. Each piece, whether music or printed word, should be a performance that serves as your audition to a worldwide audience. (While that may sound a bit nerve-racking, don't think of it as walking out on stage so much as building something fine to send into the world.) Just have fun, and your audience will enjoy the ride with you.

If you need a refresher on the basics of editing, skip back to Chapter 8 for the primers on editing with Audacity and GarageBand.

» **Open or close your podcasts with a brief, off-script commentary.** Before beginning your latest installment or after your latest chapter concludes, a brief word from the author is a nice (and in many cases, welcoming) option for a podcast's audience. This commentary gives the author a unique opportunity to connect with readers, sharing ideas about what inspired a scene, to promote an upcoming book-signing, or to give an update about what's happening in the next book's production.

This approach adds to the intimate experience of podcasting a novel, and podcast storytellers like Mur Lafferty, Philippa Ballantine, and Chris Lester use this to invite listeners into their real world after sharing the world they imagined. Let your audience members know who you are, and they'll show their appreciation through their support of your current and future works.

Podcasting continues to prove itself as a viable means of promotion for artists of any media unable to fund their own coast-to-coast tour. It may make conventional creators shake their heads at the idea of giving their works away for free, but the numbers and individual successes of authors taking this chance is the proof in this publicity. Now, before ink even hits the page, authors are building fan bases and getting their names out into the public. (And some of the lucky ones get to write books for the *For Dummies* people!)

WHERE IT ALL BEGAN . . .

Allow us a personal account of the journey from podcasting fan to full-fledged podcaster. When *Podcasting For Dummies'* own Tee Morris was in the final rewrites of *Legacy of MOREVI,* his publisher contacted him and said, "Okay, Tee, start thinking of neat promotional ideas." Around this time, Evo Terra and Michael R. Mennenga of *The Dragon Page* had just started podcasting. The more Tee found out about podcasting, the more he began planning to podcast *MOREVI* to get word out about *Legacy of MOREVI*. After all, he'd been complimented several times on his live readings. And as an actor who loved playing around with his Mac's audio and video features, he figured, *why not?*

The Prologue of *MOREVI: The Chronicles of Rafe & Askana* dropped into the Dragon Page's feed on January 21, 2005, and so began a completely new kind of promotion, different from what *The Dragon Page* had ever done before: a chapter presented every Friday, as read by the author. The feedback was instantaneous. Within weeks of Tee's first episode, two other authors stepped up and offered their works for podcast as well. One of them was Mark Jeffrey, author of the science fiction/fantasy young adult adventure, *The Pocket and The Pendant* (www.markjeffrey.net). The other author was adrenaline-hopped, in-your-face, über-intense conductor of mayhem, chaos, and carnage, Scott Sigler (www.scottsigler.com), and the book was *EarthCore*.

From here, the podcast novel — or podiobook — was born. Since then, authors both new and accomplished have turned to podcasting as a way of sharing their stories with the world.

Keeping Good Company: Community Podcasts

Slice-of-life podcasts that encourage community among listeners and among fans are podcasts that *promote.* They can promote a show cancelled too soon into production, an issue affecting the well-being of a community, or offer a voice to a cause. The promotion comes from word-of-mouth advertising *(buzz)* that these podcasters generate from their thoughts, comments, and opinions on their subject — be it traveling across Spain, daily life in New York City, George Lucas's *Star Wars,* or Joss Whedon's *Firefly.*

Slice-of-life podcasts let the world into locations and clue people into possibilities that listeners may be curious about. After a few podcasts, you can even encourage listeners to experience that corner of the world, that idea, or join the community.

Do you have a cause you want to give attention to? Do you want to raise awareness in your county or district? Do you want to share the experience of preparing for a wedding or anniversary? Consider sound-seeing tour podcasts to build an online community through your podcast.

Creating a podcast to encourage testimony

Community is synonymous with podcasting. This book talks a lot about community, establishing a connection between you the podcaster and your audience which is waiting impatiently for the next episode. Podcasts can also bring an existing community — a group with a shared interest, a community of homeowners, or a group dedicated to a cause — together and keep its members informed. The podcast can reach audiences in and outside of your community, sharing your interests and concerns with others, making your community even stronger in the long run.

The WDW Radio Show (Figure 16-2, found at www.wdwradio.com) has been a long-running podcast about planning the best trip to the "House of the Mouse," Walt Disney World. Hosted by Disney expert, author, speaker, and entrepreneur Lou Mongello, the *WDW Radio Show* has built an impressive community around this family-friendly podcast, featuring a blog, videos, and live broadcasts alongside this audio travel guide.

Travel planning is not the only topic of discussion on the *WDW Radio Show.* Lou also hosts interviews with representatives from the Walt Disney Corporation, shares comments from listeners about previous episodes or queries about best travel tips, and many personal anecdotes on everything from a favorite amusement park ride to the best Disney vacation memories. What makes the *WDW Radio Show* more of a community than just another podcast is in how its podcast works to not only inform listeners on getting the most out of a visit to Walt Disney World, but also encourage listeners to share their own tips, ideas, and stories about the best way to experience Disney, Epcot, and other properties. This community, in turn, promotes the Walt Disney image through the best of methods: word-of-mouth.

The podosphere takes great pride in its sense of community, but the podcasts showcased here are set apart because the community is encouraged to take a more active role in the issues, concerns, and points of focus the podcast is centered around. More than chiming in with feedback, the community takes an active role in participating with increasing awareness over the podcast's main subject. In some cases, the producing of the podcast brings the community together, either through listener contributions, listeners directing the course of the show, or listeners coming together for a common cause.

Podcasting for fun while promoting in the process

When it comes to promotion, no one does a better job in promoting your business than your most passionate fans.

They work for free, set their own hours, and sing the praises (if you are lucky) of whatever it is you happen to be producing. Many times, these podcasts are nicknamed *fancasts* but these are podcasts where consumers independently sit down around mics and talk about your business, be it an entertainment property, a product, or some sort of service.

But what, you may ask, is the line between a fancast and a podcast about your business?

Well, as we describe in Chapter 5, *The Expanse* has *The Churn,* produced by SyFy Wire. *The Churn* is hosted by SyFy and features as co-hosts authors Ty Franck and Daniel Abraham, who write collectively as James S.A. Corey, author of *The Expanse* novels. This makes the podcast an *official* production, and upon listening to it, you know without question that anything appearing on this show is firsthand knowledge of what is happening on the set, coming from the creators of the world, and shared from the actors bringing these characters to life.

That does not mean *The Churn* is the only podcast about this popular SyFy offering.

While SyFy hosts its own podcast about *The Expanse,* Solo Talk Media produces *The Expanse Podcast: Tales from the Rocinante* (see Figure 16-3).

FIGURE 16-3:
The Expanse Podcast: Tales from the Rocinante is a podcast by the fans for the fans.

The Expanse Podcast: Tales from the Rocinante (http://solotalkmedia.com/category/the-expanse-podcast) is hosted by Mark, a graphic designer from Ontario, Canada. Mark is not affiliated with SyFy or Universal Studios, but he is a fan of *The Expanse* and launched this podcast to share his love for the series. Along with show recaps, he reports news on *The Expanse* cast and crew and offers his own speculation on how things will unfold over upcoming episodes. Other shows like Solo Talk's include *The Expanse: The Unofficial Podcast* and *The Expanse After Show,* two podcasts independently produced from SyFy's own official podcasts. These are examples of fans who are sharing their appreciation for this science fiction series, serving as an unofficial street team for the production.

WARNING

When it comes to fans podcasting, be it about a specific property or a generic theme, don't expect all the opinions coming from the podcast to be positive. If fans don't like a direction or a decision taken in a series, they will share it on their podcast. A fan's podcast could be considered the highest form of feedback, but it should not be regarded as such. You might like the podcasts supporting your favorite sports team, show, or organization. You also might hear some opinions radically different from your own.

Between fancasts hosted by experienced journalists like Yahoo! Sports' Greg Wyshynski and Vice Sports' Dave Lozo (of *Puck Soup* at http://nerdist.com/podcasts/puck-soup, part of the Nerdist Network) or two fans passionate for the sport as in *Shut Yer Five Hole with Meg and Piper* (http://shutyerfivehole.libsyn.com), the National Hockey League receives regular promotion and attention free of charge. Irish culture is also given plenty of attention through podcasts like historian Fin Dwyer's *Irish History Podcast* (http://irishhistory.libsyn.com) and celebrated musician Marc Gunn's *Irish & Celtic Music Podcast* (http://celticmusicpodcast.com), shown in Figure 16-4. What's terrific about these podcasts is they can work to not only promote your passion but promote your own brand. Marc Gunn, for example, in showcasing Irish and Celtic music, culture, and lore on his podcast, also spreads awareness of his own brand as an accomplished musician. The podcast, blog, and companion app all offer listeners a chance to find his music alongside the music of other independent musicians featured on his podcast.

FIGURE 16-4:
Marc Gunn, in offering a platform to musicians everywhere with his *Irish & Celtic Music Podcast*, also promotes his own music brand.

Community-driven podcasts cover a wide range of audiences. However, all communities share a similar mindset, and you can apply these "sound" production principles:

» **You are the host, but it's not all about you.** Community podcasts should be *about the community.* Yes, there is room for personal thoughts and commentary, but in small doses.

The podcast is about the community and how it interacts with the world around you; that is what the content should focus on. Your podcast can feature other members of the community who share the same opinions as yours or even take opposing viewpoints (a spirited debate can up your show). Just remember that the community-based podcast is not about you personally, but about how you see the world, how that connects with the people around you in the community, and how all that comes together in the pursuit of a common interest.

>> **Avoid the negative.** It would be easy to turn a podcast into a gossip column or a personal rant against the very concept that brought the community into being. While there is no law or ethic barring you from speaking out or voicing concerns, a community is based on support. Whether you consider yourself a fan of Harry Potter, Apple Computers, or your local county, your goal in a community podcast is to remain positive and celebrate the benefits of being part of the cooperative spirit. If there is a matter of concern in your community, then there's room for debate and action, as with a political podcast — offer some possible solutions to these issues.

Regardless of the kind of community you're chronicling, your podcast should work much like glue — helping to keep supporters together in the face of problems (instead of just crying in your collective beer) and celebrating what gives them joy. Reinforce that sense of community and keep your podcast strong.

Chapter **17**

Podcasting for Passion

O ur mission from the beginning of this book has been to fill you in on what a podcast is, demystify the technical aspects of getting your voice heard on media players around the world, and assure you that those with the drive to make their message happen can do it, with the right tools. But a podcast is empty if you don't have that drive, that passion to get your podcast up and running and keep it running, whether the episode goes out every week, every other week, or every month. We drop that word a lot throughout the book: *passion*. What do we mean by *podcasting with passion*?

Okay, if you take the dictionary as a starting point, *passion* means "a keen interest in a particular subject or activity, or the object of somebody's intense interest or enthusiasm." You can have state-of-the-art audio equipment, hire the most engaging vocal talent, and employ the best engineers, but that isn't what makes a podcast a podcast. The artists and creativity behind a podcast make an investment — not simply financial or physical — and collect the windfall in listener feedback and download stats.

Yes, a podcast can make money, promote a cause, or bring attention to social issues, but without that passion, you might as well sit behind a microphone and read the instruction manual to your mobile phone. Passion is what motivates relative unknowns to slip on the headphones, step up to the microphone, and let their words fly.

This chapter won't presume to teach you how to create, cultivate, or conjure your own passion. It's something you have, or you don't, for a given topic — and we suspect everybody has it for *some* topics. Instead, we offer some real-world examples of how others apply their passions to podcasts — and we tell you about some tools to apply a little passion-power of your own.

The Philosophical Question for All Podcasters: Why Do We Do It?

It's going to come up sooner or later: Someone will question your motives, rationale, and even sanity at your investment of so much time and energy into a podcast. We highly recommend deep nonsensical answers such as "It's because of the cheese" be returned to these people. Then watch their eyes start to twitch. That never stops being funny.

The following sections tell you some of the ways you can take that passion and channel it in to a truly effective force behind your podcast.

Gaining perspective on passion

"Get some perspective!" they say. Well, we agree with them (whoever *they* are). As a podcaster, you need a firm idea of what your show is about. If you're not sure what your point is, your audience isn't going to be sure, either!

Marc Blackburn's *America at War* podcast (http://americaatwarpodcast.libsyn.com) started in February 2016 and is still a relative newcomer to the podcast scene at the time of this writing, but the content has been centuries in the making and taken decades of Marc's life to collect to tell his story about military history. Marc, a Ranger for the National Park Service, has a PhD in American Military history and has been in love with the topic since he was a teen — let's just say a "long time ago." He loves his topic and he loves to write. That's what we call a certifiable subject matter expert!

Marc was one of a dozen or so people who participated in a podcasting course offered by Chuck Tomasi in 2009 to the National Park Service western region. One day he found himself with the training, the material, and enough Amazon gift cards to get some equipment so he decided it was time to let the world know about his love for military history.

He has a well thought out method to his madness that can serve aspiring podcasters well.

>> **Learn the landscape.** Take time to find out what shows on your topic exist. Like any good prospective podcaster, Marc did some listening to other similar podcasts to understand what is out there and identify a unique place he can fill in the podosphere.

>> **Look for a unique angle.** The last things your listeners need are carbon copies of other podcasts or (perish the thought) radio shows based on a template. If your passion is commonplace, focus on a niche or small aspect that you have the most knowledge about. Many of the shows Marc heard focused on specific events, often leaving the listener desiring more context of how we got those events. Marc opted for a chronological approach starting with the settlement of Jamestown in 1607. Until we listened, we weren't aware that the reasons for our early colonists seceding from England go back so far.

>> **Make it personal.** Let's face it, history in high school was pretty dull because it was mainly facts about people and places a long time ago — okay, as teens we also had other things on our minds to distract us, too. Marc explains that it helps to make the listener feel a part of the story. He's got expertise in this area as well having interpretation training from the National Park Service. We sure wish we had someone like Marc leading our high school history classes. It would have been a lot easier to relate to what these people went through since we were the nerdier types who didn't have to think about a date on Friday night. Figure 17-1 shows Marc's *America at War* podcast.

FIGURE 17-1:
Marc Blackburn puts his PhD in Military History to good use on his show *America at War*.

Podcasting passion with a purpose

Podcasting with a purpose is an essential. By doing so, you have a destination. It doesn't matter if that destination is to educate, showcase your material, or entertain. Pick something as your core reason for speaking and don't be afraid to have fun with it and make it exciting.

That's exactly what Barry and Catherine Cohen of Phoenix, Arizona, have done with their podcast *Together 24/7* (http://together247.net). Not only are they partners in life, but also in business. They started working together in 2003. Several of their friends and colleagues kept telling them, "You two are great together and funny; you should get a show." They heard tales of people making bushel baskets of money and thought it might be worth a try. With Barry's technical background and a little research, they put together their first episode.

Together 24/7 talks to other couples in the same situation — they own their own business and live together. (God bless them!) The main purpose of the show is to be a vehicle for clients for their consulting business; however, it has turned into much more than that, bringing them friendships, fun, and yes, more together time.

Their approach to podcasting can be summed up like this:

>> **A new perspective on creativity.** As Barry and Catherine are going about their day they are constantly asking each other, "Would this be good in the show?" "We should think about adding this in a future episode," and "Do you think people on the show will find this helpful?" Tee and Chuck agree as well. It's hard to listen to another show, or watch TV or a movie without thinking about the production, editing, lighting, vocal inflections, really everything that goes in to it and try to improve their own product. That's called being professionally aware.

>> **Continuity.** Produce episodes on a regular basis with a consistent format. As Catherine stated, "If you want to make changes to your show, do it how you would cook a frog. You don't just throw a live frog in a frying pan or it will hop out. You put it in a pot of water and slowly turn up the heat." The metaphor, gross as it may seem, is also appropriate to podcasting. If you suddenly shift topics or format, your audience may think they got the wrong show.

>> **Because it's fun.** Sure, the primary purpose of the show is to drive interest with their potential clients, but it's the passion for what they do and enjoying, that keeps the show going.

Sharing your passion with friends

Enthusiasm can be infectious. Podcasting can sometimes feel like a very solitary endeavor when it's just one voice behind the mic, but as we mention in Chapter 5, getting multiple hosts around the microphone can be a challenge. However, when the mics go live and the banter begins it can be a challenge to stop talking. It's that spark that all podcasters strive for, and sometimes, with the right people, the chemistry is instantaneous.

Podcaster Tony Mast of the *Back Seat Producers* (http://backseatproducers.com) knows all about this chemistry as his first foray into podcasting over a decade ago began with *Fanboy Smackdown,* a podcast that evolved into *Back Seat Producers,* a podcast about what's at the box office, what's coming to Blu-ray, and what fans would like to see from Hollywood. "We all knew each other from our local science fiction convention, Archon," Tony recalls, "and we got together to create *Fanboy Smackdown* which launched on the week of April 30, 2006. The thing was, we could never talk about anything other than movies, so we re-branded the podcast to *Backseat Producers.*" Since then, Tony has launched other podcasts such as *SciFi Smackdown* (with Christiana Ellis and Trampas Whiteman), *Tony's Losing It* (a weight-loss podcast), and many *Backseat Producers* spinoffs like *Backseat Box Office* (still on-going with different hosts), *Backseat Quickies* (a 10-minute movie review podcast), and *Backseat Book Club.*

The original intent of Tony, a writer of fiction, and his co-hosts was to build a fanbase around their podcast and their personalities. That way, when their books went live, they would have an instant fan base. "The podcasts evolved into something much bigger," he admits. Even with the success of *Backseat Producers* and their loyal fan base (*Backseat Box Office,* for example, is produced solely by fans of the original podcast), Tony continues to podcast because of the community they have built. "When these listeners drive through town, we all get together and have drinks with them, or pie from Richmond's Proper Pie Company, in Tee's case. We've met them at cons. We call out our friends on the podcast because we know they listen."

For Tony, the podcast is a catalyst for staying in touch with friends, as well as forcing himself to slow down and treat himself to a bit of entertainment. "The reason I podcast now is that my buddies come over and we have a good time for an hour or two. Our lives get busy, and there are things that we want to do but don't make time to do. Podcasting forces us to make time with our friends, and obligates me to just stop and sit down to watch a movie, which is not a bad thing."

As for a podcast's infectious enthusiasm, as we mention earlier, the *Backseat Producers* continues to grow beyond its original founders. "We've had a lot of people come to our table every week and served as co-hosts. Right now, we are a group of four who have been consistent over the years," Tony says, chuckling a bit at being the *old man on the mic*, "but for a while we had a gentleman in his fifties joining us every week. We have David who's in his thirties, and David — everywhere we go — tells people he builds a rapport with 'Hey, we do a podcast. Show up at Tony's house Wednesday night,' and this brings a completely different set of ideas, ideals, and perspectives that keeps *Backseat Producers* fresh after 400 episodes."

When you invite friends together to launch a podcast, here are a few tips to keep in mind:

>> **Make sure to have an agenda for the night.** Coming up with a plan is more than just saying to the people you work with, "We should do a podcast because it's cool. Here's what we talk about in Episode One." A podcast's agenda, or game plan, or to-do list, should be an idea of what you will want to gather around the mics to riff about for at least five shows. If you have ideas that go well beyond Episode 10, then you might just be on to something. When getting the cast and crew together for your podcast, you will want to make sure it is clear what the topic of conversation is. Otherwise, you might find yourself recording awkward silence, and that makes for terrible audio.

>> **Make the most of your time together.** If the subject matter is not time-sensitive, or if you have mapped out evergreen topics (subjects of discussion that are relevant no matter when they drop in a show's schedule) for a few episodes, then record these episodes in one night. Granted, the ability to create a buffer for your podcast will depend on the running time for your episodes, but if possible, record several episodes in case schedule conflicts occur.

>> **Nominate one person to take the point in a conversation.** Usually in situations where many hosts are on mic, there should be one person calling the plays and prompting others for commentary. In a quick-paced, back-and-forth conversation, that might mean the lead host sits back and moderates the episode. What matters is that you stay on topic, lest your episode goes bouncing off the rails and into the great audio-video abyss. Having a lead host — and that position can vary from show to show, depending on the topic — will keep you, your cast, and your episode on track.

>> **Invite others to join in on the fun.** While there should be core hosts in every multi-mic podcast, inviting people to join in only adds to the dynamics of a podcast. It could be a formal interview, or better still, it can be an informal sit-down where everyone contributes. These sort of round-table discussions may open your podcast up for more hosts, or some hosts may offer to pick up the mantle for a spinoff podcast — much like in the cast of Tony Mast's *Backseat Box Office* — out of loyalty to and joy from the podcast. Open mics also offer different perspectives and backgrounds, providing your podcast a broader scope and reach.

A passionate love for the podcast

All successful podcasters share a true love for the podcast. Something about getting behind the mic and producing quality content is satisfying. That passion can tax you, especially if the podcast is an emotional ride; and if a podcast reaches a conclusion, it would make sense if the podcast's host decided to step away from the mic for a spell.

However, when you are one of podcasting's original voices, it is hard not to want to podcast, especially when embarking on new adventures overseas.

Such is the story of Evo Terra, a name very familiar in podcasting circles. Evo was one of the original advocates of podcasting, hosting alongside Michael R. Mennenga of *The Dragon Page* in October 2004. He launched Podiobooks.com with Chris Miller and Tee Morris, and joined Tee on the first edition of *Podcasting For Dummies*. "One thing we had going for us," Evo recalls, "is that Mike and I were already doing *The Dragon Page* as a syndicated radio show, both on Internet Radio and terrestrial radio since 2002, so we hit the ground running while many other podcasters at that time were figuring things out as they went. Many of the technical challenges of podcasting gear we already had figured out."

Evo loved podcasting so much, he brought in his wife, Sheila Unwin, when *The Dragon Page* launched a Y.A. Fiction spinoff series, *The Dragon Page with Class*. Together, Evo and Sheila podcast on *Evo at 11* and *The Opportunistic Travelers* which evolved into *This One Time. . .*; all three podcasts very different but all three very much full of the intellectual snark that Evo and Sheila are known for. "When I was asked to deliver the keynote at the very first Podcast Movement event, I was told 'You should be podcasting more. . .' but by then Sheila and I were transitioning to leave the country," Evo recalls. "I had sold most of my equipment, but I had kept my H4n, a few cables, and a pair of Shure SM58s. It occurred to me that we needed to produce a podcast to explain what we were doing. I had been listening to *The Startup Podcast* with Alex Bloomberg, and I really liked that journalistic style. So during our drive out to California, I broke out the mic and started asking Sheila questions, and that was the first episode of the *Opportunistic Travelers* (www.theopportunistictravelers.com)." As seen in Figure 17-2, *The Opportunistic Travelers,* while a dramatic change in the kind of podcast Evo was known for, still retains his signature of a lighthearted look at life and the world around it.

Sheila's own love of the podcast took root not on the technical side, but more on the content provider side. "When I first started, I was primarily voice talent, and it was a lot of fun. Initially, *The Dragon Page with Class* was an interview show, and I really loved the back stories of these books I've been reading and how they came to be." After *Evo at 11*, Sheila believed her podcasting chapter had concluded, until, "When we were getting ready to leave the country, Evo said, 'We'll update people in a blog format,' and I came back with 'That doesn't make any sense. You're a podcaster. We need to podcast this.' So we started *The Opportunistic Traveler*." Not only has podcasting made Sheila a better public speaker and presenter, Sheila gives podcasting credit for the close friendships she has cultivated over the years. "I have friends all over the world, and I've met people at different conferences, all of who know me from my appearances on podcasts."

FIGURE 17-2:
Evo Terra and Sheila Dee podcast their adventures around the world as *The Opportunistic Travelers.*

What keeps both Evo and Sheila podcasting today, on a more personal level, is their online dynamic. "Our podcasts are our personalities amped up," Sheila says. Evo agrees. "It's a project and a platform that we not only can work on together, we work on it well together."

And it doesn't hurt Evo's passion at all that it has now become a source of income. "*The Opportunistic Traveler* and then later *The Bangkok Podcast* — the #1 show produced in Bangkok, Thailand — served as showcase for me. Now I've been hired to co-host and produce. It's easier now to get people to pay you to produce a podcast because of podcasting's increased attention recently. As a podcast producer, I am hired to handle strategy, execution, and promotion."

The desire to continue recording, producing, and uploading shows simply for the love of the podcast is not uncommon. Many podcasts are created out of that need. These shows and their hosts stand out in their dedication, infusing raw enthusiasm for this medium into every new show. It is this passion that brings the podcaster back to the microphone and invites new podcasters (like you!) to take the host's chair.

Holding Interest: Keeping a Podcast's Passion Alive

You have your podcast underway. You're planning to have a weekly show. The first month in, you feel strong, confident. But this is all in the first four episodes. How do you keep the momentum going?

In the early days of a podcast, you can easily see yourself continuing banter a year from launch date — but remember that schedule you planned? Have you considered sick days? Vacation? The occasional stumbling block of inertia ("Do I really want to do a podcast today?")? Even the best podcasters need to step away from their mics, recharge their batteries, and then jump back into their recording. Personal health, well-being, and time to edit episodes if your episodes need editing (and if you're human, sometimes they do) are factors you also must consider. Add in dealing with conditions such as background noise and having to tax the strength of your voice, and podcasting can become less of a joy and more like a chore or a second day-job. Plenty of podcasts begin strong out of the box, only to have their feeds go silent, and remain so.

Even with passion, momentum is difficult to sustain. How do podcasters keep that spark alive? Well — as with the answers to "Why do we do it?" — podcasters have a myriad of opinions and thoughts. Each show applies different tactics to keep each new episode fresh; even amid diverse topics, you can find common threads between all podcasts that provide the momentum to forge ahead 50 episodes later.

Podcasting on puree: Mixing it up

After you've racked up a few episodes of your podcast, look at its format. How do you have it set up? Is it all commentary? What can you do to vary the content?

Just because this is your first, second, third — or seventeenth, eighteenth, or nineteenth — episode, that doesn't mean you've set your show in stone. (That's where you find the fossils of all sorts of creatures that didn't manage to evolve.) In this section, we look at ways to dodge that asteroid and keep your show from suffering an extinction-level event.

Don't be afraid to try different things with your podcast's format. For example, you might

>> Talk about a product, a service, or an idea that's only loosely related to your normal focus.

>> Interview a guest with a unique perspective on the focus of your show.

>> Experiment with adding a co-host, even if only temporarily.

>> Podcast from a remote location or from a studio if you normally do remote shows.

Technorama, hosted by one of your illustrious authors, has been in a near-constant state of evolution since inception in May 2005. It started with a single host and acquired a second after only a handful of episodes. Things stayed constant for a while, and then its hosts — Chuck Tomasi and Kreg Steppe — added an "On This Day in History" segment to the show to review tech, science, and geek events that happened in history on the day the show is released.

With the addition of "On This Day in History" segments, Chuck and Kreg started experimenting with production elements and other kinds of regularly occurring features in the podcast. Soon the show, described as looking at the lighter side of technology, started covering odd news in the "Hacks and Strange Stories" segment and the hosts began scratching their heads at how silly people can get over tech with the "What the Chuck?!" segment. Following the wacky wake-up morning show format, *Technorama* became a favorite in the podosphere.

Fast-forward through the years (time travel saves belaboring the point), and the award-winning show continues to offer something different than its normal fare. While taking pride in its lighter look at tech, *Technorama* has also featured interviews with Grant Imahara and Adam Savage of *Mythbusters,* oceanographer and *Titanic*-discoverer Dr. Bob Ballard, John Chatterton and Richie Kohler of *Deep Sea Detectives,* and renowned physicist Dr. Michio Kaku. The guys have also ventured in to video podcasting, on-location recordings, and elaborate audio spoofs, including "How Can You Tell He's a Geek?" (inspired by Monty Python's "How You Can Tell She's a Witch" sketch) and several parodies inspired by *Star Trek, Star Wars,* and classic TV shows.

Your show may not have to go to elaborate lengths to stay fresh, but it does need to heed the creed: *Evolve or die.* Remember Catherine Cohen's story about cooking a frog mentioned earlier in this chapter — do changes like this slowly and get feedback from your audience to see what works.

WARNING

If you decide your podcast is going to be in a constant state of flux, keep in mind that the risk of alienating your listeners is ever present. Podcasting for podcasting's sake is like improvisational comedy: It's a skill. You can keep your passion alive by continuously changing the format of your show, but you run the risk of making your show an acquired taste.

Starting a second (or third) podcast

Keeping the passion alive and well in one podcast can be found in variety, but what happens when you are finding yourself cutting off the microphones and still having a lot to say? Some podcasters decide to fire up the mics again and keep going. Sure, the occasional "super-sized" show isn't a bad thing, especially if the topic is timely and your normal running time can't cover everything you want or need to. What happens, though, when your special super-sized shows are becoming less and less special, but becoming the norm? What if your broad focus on a subject matter is becoming more and more focused on one aspect of it? Are you willing to risk overloading your podcast's audience with new content, and possibly burn out you, your co-hosts, and your audience?

It might be time for another podcast.

Okay, that may double your workload. Well, no, it *will* double your workload; but spinoff podcasts allow you to follow this new rabbit hole you've discovered while keeping the original podcast's voice true. A new podcast also keeps your perspectives fresh and excited about what unknown discussions you have yet to record for upcoming podcasts.

If your gut instinct is telling you to begin a second podcast, go for it. Variety, not only in a podcast's original content but also between the different podcasts you create, can benefit both shows. Now, instead of the same old podcast every week, you can allow yourself different avenues to explore — and maybe in the new venture, attract a whole new audience.

Podcaster Jason Gregory Banks, after launching *Talk Nerdy 2 Me* (branded with its signature show art seen in Figure 17-3 and found online at http://talknerdy2mepodcast.com) in 2012, discovered that while his co-host, Jen, and he had a lot to talk about when it came to nerd culture, anime, and comics, one podcast was not going to cover it. Along with a long drive between jobs, Jason wanted to make the most of his time, so he recorded episodes in his car. "It's not the same quality as *Talk Nerdy 2 Me*, I admit," Jason says, "but I'm more about the content and the quality of it than audio clarity; and my portable recorder is reliable, so no worries." The *Talk Nerdy 2 Me* brand expanded to the following offerings, all carrying the same signature wit and wisdom Jason and Jen established in the original show:

>> *Anime 101* (http://talknerdy2mepodcast.com/podcasts/anime-101): For anyone curious about the animated offerings coming from across the Pacific, Jason offers *Anime 101*, a deep dive into anime both familiar to mainstream audiences and unknown but worth your time and attention.

>> **Nerds on Cinema** (http://talknerdy2mepodcast.com/podcasts/nerds-on-cinema): If you are more into movies, *Nerds on Cinema* offers everything from reviews to the homegrown commentary track for what's new on Blu-ray and DVD. *Nerds on Cinema* also hosts every October the "Halloween Horrorfest" where the *TN2M* crew releases 31 consecutive days of podcasts.

>> **Talking Comics** (http://talknerdy2mepodcast.com/podcasts/talking-comics): *Talking Comics* is *TN2M*'s exclusive platform for all things Marvel, DC, Dark Horse, Valiant, IDW, and other comic creators.

>> **Big Bear's Den** (http://talknerdy2mepodcast.com/podcasts/big-bears-den): Jason's podcast encapsulating random thoughts, short fiction, and other inspirations better-suited for its own home outside of the main podcast.

FIGURE 17-3:
Talk Nerdy 2 Me is more than just one podcast — it's a *network* of podcasts.

"I produce a lot of content," Jason states, "and Jen and I know each show has its own audience. Some people just want the anime show. That's fine. Some just want *Nerds on Cinema*. That's fine. But there are those listeners who want it all," and that makes him smile. "This is why we offer a master feed where everything goes. So long as people are listening, I'll keep podcasting."

Meanwhile, out on the West Coast, *The Wekk Podcast* (http://wekkpodcast.com) launched in February 2015, intending to be a podcast about all things geek. Not an uncommon theme for podcasts (see the East Coast's *Talk Nerdy 2 Me* above), and the show's hosts — Katy, Kellie, Kevin, and Mandy — originally planned for weekly conversations on various geek interests ranging from books to board games to box office offerings. Their first episode featured the *B-17: Queen of the*

Skies board game, Rachel Morgan's *Creepy Hollow* series, and *Mr. Kiss and Tell* by Rob Thomas and Jennifer Graham. So their adventure into podcasting began . . .

. . . but then Katy, Kellie, Kevin, and Mandy found themselves with a backlog of geeky conversations they wanted to have, but could not carve out the time in the original *Wekk Podcast.* This inspired the crew to produce and feature in the same feed their first spinoff, *Wekk Whovians,* a podcast where hosts and guests could delve more into *Doctor Who* lore. Its success inspired the podcast team to create other spinoffs that dropped into the Wekk's feed, giving the listener the option to listen or skip. *Growing Up 70's* is the Wekk–produced nostalgia podcast that looks back on the 1970's and its eclectic entertainment of the day. *Wekk Conversations* is their interview show, featuring authors, podcasters, and other interviews keen to the *Wekk* hosts' interests. *Beer, Books, and Tea* is their book club offering reviews and discussions of literature over a nice Lapsang or lager. And finally, there is *Little Things* where the cast share those tiny victories that brighten a day. With so many podcasts under the *Wekk* umbrella, the original podcast continues to get its own episodes out, remaining true to its original concept while offering "bonus" content for those who want it.

If you're thinking about branching out with a new show, consider these tips:

>> **Take your audience with you.** If you're podcasting about triathlons, yet hold a secret passion for seventh-century Gaelic text, expect only a handful of folks to subscribe to both shows. However, if you move from triathlons to a podcast on sports medicine, they may find the new topic an easier pill to swallow.

>> **Cross-promote.** Even if your podcasts are quite close in scope, there will be listeners to one who aren't aware of the other. Although we caution against turning one podcast into a giant commercial for the other, plug the heck out of your other show. Within reason.

>> **Look for the niche within the niche.** If your main topic is broad, break it out into chunks and see what needs further exploration. Granted, a deep dive into the minutiae of a niche topic may reduce the size of your listening audience. But so what? This is about exploring your passion, not about gaining market share. And (we promise) there's always someone else out there who will want you to delve even deeper into the obscure topic you've just built an entire podcast around.

>> **Keep trying.** Don't expect to hit your stride in the new show by Episode 2. You must try different formats, flavors, and ideas, just the way you did to make your first podcast perfect. (Or is it? Maybe it's getting a little stale. Time to spruce that one up, too. See the following section.)

WHO'S UP FOR A CHALLENGE?

Kreg Steppe, Chuck's co-host on *Technorama*, came up with a great idea in 2012. He challenged podcasters to publish a podcast a day for the month of August. He called his challenge "The Dog Days of Podcasting" (http://dogdaysofpodcasting.com). His idea was to get back to the roots of podcasting (late 2004 and early 2005), theoretically where there were so few shows that all the podcasters seemed to be listening to each other's show and had cross-show conversations with each other. Something said on one show would get a response on another show. The early few months of podcasting really was a more intimate group. Kreg's goal was to recapture some of that community. The first year or two there were only a half dozen or so podcasters who joined in. It was easy to subscribe to all of them and keep up with each thread. However, in recent years, the group has grown to many times its original size and listening to every single episode of the show has become somewhat of a new challenge. Some of the nostalgia is hearing from some of the original podcasters from 2004 to 2005 and hearing new voices. In fact, some people like Amy Bowen and Charlotte Kennedy have used the Dog Days challenge to launch their own podcasts. Proving that you don't need a decade of experience or lots of technology to be part of this challenge. Kreg has made it easy to listen to all the podcasts without having to subscribe to each show individually with a "master feed" which includes all episode for all shows during the annual challenge.

When enjoying the journey of your first podcast, keep in mind that your *next* podcast may be closer than you think. Keep a close eye on your feedback; look for recurring themes that your audience likes to hear. If it's a broad enough topic and you can speak on it with authority, you may be able to craft a show around audience suggestions instead of having to sweat bullets to come up with something brand new every time.

Moving forward with a plan

Reinvention for the sake of reinvention isn't a bad idea, but it's so 20th century. You may find it a better idea to move forward with a plan for your rebranding, your reformatting, or your spinoff podcasts. So here are a few dos and don'ts — with the don'ts first.

What NOT to do (Ack! *Run away! Run away!*):

>> **Don't use shock-radio techniques.** Hearing a podcaster drop a few words that would make most grandmothers blush isn't anything new, and it's a cheap way to get a laugh and attention. We personally don't have any moral compunction against the more colorful aspects of the English language. If that's your style, don't change it; otherwise, try to use them sparingly, okay?

>> **Don't swing between kid-friendly and adults-only.** If you're unhappy being a family show, give some notice so folks can unsubscribe. Hell hath no fury like a mother scorned (or even unpleasantly surprised).

>> **Don't get angry when you get dissenting email.** Not everyone will be happy with your decision to change things around or to add a new segment. Deal with it and move on. You can't please everyone — or "correct" others' opinions — so don't even try.

What to DO with all your might:

>> **Cast your net wide.** Be open to a variety of new ideas and concepts and don't be afraid to try them out on your audience. Your loyal listeners will likely forgive you a few miscues along the way.

>> **Have a purpose for the change or addition.** Find the common connection with what your show has focused on before and talk to your audience about it. You can do this before or after the "newness" goes in the show, but your listeners will enjoy knowing the method behind your madness.

>> **Encourage feedback about the change.** When you do this, ask more than "do you like it?" Find out whether your audience members feel differently about your show, if they think it's "fresher" or perhaps more appealing — and ask why. The changes you put in place are designed to give your show a boost; be sure and ask for confirmation that it actually happened!

REMEMBER

If you find yourself in need of a break, there's nothing wrong with taking some time out. As a courtesy to those who are listening, however — whether it's 20 or 20,000 — let them know you're holding off on new episodes for a few weeks so you can reorganize priorities, goals, and the whole momentum of your podcast to make it even more rewarding for them to listen to. The same courtesy applies when you've had an unexpected illness: Give your listenership a quick update on what happened; reassure them that your voice is back and that your podcast is back. As passionate as you may be about a podcast, always remember your health and your voice must come first. There's nothing wrong with missing a week or two of a podcast while you get back up to par.

When Podcasting, Be like Bruce Lee

"To me, ultimately, martial art means honestly expressing yourself. Now it is very difficult to do. I mean it is easy for me to put on a show and be cocky and be flooded with a cocky feeling and then feel, then, like pretty cool. . . and be blinded by it. Or I can show you some fancy movement. But, to express oneself honestly, not lying to oneself — and to express myself honestly — that, my friend, is very hard to do."
— BRUCE LEE, FROM AN INTERVIEW ON THE PIERRE BURTON SHOW

When Tee was writing the first draft of this chapter back in 2006, he had playing in the background *Bruce Lee: The Way of the Warrior*, a (really cool) documentary featuring recently discovered footage from Bruce Lee's then-work-in-progress *Game of Death*, rare commentary from The Dragon himself, and interview footage. In one of the interviews came the preceding quote — a compelling moment when Bruce Lee sums up, in his own words, what the martial arts mean from his perspective. As Tee pondered his words, it struck him that Bruce was basically saying, *Martial arts are all about keeping it real.*

And (for whatever reason) he blurted out loud, "If Bruce Lee were alive today, he would have a podcast!"

Part of the passion in a podcast is cultivating honesty with yourself and your audience, and that honesty in your podcast is what keeps listeners coming back. "To thine own self be true . . ." — one of Shakespeare's most-quoted lines from *Hamlet* — holds as true for podcasting as it has for every other intensely personal creative activity; let it serve as a mantra that fires up your drive to produce a terrific podcast. Honest passion, and honesty in general, cannot be faked in a podcast because many podcasters are producing their audio content without any other compensation save for ratings on various directories and analytics through Google, some feedback from listeners, and perhaps a Patreon donation. On the larger scale, podcasters, regardless of their agendas or goals, are on the podcasting scene because they want to be there, and if that honesty in wanting to deliver new content is even remotely artificial, listeners will lose interest in your podcast.

It's okay to ask yourself, before hitting Record, "Do I know for sure what I'm getting into?" — or, more to the point, "Do I really want to do this?" — but never ask yourself whether you *can* do this. That isn't even a question to consider. Podcasting welcomes voices of all backgrounds, all professions, all experience levels (be they professional, semiprofessional, or amateur). You can do this — and you have as much right to as any of us. All you need is a mic, an application, a feed, and a server host. From there, it all rests on you. And once you start podcasting, produce your podcast because you *want* to, not because you *have* to.

REMEMBER

Podcasting is a commitment of time and resources — to yourself and to your listeners. It's a promise you make to bring to the podosphere the best content you can produce — and with the right support, passion, and drive, your podcast will evolve, mature, and move ahead with the same zeal that inspired the first episode. Accomplishing this feat rests on remaining honest in your desire to sit behind the microphone and produce your next show. If you're not sure about the answers to "Do I know for sure what I'm getting into?" or "Do I really want to do this?" ask yourself, "If I don't want to be here, then why would listeners want to hear my latest episode?"

"To express myself honestly — that, my friend is very hard to do." Tee believed back in 2006 Bruce Lee would have produced an incredible podcast.

Ten years later, Tee got his wish realized as Bruce Lee's daughter launched the *Bruce Lee Podcast* over at `http://www.brucelee.com/podcast` in 2016. Lee's philosophy and disciplines, reviewed weekly.

And yes, it's an incredible podcast.

6
The Part of Tens

Discover favorite types of podcasts from the authors of *Podcasting For Dummies.*

Learn tips and tricks from podcasters who have been in the game from the beginning.

Find out why podcasting is the thing to do.

Chapter **18**

Ten Types of Podcasts to Check Out

A h yes, narrowing down the thousands upon thousands *upon thousands* of podcasts out there to an elite ten: The Top Ten Podcasts You Should Be Listening To. The Best of the Best. The Select Few to Follow.

No pressure.

Where to begin? Where to begin? With each edition of *Podcasting For Dummies*, your humble authors sat down and put together our own top ten lists of podcasts, and here's what we have noticed: There are a *lot* of podcasts out there. While some of our listening habits have remained steady and constant as the North Star, our taste can sometimes shift into unexpected offerings . . . which if you listen to *Astronomy Cast*, you would know Polaris is not *that* constant. We have found, over our years of podcasting, that we listen to a solid cross-section of *types* of podcasts, not just in the way of genres but in production values. So, with a quick edit of the outline and a change of mindset, we present Ten Types of Podcasts to Check Out.

There are other kinds of podcasts that are, perhaps, not showcased here; but with these ten kinds of podcasts as a starting point, you can easily begin to fill your media player with a variety of offerings. When you're comfortable with what you hear, you can then follow podcasts that podcasters will recommend. Feeling even braver, you can delve into the many directories out there, some of which offer suggestions based on your listening habits.

Here's your starting point for podcasts to seek out and consume. We are confident that from the list given in this chapter, you can sample a wide cross-section of interests, passions, and projects. Relax, download, and give your eyes and ears a treat.

TIP

Always check podcasting directories to see how active these shows are before you subscribe. The podcasts in this section are constantly changing. They were actively producing content when we wrote this book, but printed material is never as up to date as a good podcast directory.

Tech Podcasts

If you're thinking about podcasting, you likely have a comfortable knowledge of computers, the Internet, and blogging. But regardless of how technologically savvy you are, like any aspect of life, you can never stop learning. That's why your aggregator should be catching at least one *tech podcast.*

The agenda for a tech podcast is (surprise!) technology. All geek, all the time. Geeks, nerds, wizards, and Tech Help gurus sit behind a microphone and pull back the curtain on how your computer works, how a podcast's RSS feed can be better, and how to make your time behind the keyboard more efficient.

Tech podcasts come delivered to you in a variety of skill levels and on a variety of topics:

» **Macs:** Some excellent podcasts for Mac users include *The Mac Observer's Apple Context Machine* (shown in Figure 18-1 and available at https://www.macobserver.com/show/apple-context-machine) and the *iMore Show* (http://www.imore.com/podcasts), or for the more retro Mac user *Open Apple* (www.open-apple.net) that covers all things Apple II.

» **PCs:** *Windows Insider Program* (http://windowsinsider.mpsn.libsynpro.com) is an ambitious effort spearheaded by Windows Insider chief Dona Sarkar to podcast updates from within the Windows Insider community.

The *MSPoweruser Podcast* (`https://mspoweruser.com/podcast`) is more end-user/consumer focused to help you be more productive on your PC (and all things Microsoft).

» **General computing:** Many of the tech podcasts out there like *This Week in Tech* (or TWiT, as it is so lovingly referred as by its hosts and listeners, available at `www.twit.tv/twit`) or *Daily Tech News Show* (`www.dailytechnewsshow.com`) are generic in their approach to operating systems, following a mindset that a computer is a computer and the rest is mostly bells and whistles.

» **Technology perspectives:** *Computer Talk Radio* (`http://computertalkradio.com`) and *Technorama* (`http://www.chuckchat.com/technorama`) give personal and (in many cases) lighthearted perspectives on technology in society and go beyond the geek-speak, giving their own perspectives on issues and how technology can affect just about everything.

Whichever podcast you feed into your podcatching client, find a tech podcast that's right for you and either enjoy the new perspective or allow yourself to grow into your geekdom. There is a lot to learn about computers, smartphones, the Internet of Things, and other cool Q Branch gizmos that are available at your local electronics store. When you have the basics down, these podcasts allow you to unlock their potential and go beyond your expectations.

FIGURE 18-1:
The Mac Observer's Apple Context Machine is one of many podcasts offered to Mac users to get the most out of their iPads or MacBooks.

Independent Media Podcasts

Podcasting is audio and video content on demand, and after taking in what is being offered on the radio, that is a very good thing. Maybe it's a hazard of getting older, but some of us just aren't hearing anything on the air that's all that interesting or exciting. Unless you are really into auto-tune or hungry for yet another hacker-crime-investigation-unit-comprised-of-incredibly-pretty-people series.

The good news is that media mavericks are alive and well and doing just fine in the 21st century, finding a new promotion channel with podcasting.

Independent labels, where the artists also work as promoters, producers, and holders-of-all-rights, have control over where their music plays, how often it is played, and how much it will cost you. Many indie musicians who are having trouble getting exposure and radio airplay will grant permission for podcasters to use their music. What does this cost the podcaster? A few moments of time and a spot or two, such as, "This music is brought to you by . . ." and "Visit this band online at w-w-w-dot . . ." And in return, the musician is exposed to a worldwide audience.

Musicians such as The Gentle Readers, Michelle Malone (both featured on *Evil Genius Chronicles* at www.evilgeniuschronicles.org), George Hrab, and Rubber Band Banjo (both featured on Tee's Parsec-winning podcast *Billibub Baddings and The Case of the Singing Sword*) have all enjoyed the benefits of associating themselves with a podcast. Catching wind of this, indie artists of all backgrounds are turning to podcasts to spotlight their independent works whose vision might go against the corporate entertainment industry's notion of "what the public wants." Here are few such podcasts you may want to check out:

>> *Welcome to Night Vale* (www.welcometonightvale.com): Best described as *A Prairie Home Companion* meets The *Twilight Zone* and known for its quirky, sometimes sinister storytelling, the popular podcast has proven itself a fantastic platform for independent label music. Whenever Cecil announces the Night Vale weather report, listeners are treated to music from artists such as Anais Mitchell, Robin Aigner, daKAH Hip Hop Orchestra, Destroyer, Daniel Knox, Toys and Tiny Instruments, and Eliza Rickman, just to name a few.

>> *Irish & Celtic Music Podcast* (http://celticmusicpodcast.com): Celebrated musician Marc Gunn hosts *The Irish & Celtic Music Podcast*. It's all in the title. Marc offers his podcast as a spotlight for the best in Irish and Celtic culture and sound; and with over 20,000 downloads per episode, multiple wins for

"Best Podsafe Music" from the People's Choice Podcast Awards, and a consistent spot in iTunes' "What's Hot" directory for music podcasts, The Celtfather shows no signs of stopping.

>> ***Making Movies is HARD!!!*** (`http://spindryproductions.com/podcast generator`)**:** The independent film industry — particularly with the popularity of video podcasting, YouTube, and other online video providers — is embracing podcasting platforms as not only a place to promote but a place to educate. *Making Movies is HARD!!!* (shown in Figure 18-2), hosted by Timothy Plain and Alrik Bursell, discusses independent filmmaking, but not just shooting and editing a film. Timothy and Alrik deep dive into all aspects of filmmaking. Writing. Producing. Directing. Even how you take care of your cast and crew. Timothy and Alrik also cover the downsides of making movies: hours of investment, rejection, lost opportunities, self-doubt. It's all here.

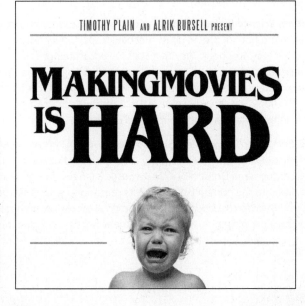

FIGURE 18-2:
From screen-writing to film editing to managing cast and crew, *Making Movies is HARD!!!* takes an honest look at the independent filmmaking process.

>> ***Film Trooper*** (`http://filmtrooper.com`)**:** Scott McMahon, following two decades of working in the entertainment industry through gaming, film, TV, and video production, delved into independent filmmaking, creating for $500 a short film called *The Cube*. Now, he hosts *Film Trooper*, a resource for up-and-coming filmmakers who want to know more about the business. *Film Trooper* features interviews with performers, directors, musicians, and other creative minds involved in making independent movies as well as step-by-step tutorials on how to get your movie from concept to cinema screen.

Science Podcasts

The approach to science made popular by Bill Nye the Science Guy, Mr. Wizard, and the Mythbusters, is rampant in the podosphere. Here are some science podcasts that we recommend:

» **Astronomy Cast** (http://astronomycast.com): If you've always wondered about what's really going on beyond our atmosphere, take a listen to a podcast descendant of Carl Sagan's *Cosmos* concept. For those who would never leave the planet without their attitude, Fraser Cane and Dr. Pamela Gay dubbed the show *Astronomy Cast.*

» **Skepticality** (http://skepticality.com): This Parsec-winning podcast looks deeper into the news too weird for mainstream media, and it takes a critical microscope to the pseudoscience of the paranormal, the supernatural, close encounters, and urban legends.

» **The Brain Science Podcast** (http://brainsciencepodcast.com): When it comes to the human brain and its mechanics, Dr. Ginger Campbell, MD, knows her way around it. *The Brain Science Podcast* features the latest books about neuroscience as well as interviews with leading scientists from around the world. Neuroscience, you might think, would appeal to a niche audience; but with over 7.5 million downloads, Dr. Campbell's podcast continues to educate the world about how our brains work.

» **Headshots** (http://www.headshotspodcast.com): Part of the Geek Therapy Network (http://www.geektherapy.com/PodcastNetwork) and hosted by Josué Cardona and Dr. Kelli Dunlap, *Headshots* (shown in Figure 18-3) takes a deep dive into the human psyche and its reaction to games like *Destiny, Zelda, Halo,* and *Overwatch. Headshots* offers a clinical (as well as comical) observation at how people game, and analyzes the way gaming, game mechanics, and gaming concepts impact behavior, emotion, and social interaction.

FIGURE 18-3:
The intersection between psychology and gaming is explored in *Headshots,* hosted by Josué Cardona and Dr. Kelli Dunlap.

Science shows are good for you — like vegetables, only better. Not only can you learn something new or broaden your scope in a field you may regard as a hobby, but you can marvel at how the hosts demystify concepts once comprehensible only to PhDs and keep the ideas easy to grasp.

Self-Development Podcasts

Why not broaden your horizons — personal or professional — with podcasting? For example, say you've always wanted to learn Spanish. You could shell out some bucks for the "Teach Yourself Spanish" series, or you could to listen to the free *SpanishPod101 podcast* (`https://www.spanishpod101.com`). *SpanishPod101* is a podcast that is part of a multiple device approach across PDFs, online forums, and smart devices that culminates into a survival guide for a new language. With its podcast as the first step, *SpanishPod101* helps you navigate situations at the restaurant, at the bank, or if your car breaks down.

If you aren't interested in learning another language, look at some of the other subjects offered in the podosphere. Here are just a few examples of what's available:

>> **Education:** Podcasts can be like your favorite class after the bell has rung, offering material completely devoted to what you might not have heard while in middle and high school. *Stuff You Missed in History Class* (`http://www.missedinhistory.com`), hosted by Tracy V. Wilson and Holly Frey, offers details behind Lady Jane Grey, Executive Order 9066, or comedians Abbott & Costello, each episode an in-depth look at events from our past. Instead of history, you want to know the origins of stories like "The Legend of Sleepy Hollow," *Aladdin and His Wonderful Lamp*, or *King Arthur and the Knights of the Round Table* (including Camelot, a silly place). This means *Myths & Legends* (`http://www.mythpodcast.com`) is the podcast you need to subscribe to.

>> **Career Development:** Are you looking to make a jump from working stiff to corporate raider? Have a listen to *Mechanic to Millionaire* (`http://www.mechanictomillionaire.com`), a podcast about making the right steps forward in a career no matter what place in the office you occupy. For female entrepreneurs, the *She Did It Her Way* podcast (`http://shediditherwaypodcast.com`) features interviews with risk-takers who worked hard to bring their ideas to reality. And when it comes to incredible visionaries — Elon Musk, Norman Lear, and Michelle Obama, to name a few — the *TED Talks* podcasts (`http://www.ted.com/talks`) offer up all kinds of great career advice from those who shape the world.

>> **Personal Development:** *TED Talks* don't just stop at Career Development (as there are *many* podcasts TED produces), but also help you better yourself and your life. Are you looking to change your eating habits or maybe just find calm within the stress of daily life? Podcasting can bring a healthy alternative to your current digital lifestyle, and maybe even lower blood pressure and cholesterol points in the process. To find a bit of health and harmony in your life, give *The Ultimate Health Podcast* (http://ultimatehealthpodcast.com) or *The Healthy Moms Podcast* (https://wellnessmama.com/podcast) a listen. Get more background on the martial art you study (or are thinking about studying) from *whistlekick Martial Arts Radio* (http://www.whistlekickmartialartsradio.com), or learn more about the philosophy of martial arts applied to life from one of the legends. *The Bruce Lee Podcast* (shown in Figure 18-4 and found at https://www.brucelee.com/podcast), hosted by the Dragon's daughter Shannon Lee and culture analyst Sharon Ann Lee, centers around the life and lessons of the iconic Bruce Lee.

FIGURE 18-4:
The Bruce Lee Podcast, hosted by Shannon Lee and Sharon Ann Lee, goes deep into the philosophy martial arts icon Bruce Lee practiced every day.

>> **Money management:** If you're looking for advice on managing your money, check out *Money Girl* (http://moneygirl.quickanddirtytips.com). Or if you are trying to manage finances after you have made the ultimate life investment (Hint: It involves the words "I do" or a variant of that), try *His & Her Money Podcast* (http://www.hisandhermoney.com/category/podcast), which focuses on joint financial plans and their balance in a strong marital relationship.

There is a lot to learn from the world, and whether you're tuning in to one of numerous podcasts sponsored by universities and colleges or to an enthusiast who wants to share and swap resources with you, all this continuing education is available online, in audio, and at no charge.

Comedy Podcasts

There are times in life when you just need a good laugh. A real bonus with comedy podcasts is having those good laughs categorized, digitized, and waiting for you, only a tap or click away.

Humor, though, is in the eye of the beholder and the ear of the listener. Performing a search on "Comedy Podcasts" will offer you many, many choices, ranging from kid-safe comedy to performing arts to adults-only discussions with an irreverent approach. Comedy covers a lot of ground, but straight-up comedy podcasts are not intended to do anything other than entertain.

The way these podcasts make you laugh covers a wide spectrum of how humor is defined. Here are a few comedy podcasts that we enjoy:

>> *The Bitterest Pill* (http://thebitterestpill.com): Perhaps you like your humor dry, witty, and maybe just a touch smarmy. Dan Klass and his award-winning podcast, *The Bitterest Pill,* shown in Figure 18-5, should do the trick. With his background in stand-up comedy and over a decade of podcasting under his belt, Dan's delivery is edgy and relentless. He takes a hard, cold look at the world and makes observations that you might think but would not have the courage to express openly. Dan not only gives you his opinions but also podcasts them for the world to hear.

>> *Comedy4Cast* (www.comedy4cast.com): The unpredictability from *Comedy4Cast*'s host, Clinton, is one of the elements that adds charm to the show. Sometimes you get a tongue-in-cheek review of an electronic gadget, another time you hear a parody of another popular podcast, or Clinton could be offering a comedy serial. Whatever is on the menu provided by cast and crew, *Comedy4Cast* has but one goal: having you pull over to the side of the road so you don't drive in to the ditch, or setting the hot coffee aside so as not to spit it on your keyboard. DISCLAIMER: *Comedy4Cast* is not responsible for damages incurred while listening.

THE BITTEREST PILL

FIGURE 18-5:
The Bitterest Pill is the award-winning podcast hosted by humorist and actor Dan Klass.

>> **The FuMP** (www.thefump.com): *The FuMP* stands for "The Funny Music Project" and features a cavalcade of comedy musicians that include Devo Spice, the great Luke Ski, Worm Quartet, Power Salad, Nuclear Bubble Wrap, Carrie Dahlby, Carla Ulbrich, Robert Lund and Spaff, Raymond and Scum, and more! All the music showcased in *The FuMP* is protected under a Creative Commons license so listeners know they can share the music or even make their own music video to it, so long as no one makes money at it. *The FuMP* also operates as a network, offering to website visitors links to the Artists pages for additional laughs beyond the podcast.

>> **Alison Rosen Is Your New Best Friend** (www.alisonrosen.com/ariynbf): This podcast began as an online talk show, streamed from journalist Alison Rosen's Brooklyn apartment. This window into a comic writer's life evolved into interviews that center around people's genuine struggles, both in New York City and in the world. *Alison Rosen Is Your New Best Friend* has been described as a marriage between *Seinfeld* and *Charlie Rose*, but Rosen considers her podcast as a chronicle of daily life and how we tend to laugh at what we as humans deal with.

>> **The Geologic Podcast** (www.geologicpodcast.com): No, wait, *The Geologic Podcast* is a podcast featuring the music of musician and author George Hrab! Hold on — *The Geologic Podcast* is a scientific and skeptic podcast featuring the musings of musician and author George Hrab! Actually . . . yes, *The Geologic Podcast* is all this and a comedy podcast guaranteed to get you thinking all while rocking your socks off. There is a lot happening in this podcast, so best hold on to something when you dive in.

Slice-of-Life Podcasts

Comedy is prevalent in all the various genres of podcasting, especially with the podcasts that just take a look at life and give it a perspective. Sometimes you need humor to deal with loved ones, life's unexpected pitfalls, or just the world on a whole. Slice-of-Life podcasts offer audiences a chance to laugh at the headlines, slow down with an in-depth look at a specific topic, or offer a look at a lifestyle. The subjects covered are varied, but the podcasts serve as windows into the hosts' world. True, most podcasts are; but in these podcasts, it's about the moment, the here and now, and what is happening in their lives. From this casual and candid approach comes a podcast that might make you laugh, might make you cry, and maybe — just maybe — make you think.

>> *Black Girls Being* (www.blackgirlsbeing.com): Conceived and recorded (most of the time) from Brooklyn, New York, *Black Girls Being* is a weekly podcast about black girls being intelligent, loving, ambitious, funny, artistic, angry, joyful, and everything in between. With Amira, Tyler, and Sophia as your hosts, this podcast gives a candid look into the multifaceted lives of young black women in America. *Black Girls Being* and its companion blog also showcase artists of any and all media to share their passions openly and honestly.

>> *The Way I Heard It with Mike Rowe* (http://mikerowe.com/podcast): Mike Rowe, best known for his snarky-but-sincere approach to America's working force in *Dirty Jobs*, brings all his dry wit and endless charm to *The Way I Heard It*. This podcast tells new and slightly unexpected stories of celebrities, history, and icons of culture, passed on from person to person, generation to generation. It's a quick listen — usually under ten minutes per episode.— and guaranteed to make you smile.

>> *Note to Self* (www.wnyc.org/shows/notetoself): Produced by WNYC Studios, Manoush Zomorodi hosts a weekly look at the boundaries between connecting online and connecting with the real world. This may sound like a podcast better suited for our Tech Podcasts section, but Manoush's podcast is more about how our culture and its values — privacy, empathy, personal relationships, and perception of current events — are affected by technology. *Note to Self* emphasizes the importance of remaining human while taking advantage of the latest digital innovations.

WARNING

As it goes with slice-of-life podcasts, the general content can go in any way: G, PG-13, to *"What did they just say?!"* Always check the podcasts' listings (in directories or on their websites) for an "Explicit" tag to see how "playfully blunt" these podcasts can get.

Gaming Podcasts

You might think that podcasts about games and gaming would be something better suited for the Slice-of-Life, Geek, or Comedy sections, depending on how lively these style of podcasts get. Long-form and serialized productions of friends gathering together to crawl through a dungeon, claim the title of *King of Tokyo*, or share strategies and latest news from *World of Warcraft* or *Minecraft* stand in a class all their own. Gaming podcasts are quite popular, and the skill levels featured on these podcasts range from the professionals appearing on the circuit to the novices purely in it for the fun.

» **ESPORTS Podcast** (www.espn.com/espnradio/podcast/archive/_/id/ 16788274): You may not believe that eSports — professional teams with such names as Cloud9, Evil Geniuses, and Digital Chaos that come together to play video games — is a thing, but it is. It is a *serious* thing. So serious that ESPN Radio hosts the *ESPORTS Podcast,* featuring interviews with outstanding athletes from the digital octagon, latest news and results from recent tournaments, and breakdowns of how teams performed.

» **Dumbbells & Dragons** (http://dumbbellsanddragons.com): When it comes to *Dungeons & Dragons* and other role-playing games, a stereotype has developed over the years of players consuming pizza, Cheetos, and Mountain Dew — personal fitness is not viewed as a priority when it comes to looting a necromancer's chamber for treasure. However, there are gamers who care about health, exercise, and diet, and how taking care of yourself makes you a better player. That was Kenny Rotter's intention with *Dumbbells & Dragons*, a podcast combining his love of Tough Mudders with casting magic missiles. With many others contributing to Kenny's world where fitness and nerdiness collide, *Dumbbells & Dragons* strives to live up to the podcast's popular theme, "Work out. Nerd out."

» **The Steamrollers Adventure Podcast** (http://riggstories.com/the-podcast): Michael J. Rigg loves to write. Michael J. Rigg loves role-playing games. And Michael J. Rigg loves steampunk. When Mike wrote his debut novel, *Clockwork Looking Glass*, he wanted to delve even deeper into his world, but invite his friends along for the ride. This inspired Mike to design a d20-style role-playing game around his steampunk universe. *The Steamrollers Adventure Podcast* provides an immersive RPG experience for its audience as Mike provides music and sound effects associated with events in-game. There is also a lot of inappropriate humor peppered throughout which has been known to happen during RPG sessions, but "Storycrafter Mike" keeps the action going as he pulls his friends and special guests deeper into a Wonderland of his own making.

>> **Happy Hour from the Tower** (www.happyhourfromthetower.com)**:** If you enjoy video games, you have a lot of podcasts to choose from. There are podcasts that just talk about console gaming on a whole, and then you have podcasts that focus on one game like *Halo, Mass Effect,* or *Call of Duty.* Then there's *Happy Hour from the Tower* (shown in Figure 18-6), hosted by Tee Morris, Ron Dauphin, Nick Kelly, and Brandon Kelly. The hosts may not be the best players at Bungie's science fiction, first person shooter *Destiny,* but they genuinely love the game, the lore behind it, and their own experiences within it. *Happy Hour from the Tower* also features the latest news from Bungie, gameplay video, and original fiction. If you are wanting more after listening to these Guardians, have a listen to other *Destiny*-centric podcasts like *Destiny Reset, DCP: The Destiny Community Podcast, Fireteam Chat,* or *R2O: Return to Orbit.*

FIGURE 18-6:
Happy Hour from the Tower features three generations of console gamers who get on mic for the love of the game.

Podcasts of the Pen

As you know, Tee stepped into podcasting with an idea no author had yet set out to do: serialize a novel in podcasts. When the podcast of *MOREVI* ended for Tee in the summer of 2005, he looked at the audio equipment he had and asked himself, "So . . . what do I do now?" By this time, there were a few writerly podcasts out there all talking about the *craft* of writing, but there were no active podcasts on the *business* of writing books. To fill this void, Tee launched in September 2005 *The Survival Guide to Writing Fantasy*, a podcast about the everyday operations of a writing career.

The last episode of *The Survival Guide to Writing Fantasy* aired in 2009, but many more podcasts have appeared that cover all aspects of writing from the business to the basics behind getting the work done to marketing and promotion that works.

» ***The Creative Penn Podcast*** (www.thecreativepenn.com): *New York Times* and *USA Today* bestselling thriller author Joanna Penn has developed quite a reputation with *The Creative Penn*, a podcast (and companion blog) that goes into all aspects of writing. Business. Creative demands. Time management. If you have questions about the writing industry, Joanna is a one-stop shop of knowledge. Her podcast also features interviews with authors of all backgrounds and all genres, so if you are looking for help in your writing career or creative project, *The Creative Penn* may be your first stop.

» ***Writing Excuses Podcast*** (www.writingexcuses.com): A Hugo-winning podcast featuring seven professional authors and 12 seasons of interviews, advice, and back-and-forth banter, *Writing Excuses* is a fast-paced, weekly podcast for writers, by writers. They like to say, "Fifteen minutes long, because you're in a hurry, and we're not that smart. . ." but if you get them going, the show may run a little longer. *Writing Excuses* wants to help its audience become better writers, regardless if the end goal is writing professional or writing for the soul.

» ***The Shared Desk*** (www.theshareddesk.com): Tee Morris and Pip Ballantine love writing together, and you get the idea they enjoy podcasting together when you hear them on *The Shared Desk*. When Tee and Pip turn the mics on, their topics of discussion cover collaborative projects of all kinds, what's happening in the publishing industry, and go into what is happening with their individual works as well. Whenever possible, Tee and Pip bring guests in studio to pick up different perspectives on writing.

» ***The Everyday Novelist*** (http://everydaynovelist.com): J. Daniel Sawyer has penned 24 books and over 30 short stories. While working on his next work-in-progress, Dan hosts *The Everyday Novelist*, a daily writing podcast about taking your writing passion to the next level. Within a few minutes, *The Everyday Novelist* tackles a new topic presented by Dan, a special guest, or his listeners. It's a podcast that serves as your daily affirmation for what you want to accomplish as a writer.

Geek Podcasts

If you have ever attended a Comic Con or a science fiction-fantasy-horror convention, you may have witnessed first-hand passionate individuals who love to talk about their favorite movie, television show, or game. Or maybe you caught a live interview with an actress or writer that you love, and heard that Nathan Fillion is a comic book nerd or that Erin Grey is big into Tai Chi. Truly one of the joys of podcasting is capturing good laughs between friends, luminaries, and a room full of fellow geeks attending a con and riffing on the mics.

This is the joy you hear in these podcasts. A love and a passion for all things geek. (There it is again! The *P* word — passion.)

>> ***The Nerdist Podcast*** (http://nerdist.com): Proud nerd and wordsmith Chris Hardwick hosts *The Nerdist*, a podcast celebrating pop culture and the geekier side of entertainment. Whether it is the latest in technology, an interview with actors and directors like Danny Boyle, Brandon Routh, Alan Tudyk, or the cast of *Silicon Valley*, *The Nerdist* is a sit-down with Chris, Chris' co-hosts Jonah Ray and Matt Mira, and guests who are happy to let their geek flag fly high and proud.

>> ***Geek Radio Daily*** (www.geekradiodaily.com): *Geek Radio Daily* featuring The Wonderful Billy Flynn, Podcasting's Rich Sigfrit, and The Flynnstress provides a daily (yes, *daily)* dose of geek every weekday. **Mondays** highlight the weekend box office results, **Tuesdays** cover what's out on Blu-ray, **Wednesdays** is New Comic Book Day, **Thursdays** are all about new video game releases, and **Fridays** offer up what is opening at theaters everywhere. Then there is the *GRD sWeekly* super-sized show — in many cases, recorded live at a convention — featuring special guests and in-depth discussions on how to get your geek on.

>> ***The Geek Wolfpack Podcast*** (www.geekfamilypodcast.com): The Geek Wolfpack is the Kelly Family: Nick, Stacia, and Brandon Kelly. Nick and Stacia are both science fiction writers while Brandon is an avid console gamer. Together, these three settle around the mics to talk about their passions as a family in their travels, what they are watching on Netflix, and what new app they are currently mastering on their smartphones. The second half of each episode features *ADHDD&D*, a dungeon crawl with a team of adventurers who have to work really hard to stay focused on the task at hand. This is a podcast about keeping it geeky in the family, and the fun to be had when you do.

SOMETIMES, OPPORTUNITY PRESENTS ITSELF. TAKE IT.

This is Tee Morris and Jack Mangan interviewing *Battlestar Galactica*'s Richard Hatch in February 2006 at Farpoint, a science fiction convention in Baltimore, Maryland. You'll notice that Richard is wearing a coat. He wasn't cold. He had a plane to catch, but he made time before leaving to sit down and talk on the mic about his experience between the BSG of the 1970s and of the 2000s. With *Battlestar Galactica* being a hot property once again, it was a real treat for Tee and Jack, two fans of both renditions of the epic space opera, for Richard to give them time, but how did they do it? How did two podcasters — at a time when podcasting was still a new media — land an interview with one of *BSG*'s regular players?

Simple: Tee and Jack asked.

We go into more detail on approaching people about interviews in Chapter 6, but there are those opportunities that present themselves in the moment. There is nothing wrong with asking experts and special guests relevant to your podcast's subject matter if they would like to take a few minutes to talk. There is a strong possibility that this favorite writer, actor, performer, or comic book artist will have time to sit down for a few minutes to talk, but you will never know if you don't ask. The worst thing a potential guest on your podcast could say to you is "No."

But if they say "yes" then be ready to go. And as we say in Chapter 6, be ready with solid, intelligent questions. Then let the magic happen.

Podcasts about . . . Podcasting

It may sound redundant and feel a little odd to listen to a podcast about podcasting. It would be like having an electrician come over to another electrician's house to fix faulty electric wiring. But why not?

>> *The Feed* (`http://thefeed.libsyn.com`)**:** When it comes to podcast tutors, you want to work with people who have trustworthy track records (and thank you for trusting us!); and when it comes to trustworthy track records, Elise Escobar, Rob Walch, and Libsyn are responsible for many podcasts available today. *The Feed* is LibSyn's official podcast, covering podcast strategy, tips, media hosting and all things LibSyn (see Chapter 3 for more). As *The Feed* is a community-driven show, topics go beyond getting a podcast off the ground. Rob and Elise go deep into ways of growing your audience, promotion that won't come across spammy, and crafting a strategy for your podcast, whether it is a casual endeavor or a professional venture.

>> *The Audacity to Podcast* (`http://theaudacitytopodcast.com`)**:** Podcaster Daniel J. Lewis is your host for *The Audacity to Podcast,* an award-winning podcast all about podcasting using Audacity and WordPress. Along with those foundations, Dan recommends audio gear, suggests good podcast habits, and reminds you of the reasons why you podcast in the first place.

>> *The Podcast Report* (`http://thepodcastreport.com`)**:** Google the name "Paul Cooligan" and you will see a few bylines and podcasts associated with it. Paul is another one of those podcasters who brings over a decade of experience to the microphone. *The Podcast Report* is his continuing podcast offering both tutorials on how to launch a podcast and keep it running, as well as the latest news and developments on how podcasting is evolving. The landscape of this medium is in constant flux, and Paul is out there to help you keep pace with the technology and reach new audiences.

Chapter **19**

Top Ten Reasons Why to Podcast

"**P**odcasting is just a fad."

"*I've listened to a few podcasts, and I'm not impressed.*"

"*This is nothing more than streaming media, and that really hasn't gone anywhere.*"

The naysayers of podcasting (especially those who have no idea what it is, have never listened to one, but are the first to dismiss it) have a plethora of reasons why podcasting will fail or never *really* catch on in mainstream media.

And yet, here we are a decade later — naysayers still talking smack about podcasting, even though podcasting is more popular than ever.

We podcast for a great many reasons. You have heard us talk about those reasons, but this chapter — this final word from your authors — is our hard sell. We love doing this. We returned to *Podcasting For Dummies* because we enjoy podcasting that much. Heck, Tee launched a *brand new podcast* right after completing the first deadline for this book, Chuck started a new *Star Trek* podcast called *The Topic is Trek* (http://thetopicistrek.com) during final edits, and Chuck and Tee *are resurrecting another podcast* after finishing this edition!

So, yeah — there is something to podcasting, and there are some good reasons to jump into the podosphere with us.

Here are a few (ten, to be exact) reasons why.

You Are Considered a Subject Matter Expert

Guy Kawasaki is a name you should know in social media circles. As if his time with Apple Computers (where his team was responsible for the marketing of the Macintosh back in 1984), his *New York Times* bestselling titles (like *The Art of Social Media, The Art of the Start 2.0, Reality Check,* and *Rules for the Revolutionaries*), and how his blogs remain in the Top 100 visited blogs in the world wasn't enough to make him a name in tech circles, Kawasaki has cemented himself as something of an oracle when it comes to influencing, both online and in the walking world. Some of his advice? Rock solid. Other bits of it? Worth questioning. However, in one of his most loved/hated of blogposts, "Looking for Mr. Goodtweet" (https://guykawasaki.com/looking-for-m-1), Kawasaki had this to say:

"**Establish yourself as a subject expert.** One thing is for sure about Twitter: There are some people interested in every subject and every side of every subject. By establishing yourself as a subject expert, you will make yourself interesting to some subset of people."

Yes, Kawasaki is talking about Twitter but this rule does apply to podcasting quite aptly. When you launch a podcast, you are establishing yourself as a voice in the subject matter of your podcasting. When it comes to writing, Joanna Penn on *The Creative Penn* brings her experience as a *New York Times* and *USA Today* bestseller along with her own experiences promoting her works and her brand. The *Spy Cast* (https://www.spymuseum.org/multimedia/spycast), shown in Figure 19-1, the official podcast of the International Spy Museum, was started by and hosted for years by ISM's Executive Directory and 36-year spy veteran Peter Earnest. When Peter decided to step down he wanted to ensure the expertise remained so he turned the mic over to Dr. Vince Houghton, historian and curator at the museum, his specialty being in intelligence, diplomatic, and military history, with expertise in late World War II and the early Cold War. Then you have Cliff Ravenscroft, the

Podcast Answer Man (http://podcastanswerman.com), who started his journey with podcasting over 500 episodes ago and he continues to help others find their feet in media production.

FIGURE 19-1: The *SpyCast* is hosted by Dr. Vince Houghton, historian and curator at the museum.

When you launch a podcast, you speak with the voice of authority. You speak as an expert in your field, as someone who has a proven track record and an individual who knows a thing or two about the topic of discussion. Speak with confidence. You have a lot to say, and what you have to say makes a lot of sense.

You Are Passionate about the Subject

You may not be the world's greatest gamer. You may not be the best at crafting costumes. You may not be the world's fastest runner. But if you are passionate about a sport, if you are passionate about creative endeavors, if you are passionate about a board, card, or console game, then yes, you should be podcasting about it.

It is a reoccurring theme in this book, and it bears repeating as many people want to podcast about something they love but are intimidated by the amount of work that *could* go into a podcast. Another obstacle for passionate people who podcast is to compare themselves to more polished, professional podcasts that gather the best and the brightest guests in-studio. How do you compete with productions like that?

Well, Chuck and Tee have seen professional podcasts come and go, sometimes after eight episodes. Sometimes, after four. Why do productions like this *podfade* so quickly? In many instances, podcasts are regarded as revenue generators. In other words, these hosts are in it for the money. Podcasting can be a money-making venture (as discussed in Chapter 15) but that "overnight success" rarely happens. Eventually, the studio lights are turned off and the equipment is packed away.

Sure, there are plenty of podcasts out there for Bungie's video game, *Destiny,* but Tee, Nick, and Brandon love the game. They are not experts (although Brandon is ruthless in the Crucible), but it was their passion for *Destiny* that led to *Happy Hour from the Tower.* With so many podcasts out there about technology, why do Chuck and Kreg continue to podcast *Technorama* since 2005? Because after 500 episodes, *Technorama* continues to nurture that passion. No show ever sounds forced or trite. There's a genuine joy within every podcast.

You can be an expert in your chosen field, or you can just be a huge fan. Passion should be at the core of every podcast. Without that, you can't really find the drive to sit yourself behind the microphone and record, only then to edit and produce the final work for your audience. So if you feel the drive to podcast, do so. It will take you far.

You've Got a Creative Itch to Scratch

Maybe you never thought of yourself as a creative person, or maybe you were a creative person when you were younger. Maybe there's been an inspiration working at the back of your mind, and you've been wanting to explore it. The weird thing about this idea, this unexpected muse that has grabbed hold, is that you may need to pick up some skills that you don't know. Audio editing. Video production. Is this creative endeavor something that can really happen? And can you afford it?

Podcasting, as we have shown, is not only something you can pick up quickly, but it is an affordable venture.

Science Fiction-Fantasy author Aly Grauer and game connoisseur Drew Mierzejewski took a few brave steps into podcasting with *Dreams to Become* (http://dreamstobecome.com). It began with *The Disney Odyssey* where Aly, Drew, and special guests joined them in their personal journey through every animated feature film from Walt Disney. They were enjoying this adventure so much, they launched an additional podcast, *The Night's Rewatch,* a step back to the beginning of HBO's

Game of Thrones. But still this wasn't enough so *DND20 Public Radio,* a sketch comedy created at the intersection of NPR, *Dungeons & Dragons,* and *Waiting for Guffman* launched, all under the *DTB* feed.

Within their first year of podcasting, Aly and Drew shut down their *DTB* feed, and brought all their creative inspirations — writing, gaming, fantasy, and theater — together to launch, *Welcome to Warda* (`https://welcometowarda.com`), shown in Figure 19-2. This production could be best described as a transmedia FATE-core RPG experience, telling the story of the far-off fairy realm of Warda through gaming, podcasting, and live stream actual play on Twitch's channel One Shot Podcast Network (`http://oneshotpodcast.com/`).

FIGURE 19-2: Creative power couple Aly Grauer and Drew Mierzejewski bring all their loves together in *Welcome to Warda.*

Once you have your studio, be it a simple audio setup or a complex video production, a podcast serves as your blank canvas for whatever creative endeavor you're about to embark on. This could be a throwback to the days of radio theater or this could be a personal journal for you accomplishing a life goal, be it physical fitness, a college degree, or a trip across the country. This podcast is where you share your creation with the world. Regardless of whether your feedback is positive or negative, this is your stage. Make the most of it. Assure your audience what they can expect from your feed, and then allow your creativity to run. This is your creative corner of the Internet. Make the most of it.

You Like Playing with Tech Toys

So let's just be honest: The toys a podcaster gets to play with are just so cool.

Microphones. Mixer boards. Gadgets for going portable. Software. The tools of the trade, while sometimes coming with steep price tags, are absolutely tempting. Not only do some of these technical gadgets stimulate the creative juices within your brain, but they can also be quite the showstoppers with the company you keep.

Tee has a terrific story about when he sat down in 2007 to interview Peter Earnest, executive director of the International Spy Museum. At that time, Peter was the host of the aforementioned *SpyCast*. Tee was using a Zoom H4 for the interview, the predecessor to the H4n mentioned in Chapter 4. While both models differ in features, the H4 was of a similar design. In other words, it looked a bit like a taser. This *fascinated* Mr. Earnest, and before the H4 went hot, Peter asked Tee many questions about the device, its many features, and the quality of its recordings.

Think about that for just a moment: The curator of a museum that features a lipstick pistol, an Enigma machine, the Model F-21 buttonhole camera, a rectal toolkit (yes, you read that right), and the "Bulgarian Umbrella" used to fire a tiny pellet filled with poison, was completely captivated by this portable audio recorder of Tee's. Considering Peter's background, that is saying something about the allure of audio gear.

If there is something to the latest technology that makes you happy and gets your blood pumping, whether it is an all-in-one recording device like a Zoom H6 Handy Recorder or an accessory like the MXL Mic Mate Pro (see Figure 19-3) that offers you recording options, consider all the wonderful toys you find in podcasting. While this may sound like a frivolous reason to think about launching your own show, consider how your skill set also broadens. Working with gear like condenser and dynamic microphones, portable digital recorders, software packages from Adobe and Ambrosia Software, and producing audio or video presentations will only serve to your advantage when called on to create something special for an office demonstration or for a special event at home. It might surprise you, as well, what kind of skills you pick up in producing a podcast in the ways of planning, project management, presentation skills, resource budgeting, and time management.

And to think it all starts with the tech toys.

FIGURE 19-3:
MXL's Mic Mate Pro takes any XLR microphone and converts it to a USB microphone, making it ready for podcasting on-the-go.

Bring Your Friends Together

You are putting together your notes for your podcast. It could be your first podcast. It could be a new podcast to add to your portfolio of podcasts. Whatever the case, you decide that instead of your voice being the only voice on the show, you reach out to a few friends in the area or online that you know are just as passionate about the subject you plan to podcast.

Maybe this podcast is a Dungeons & Dragons session, or perhaps you want some fellow Chicago Cubs fans or L.A. Kings fans to get around the mics and talk about the last game. Or you invite some friends who all share an interest — writing, period costume productions, movie soundtracks — to come on over and riff about it on pod. With schedules agreed upon and set, you settle in with your friends either in real time or over Skype, Google, or your favorite online conference network of choice and record. Maybe you don't realize it, but your recording sessions are more than just your chance to herd content and build up a buffer for your show. The podcast is your guaranteed connection with you and your friends. Tony Mast even mentions this in Chapter 17. His podcast *Back Seat Producers* is a "locked-in" time when good friends know they are getting together to have a little fun and share some quality time around microphones.

Another great thing about podcasting with your friends is that the podcast becomes a journal — a testament — of your friendship. That's worth the time, especially when you do retrospective episodes.

All the Cool Kids Are Doing It

Kevin Smith.

Katie Couric.

Neil deGrasse Tyson.

And you.

It's a little humbling how many high-profile journalists, celebrities, and industry influencers are turning to what was once a platform for indie artists exclusively. What is most satisfying is, after a decade and some change, podcasting is still a fantastic platform for independent creatives. For the NPR, network television, AMC, and ESPN types, the podcast also serves as a fantastic opportunity to go beyond their time on stage, screen, or a sports event. Podcasting is something akin to a great equalizer as, regardless of the production values, we are all doing the same thing here: getting in front of the camera or on the mics and sharing what's on our minds.

This is some great company to be in, so why don't you go on and get your podcast up and running? It's okay. There's plenty of room in the podosphere for what you've got. Bring your best, put your heart into it, and get your pod on!

I Can Do More

In the 2009 edition of *Star Trek*, Captain Christopher Pike says to young upstart James T. Kirk:

"Your father was the captain of a starship for 12 minutes. He saved 800 lives, including your mother's and yours. I dare you to do better."

Now what exactly does the reboot of a popular science fiction series have to do with podcasting? Pike's words serve as a great mantra for podcasters as with every show produced, podcasters look to do better. We look to improve. We look to grow. Some podcasters, after running a show for a time, love to look back on early shows and see the progress made from those first steps. It is said among some podcasters that the first five episodes of any podcast (even those done by experienced hosts) will suck, but they are allowed to suck.

Chuck and Tee do not necessarily adhere to or believe in that rule as some podcasts find their voices straight away within two or three episodes. Others, we have found, record an "Episode 0" just to see if the idea looking awesome on paper translates as well to media. Then you have shows that find a groove once the mics are hot or the camera goes live. Whenever you find your voice, creating something that people react to is truly special and worth the time and effort. The slippery slope in podcasting, though, is that drive and desire to do more.

Take a look at Tee, for example. He's the first author to podcast a novel from cover to cover. He took what started as a marketing strategy and turned it into a book. Then he goes on and creates a podcast about the business side of writing, launches companion podcasts for his books in social media, and helps establish a website where other podcasters can podcast their own novels and collections.

And yet, he wanted to do more.

Tales from the Archives is launched, opening up the steampunk universe he created with his wife to other authors and to wider audiences. *The Shared Desk* is soon launched after this, offering commentary on the latest news in the publishing industry as well as a behind-the-scenes look at an author's life. While delving into the current edition of this book, Tee follows an impulse and launches *Happy Hour from the Tower,* a loving nod to the Bungie game *Destiny,* alongside his friends Ron Dauphin and Nick & Brandon Kelly. All this, and he still hosts alongside Chuck *Podcasting For Dummies: The Companion Podcast* in order to keep this book fresh and up-to-date.

This may seem like a lot for Tee to take on, but for Tee this is a real love for the platform and the medium. He challenges himself to do better. He desires to do more.

This is the drive behind a podcaster.

Bring Out the Best in You

When you sit down to create a podcast, you want the production to rival that of professional broadcasting. No, you don't have that budget but that doesn't mean you don't strive for that level of polish and professionalism. Even with a show like *Technorama,* which comes across as spontaneous and off-the-cuff (and for the most part, it is!), Chuck and Kreg work to make their show a production that podcasters and radio show hosts all strive to reach, if not surpass. There is a sense of accomplishment and achievement in producing a podcast that gets people to stop and ask "Wait, hold on—you do this in your home?"

Sometimes, we do. Sometimes, we take our act on the road. It all depends on where we can kick up the most trouble!

Podcasting encourages by its artistic and technical nature to compel producers and show host to create the best podcast in whatever subject the producers and hosts pursue. Does that mean it will be regarded by audiences worldwide as the best? It depends on how you measure your success. Most podcasters measure the impact of a podcast on ratings and rankings. Others care more about feedback from their listeners. Some measure their podcast's success by how long their show runs after the premiere episode drops. This also compels producers and hosts to insist on creating the best podcast they can. This is how podcasting engenders a real desire in those involved to offer a show that is as much fun for audiences to listen to as it is for the podcast's crew to record, edit, and release.

Let podcasting bring out the best in you.

Talk to Interesting People

Bugs Bunny was right:

"My, I bet you monsters lead iiiinnnnnteresting lives. I said to my girlfriend just the other day 'Gee, I bet monsters are iiiinnnnnteresting,' I said. The places you must go and the things you must see — mmmyyyyy staaaaarrrs. And I bet you meet a lot of iiiinnnnnteresting people, too. I'm always interested in meeting iiiinnnnnteresting people."

BUGS BUNNY, *HARE RAISING HARE* (1946)

Now while Bugs was referring to monsters, Chuck and Tee refer to really *iiiinnnnnteresting* people. Some of the people the authors of this book have met over the course of podcasting include authors who have made an impact in their genre (Robert J. Sawyer and Terry Brooks); actors who have plenty of stories from behind the scenes (Richard Hatch and Lani Tupu); other podcasters who have made lasting impressions in and beyond the podcasting community (Grant Baciocco and Dr. Pamela Gay); and even scientists who have changed the world in what we know about it (Dr. Robert Ballard, discovered the *Titanic* wreckage in 1985). Both Tee and Chuck consider themselves fortunate for meeting a wide range of guests in their years of podcasting.

Sometimes, though, you are lucky enough to talk to guests who wind up becoming far more familiar than just guests on your podcasts. A perfect example is Chuck and Tee. In the infancy of podcasting, Tee reached out to Chuck, asking to be on *Technorama* as a guest. Tee returned for other promotional opportunities, at first, but those return trips led to meetups at conventions which led to friendship, which eventually led to this book's second edition as well as the edition you are reading now.

Not all the people you meet will lead to lifelong friendships, but through podcasting you will meet a lot of *iiiinnnnnteresting* people who will in some way impact your life. Some of those impacts you will notice straightaway. There will be those discussions you have with people that become a more subtle touch on your life, and you might not notice it until years down the road. Each person you meet, though, is part of a network; and that network — personal or professional — will at the very least broaden your view of the world. As an example, the P. G. Holyfield Meat & Greet, shown in Figure 19-4, was a yearly meetup hosted at Balticon to remember this fallen podcaster and friend, and the lives he touched.

FIGURE 19-4:
The P.G. Holyfield Meat & Greet was a yearly meetup hosted at Balticon to remember this fallen podcaster and friend, and the lives he touched.

At the most, it will enrich your life for years to come.

The Ultimate Thrill Ride

There is something scary, humbling, and intimidating about taking something you have created and releasing it to the world. You think it's good. Good enough to share, even. But once you release your podcast out into the world, it is out there. For everyone to consume. And for everyone to critique, criticize, and dissect. This is a whole new level of fear when your first show goes live.

It is, also, an amazing rush of adrenaline, euphoria, and accomplishment.

Tee has been podcasting for over a decade. This is nothing new to him, and yet he can attest on launching *Happy Hour from the Tower* while writing this edition that he was terrified beyond reason. Why? This was a whole new kind of podcast for Tee. He had never podcasted about video games before. This was his first regular show with co-hosts relatively new to podcasting. And when it came to a subject matter — Bungie's award-winning video game, *Destiny* — Tee was not the best of players, let alone "well known" in the community. Oh, and as the show's launch date was less than a month out from Bungie revealing details of *Destiny 2*, it just seemed a bit late to launch a new podcast about a game that had been out since 2014.

Still, Tee launched the podcast, and he's been enjoying the ride since that first show dropped.

Podcasting, whether on the grand scale or a small, personal stage, is an adventure. The longer you podcast, the bolder you become. The bolder you become, the more you want to test your limits. You find yourself reaching out to experts in the subject matter of your podcast, or maybe you reach out to podcasts similar to your own. You invite others to appear on your show. Or you find yourself carrying recording equipment everywhere, much like a photographer does with camera gear. You set up your portable studio, fire up the mic, and begin documenting. You talk. You meet new people. People with stories to tell. Suddenly, you find your own personal network growing. Your network grows closer, and those contacts become friends. Then, if you are lucky, those friends become family.

Podcasting is an incredible ride, and it can take you to unexpected places. It isn't easy. Not by a longshot. It is rewarding, even the podcasts that never seem to take off. They are an education of what to do differently and how to improve. Possibilities are endless, and the unexpected — regardless of how much you plan — will happen. This only adds to the fun ahead.

Now it's your turn. You've got an idea. The microphones are waiting. Go on and hit Record.

And hold on. Your adventure is officially underway.

Index

N

Name ID3 tag, 203
naming podcast, 143
Napster, 106–107
National Hockey League, podcasts about, 319
NCH Swift Sound SoundTap, 121
negative comments, reacting to, 263, 265
Neosounds, 107
The Nerdist Podcast, 355
Nerds on Cinema podcast, 332
networks, social. *See* social media
niche topics, creating new podcast about, 333
No Derivative Works permission, CC licenses, 110
Nobilis Erotica podcast, 74, 75
noise floor, 146
Noise Reduction function, Audacity, 146
noise-cancelling headphones, 49
noncommercial permission, CC licenses, 110
non-hosted model blog, 65
nonlinear video editing, 168
Note to Self podcast, 226, 296, 351
novels, podcast. *See* podiobooks

O

Obama, Barack, 312
omnidirectional microphones, 36–37
on the road interviews, 126–127
on-air personalities, 89
One America Committee Podcast with John Edwards, 311–312
one-line summary, in show notes, 226
The Onion Radio News podcast, 209
online forums
  free, hosted, 247–249
  generating buzz on, 283
  moderating, 251
  overview, 247
  paid solutions, 249–251
  searching for comments about podcast, 262
on-location podcasting. *See* portable podcasting
Open Apple podcast, 342
open source forum software, 250–251

open-ended interview questions, 116–117
opinions, focusing on in political podcasts, 311
The Opportunistic Travelers podcast, 327–328
O'Reilly, Bill, 308
outline, determining need for, 96–98
outros
  catch phrase sign off, 164
  credits, 164
  leaving audience wanting more, 163–164
  overview, 163
  previews for future podcasts, 165
over-enunciation, 139

P

P. G. Holyfield Meat and Greet, 369
pacing, 138–141
paid advertising
  Facebook, 270–274
  Instagram, 274–277
paid forum solutions, 249–251
passion
  additional podcasts, starting, 331–334
  Dog Days challenge, 334
  gaining perspective on, 322–323
  honesty, relation to, 336–337
  keeping alive, 329–335
  mixing it up, 329–330
  overview, 321–322
  podcasting with purpose, 324
  as reason to podcast, 361–362
  reinvention, tips for, 334–335
  role in efficient preshow prep, 98
  sharing with friends, 325–326
  true love for podcasting, 327–328
Patreon, 301–304
Paul, Ron, 312
pay-for-podcasting, 305–308
Payment page, Patreon, 303
Payout Preferences, Patreon, 303
PayPal, 298–301, 304
PCs. *See* computers; Windows PCs
Penn, Joanna, 354, 360

About the Authors

Tee Morris is social media professional based out of the Washington, D.C./Virginia/Maryland metro area, and an award-winning author of science fiction and fantasy. Tee's writing career began with his 2002 historical epic fantasy, *MOREVI: The Chronicles of Rafe & Askana*, published by Dragon Moon Press and the first novel to be podcast from cover to cover. It was *MOREVI's* podcast that led to this team-up with podcaster Evo Terra for the original *Podcasting For Dummies* in 2005. Since then, he has written four other titles for social media professionals, including *Social Media for Writers*, penned with his wife, Philippa Ballantine. Both Tee and Pip continue to podcast together with their Parsec-nominated podcast *The Shared Desk*, and continue to write together in *The Ministry of Peculiar Occurrences*, a steampunk series that has won several Parsec awards as well as numerous literary awards, including RT Reviewer's Choice for Best Steampunk of 2014.

Find out more about Tee Morris at www.teemorris.com and at www.ministry ofpeculiaroccurrences.com.

In "real life," **Chuck Tomasi** is an IT professional with over 35 years of experience. He is currently employed as a Pre-Sales Platform Architect for ServiceNow, a cloud enterprise software company. Currently residing in Phoenix, Arizona, he is a devoted husband and proud father of two beautiful girls. As for his alter ego . . . Chuck was bitten hard by the podcasting bug (there's an understatement). He was so eager to get started in late 2004 that he made a few tweaks to his self-written blog software and had the feed ready to go. Since then, he has migrated to WordPress and produced over 1,000 episodes across multiple shows. The longest running being Technorama, a light-hearted geek show that he co-hosts with Kreg Steppe. In 2011, Technorama took home a Parsec Award for best comedy/parody. Chuck has also been given license to employ his podcasting talents at work, garnering notoriety with a series called *TechNow*. This show is targeted toward ServiceNow administrators and developers and is co-hosted with Kreg Steppe and Dave Slusher (also podcasters). When people talk about podcasting with passion, Chuck's enthusiasm comes to mind.

Learn more about Chuck at his website: www.chucktomasi.com.

Authors' Acknowledgments

Due to the complexity of the issue and the incredible growth in the community, it would be impossible to properly express our thanks to all the parties who were of great help with this book. So with that . . .

To our wives, Donna and Pip: Thanks for not strangling us for our constant "Oh! We've got to add that to the book!" and "Come on, honey, we have to record this for the book!" moments. We deeply appreciate the averted gazes of death when we answered that no, unfortunately we would not be coming to bed, no, I forgot to scoop the litter boxes because we had one more chapter to write, and that yes, we did realize it was three o'clock in the morning.

To the podcasters that provided not only inspiration, but also camaraderie and friendship along the way. Through listening to you all and talking to many, you served as a constant reminder of why we were pouring our hearts and souls into this text.

Finally, a special nod to Michael R. Mennenga for passing along that e-mail on October 12, 2004, that opened a door to a world of time-shifting, kick ass mystic ninjas, podiobooks, and science fiction and fantasy geeks around the world interested in what we have to offer.

Publisher's Acknowledgments

Executive Editor: Steve Hayes

Project Manager: Colleen Diamond

Development Editor: Colleen Diamond

Copy Editor: Colleen Diamond

Technical Editor: Rich Sigfrit

Editorial Assistant: Owen Kaelble

Sr. Editorial Assistant: Cherie Case

Production Editor: Magesh Elangovan

Cover Photo: © arinahabich /iStockphoto

PERSONAL ENRICHMENT

9781119187790
USA $26.00
CAN $31.99
UK £19.99

9781119179030
USA $21.99
CAN $25.99
UK £16.99

9781119293354
USA $24.99
CAN $29.99
UK £17.99

9781119293347
USA $22.99
CAN $27.99
UK £16.99

9781119310068
USA $22.99
CAN $27.99
UK £16.99

9781119235606
USA $24.99
CAN $29.99
UK £17.99

9781119251163
USA $24.99
CAN $29.99
UK £17.99

9781119235491
USA $26.99
CAN $31.99
UK £19.99

9781119279952
USA $24.99
CAN $29.99
UK £17.99

9781119283133
USA $24.99
CAN $29.99
UK £17.99

9781119287117
USA $24.99
CAN $29.99
UK £16.99

9781119130246
USA $22.99
CAN $27.99
UK £16.99

PROFESSIONAL DEVELOPMENT

9781119311041
USA $24.99
CAN $29.99
UK £17.99

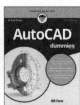
9781119255796
USA $39.99
CAN $47.99
UK £27.99

9781119293439
USA $26.99
CAN $31.99
UK £19.99

9781119281467
USA $26.99
CAN $31.99
UK £19.99

9781119280651
USA $29.99
CAN $35.99
UK £21.99

9781119251132
USA $24.99
CAN $29.99
UK £17.99

9781119310563
USA $34.00
CAN $41.99
UK £24.99

9781119181705
USA $29.99
CAN $35.99
UK £21.99

9781119263593
USA $26.99
CAN $31.99
UK £19.99

9781119257769
USA $29.99
CAN $35.99
UK £21.99

9781119293477
USA $26.99
CAN $31.99
UK £19.99

9781119265313
USA $24.99
CAN $29.99
UK £17.99

9781119239314
USA $29.99
CAN $35.99
UK £21.99

9781119293323
USA $29.99
CAN $35.99
UK £21.99

dummies.com

dummies
A Wiley Brand